Additional Parenting Books From the American Academy of Pediatrics

Caring for Your Baby and Young Child: Birth to Age 5
(English and Spanish)

Mommy Calls: Dr. Tanya Answers Parents' Top 101 Questions
About Babies and Toddlers

The Wonder Years: Helping Your Baby and Young Child Negotiate
the Major Developmental Milestones

Raising Twins: From Pregnancy to Preschool

Your Baby's First Year *(English and Spanish)*

New Mother's Guide to Breastfeeding *(English and Spanish)*

Food Fights: Winning the Nutritional Challenges of Parenthood
Armed With Insight, Humor, and a Bottle of Ketchup

A Parent's Guide to Childhood Obesity: A Road Map to Health

Guide to Your Child's Nutrition

ADHD: A Complete and Authoritative Guide

Waking Up Dry: A Guide to Help Children Overcome Bedwetting

A Parent's Guide to Building Resilience in Children and Teens:
Giving Your Child Roots and Wings

Sports Success Rx!—Your Child's Prescription for the Best Experience

Less Stress, More Success: A New Approach to Guiding Your Teen
Through College Admissions and Beyond

Mental Health, Naturally: The Family Guide to Holistic Care
for a Healthy Mind and Body

Caring for Your Teenager

Guide to Your Child's Allergies and Asthma

Guide to Toilet Training *(English and Spanish)*

For more information, visit the AAP Web site for parents,
healthychildren.org/bookstore.

Heading Home With
YOUR NEWBORN

FROM BIRTH TO REALITY

SECOND EDITION

Laura A. Jana, MD, FAAP
Jennifer Shu, MD, FAAP

American Academy of Pediatrics
DEDICATED TO THE HEALTH OF ALL CHILDREN™

AAP Publishing Staff

Director, Department of Marketing and Publications
Maureen DeRosa, MPA

Director, Division of Product Development
Mark Grimes

Manager, Consumer Publishing
Carolyn Kolbaba

Director, Division of Publishing and Production Services
Sandi King, MS

Manager, Editorial Services
Kate Larson

Print Production Specialist
Shannan Martin

Manager, Graphic Design and Production
Peg Mulcahy

Manager, Consumer Product Marketing
Kathleen Juhl

Published by the American Academy of Pediatrics
141 Northwest Point Blvd, Elk Grove Village, IL 60007-1098
847/434-4000
Fax: 847/434-8000
www.aap.org

Cover design by Stephen B. Starr Design, Inc.
Pencil drawings by Anthony Alex LeTourneau
Book design by Linda J. Diamond

Library of Congress Control Number: 2004111854
ISBN: 978-1-58110-444-8

CB0060

9-266/0710

1 2 3 4 5 6 7 8 9 10

CRITICAL ACCLAIM FOR HEADING HOME WITH YOUR NEWBORN

- Exclusively featured in the Babies R Us parent resource guide, *Becoming Us*
- Extensively excerpted with more than 1 million copies in print

AWARDS

Best in Parenting—Benjamin Franklin Award, The Independent Book
Publishers Association
First Place—Diet/Health/Fitness, Midwest Book Award
Book of the Year—Gold Award, *ForeWord* magazine

WHAT PEOPLE ARE SAYING

One of the "best guides to the first year of your baby's life."
Parents magazine

Heading Home With Your Newborn is one of the very best books for parents that I've
run across in the 24 years that I have been reviewing parenting books. Written with
great heart and soul, it provides up-to-date medical information. These two pediatrician
authors are both smart and compassionate, and it's obvious that they remember just
what it feels like to bring home a brand-new baby.
Bobbi Conner
Creator and host of *The Parent's Journal* nationwide public radio program

This book packs the advice of a parenting class, a doctor's visit, and a best friend into
one indispensable package.
Library Journal

A special book that new parents will want to read cover to cover before their little one
arrives. No matter what challenges new parenthood throws your way, Drs Jana and Shu
are sure to leave you feeling both confident and competent. *Heading Home* is the perfect
shower gift!
Barton Schmitt, MD, FAAP
Professor of Pediatrics at the Children's Hospital of Denver

In short, easy-to-read chapters, these pediatrician authors explore all the topics…
which are part of every new baby's life. Their sections on car seat safety and traveling
with an infant are especially informative and up to date. The authors' supportive
reassurances and sensitive advice will be particularly helpful to parents whose baby
does not fit the norm. Without a false note anywhere, the authors have made a gift to
parents of their own confidence and experience. This book is a fresh contribution to
adults just beginning the parenting journey.
Molly Frederick
Senior Associate Editor, formerly of *Contemporary Pediatrics*

Funny yet sage…having this book in the house is like having a doctor on call (without the co-pay).

ePregnancy magazine

This book will lower your stress about raising your child. It is a wonderful narrative that reads as if it was a conversation among friends…. You can have a shared learning experience with the authors who are moms, docs, and daughters and really do know.

George A. Strait
Former Medical Correspondent, *ABC News*

In an era of one-size-fits-all parenting advice, this book truly stands out. Doctors Jana and Shu offer the kind of advice that will help new parents keep their expectations reasonable, while giving them the confidence and encouragement they need to be great parents, and to have fun at the same time.

Armin Brott
Author of *The Expectant Father* series

I LOVE, LOVE, LOVE the humor in *Heading Home!* Very entertaining and informative. I am now recommending that all my new parents get a copy, whether they are on their first or fourth baby.

Dan Brennan, MD, CLC, FAAP
Sansum Clinic, Santa Barbara, California and contributing writer for *Santa Barbara Parent* magazine, the *Daily Sound,* and the *Goleta Voice*

A family-friendly, easily read…guide to the unique experience of caring for a newborn that is both practical and medically sound.

Lillian Blackmon, MD
Former Chair, American Academy of Pediatrics Committee on Fetus and Newborn

The advice you'd get from your sister or best friend, if she had her baby only last year.

Gil Fuld, MD
AAP News Editorial Advisory Board

Its spirited, light, and conversational tone makes readers feel like they are talking to a trusted good friend who just happens to be a pediatrician.

John C. Nelson, MD, MPH
Obstetrician-gynecologist
Past President, American Medical Association

To everyone who humored us when we told them we were writing a book, to those who actually took us seriously and, most importantly, to all of you who welcome us into your homes and share this unforgettable part of parenthood with us.

—LJ and JS

ACKNOWLEDGMENTS

As we marvel at the fact that *Heading Home With Your Newborn* has touched the lives of more than a million families over the past several years since the first edition was published, we realize just how fortunate we've been to be able to share in what we truly consider to be one of the most momentous occasions of parenthood. We are also reminded of how grateful we are for our own family, friends, and colleagues. As cliché as it may sound, this book wouldn't exist without their love, support, understanding, and ongoing reassurances that what we have to say continues to be worth putting into print. For that they are deserving of both recognition and our sincerest thanks.

First and foremost, we are thrilled to be in this partnership with the American Academy of Pediatrics (AAP). After years of hard work and climbing our way up the steep learning curve in the world of publishing, we couldn't have found a more perfect fit. Executive Director Errol Alden, MD, and Past Executive Director Joe Sanders, MD, offered us an incredible opportunity to work with the AAP, which we truly believe represents the gold standard in caring for children. Past President Louis Z. Cooper, MD, was instrumental in getting our book in the right hands to make it to the publishing stage. Also indispensable have been Mark Grimes, Director, Division of Product Development; Kathleen Juhl, Manager, Consumer Product Marketing; Carolyn Kolbaba, Manager, Consumer Publishing; and Maureen DeRosa, MPA, Director, Department of Marketing and Publications.

We also owe our gratitude to all of the many expert colleagues who reviewed our text for technical (and practical) accuracy over the years. For this second edition, we would like to extend our special thanks to Dr Emilio Arispe, Dr Tanya Remer Altman and Dr Dan Brennan for their thorough review of the entire book, and to Dr Ari Brown, Dr Ben Hoffman, Mr Sandy Sinclair, Ann King Brunzell, Jeanne Anderson, and Stephanie Nelson.

Personal Acknowledgments

Laura Jana, MD: I have been fortunate to have crossed paths with several people whose faith in my abilities has helped me to believe in myself. Perhaps one of the most influential people early in my career was Dr Benjamin Spock, who not only took me seriously years before I had a degree behind my name, but was an incredibly insightful man whose love of life and understanding of both children and parents continues to inspire me. I also want to thank pediatricians Dr Robert Needlman, who first demonstrated to me how to practice the art of pediatrics, and Dr Barton Schmitt, whose kind words of support meant far more to me than he probably realized. And finally, I owe a special thanks to Dr Georges Peter, whose commitment to involving young pediatricians and women in the AAP is what brought me back in touch with Dr Jennifer Shu years after we trained together at the University of California–San Francisco. I feel so fortunate to have Jennifer as one of my closest colleagues and friends, as our partnership has unquestionably changed my life.

My 3 precious children—Bethany, Alex, and Ryan—help remind me every day what is truly important in my life, and I am forever grateful for their willingness to let me test out (and fine-tune) my parenting techniques before sharing them with others. My twin sister, Ellen Levy, did far more than her fair share in making sure that this book would be published and as a new mom herself has added valuable insights to this second edition, while my brother Philip Levy's repeated votes of confidence in my abilities, as well as his editing skills, have been invaluable. My mother, Dr June Osborn, has always done everything in her power (and then some) to make sure that I was able to pursue my dreams, and my father, Dr Jay Levy, has made sure his pride in my accomplishments is ever-apparent. Above all else, I want to acknowledge my best friend and husband of 15 years, Dr Ajoy Jana, who has not only given me his unwavering support, but his unconditional love. To his parents, I am eternally grateful for raising such a wonderful son and for including me in their family, because it is the life and family we have created together that define who I am and are my greatest accomplishments.

Jennifer Shu, MD: Space prevents me from personally listing all the important people with whom I have crossed paths in life. Many of you have given me the encouragement and confidence to become the person I am, and for this I am most grateful. I would like to give my utmost appreciation to my husband and son who patiently supported a book that took more than 3 years to come to life; you are truly my best friends. Thanks to my parents, who taught me to believe that I could be anything I wanted to be. A big shout-out goes to my sisters, who have been my peppiest cheerleaders. To my extended family of in-laws: Thanks for welcoming me into your lives as a daughter/sister/friend. My 10th-grade English teacher, Mr Paul Lankford, told me that I would be a star no matter where I went, and I was naíve enough to believe him—I know he has similarly influenced many other students in a tremendously positive way and I would like to recognize the impact he has had. My heartfelt thanks go to my pediatric colleagues, coworkers, and mentors, who have guided me in this ongoing quest to be a better pediatrician. My friends from all the stages of my life have been incredibly supportive and tolerant of my quirks and tendency to share my excitement about our books. I would also like to extend my gratitude to all my patients, who have taught me just about everything I know about newborns. And lastly, a big woo-hoo to my coauthor Laura—we not only finally finished it, but now get to watch it grow; I'm glad we get to go through this amazing experience together!

TABLE OF CONTENTS

The Current State of Parenting Affairs

If you're standing in a bookstore as you read this, it will be obvious to you that we are by no means the first authors to write about the wondrous but admittedly daunting journey called parenthood. The fact of the matter is that we live in a time where parenting experts all but grow on trees, and parenting books, magazines, and Web sites are overflowing with advice. Given the sheer magnitude of information already available, you may wonder why we ever decided to toss our hats into this overcrowded ring and set out to write books on the subject of raising children in the first place. To be perfectly honest, we almost didn't.

A Journey of Our Own

Originally, we set out in search of what we knew parents (our patients, our friends, and ourselves) wanted—a parenting book that was informative and practical, that offered explanations right alongside recommendations and, most of all, that was firmly grounded in the realities of modern-day parenting. At the end of the day (or several years later, to be more exact) and hundreds of parenting books, patient visits, baby showers, and play groups later—not to mention several children of our own—we still hadn't found a book that reflected our own unique perspective on parenting. In fact, what we discovered was that new parents were reading "all of the baby books" and were still left with questions about the realities of caring for their newborns. It was then that we decided that there was room for at least one more parenting book on the shelf, and we set to work creating a book that would specifically focus on the first few weeks of parenthood.

Following the Rules: Parenting by the Book

Nowadays it seems you can find well-defined rules about everything from feeding and sleeping schedules to dressing, diapering, and discipline. As convenient as it may seem to have someone write out for you an exact recipe for parenting success, we believe that there is not just one right way to do things. As with diapers and baby clothes, we are convinced that parenting techniques are not simply one size fits all. Our goal is to help familiarize you with the basics of baby care, and even more importantly to build your confidence as a parent right from the beginning during what many consider to be an overwhelming time—the newborn period. With a little knowledge and a positive attitude, you will find that you are very capable of anticipating and reasoning your way through even the most challenging aspects of what lies ahead. It's a great feeling to find yourself comfortable enough in your parenting abilities that you don't have to live life with a quick reference guide—ours or anyone else's—tucked in your back pocket.

Parenting With Style

We have found that it is a rare parent—new or seasoned—who isn't also on the constant lookout for good, practical parenting advice to make life a bit easier, less expensive, safer, or simply more fun. We like to think of these little pearls of wisdom as parenting revelations—the "wow, what a good idea…I never thought of that" or "you know what, that really makes sense—I wish I had thought of that sooner" kind of revelation that comes when fellow parents share their insights—or, in this case, when we share ours. After all, we firmly believe that parenting is not only a lifestyle, but that it can be done in style.

From Birth to Reality

As parents ourselves, with 4 children between us, we have firsthand knowledge of what parenting questions tend to arise and what dilemmas have a way of presenting themselves in the course of a typical day—or night—with a newborn. Opportunely enough, we both also happen to be pediatricians. The years we have spent in pediatric training and practice have provided us with an added understanding of babies, children, and parents—not to mention what obstacles they (and you) are likely to run into along the way. We have had the opportunity to talk and listen to thousands of parents just like you—and believe us we have listened! Not only have we listened in our offices to concerns about first fevers, flat heads, and breastfeeding and helped parents sort out their babies' common (and not so common) medical ailments, but we have answered questions about everything from the family bed, first airplane trips, and installing car seats to choosing child care and infant attire.

Parent-Tested, Pediatrician-Approved

And now we're happy to be sharing with you what we've learned over the years—not just in medical school, but also from everyday life and everyday parents just like you—as we guide you through the transition from birth to the reality of being a parent. While we have complete faith in your ability to figure things out for yourself, we thought you might find it helpful to hear our thoughts *before* you have to do it all on your own! *Heading Home With Your Newborn* represents a blending of our experiences and brings you the best of both worlds—a book that presents the *reality* of parenting from a parent's perspective, but with a pediatrician's stamp of approval. Instead of being "kid-tested, mother-approved," our book is "parent-tested, pediatrician-approved" all wrapped into one convenient package.

Anticipating Change

You may have heard people say that life is never the same after having a baby. Until you have lived through the experience yourself, it may be difficult to truly imagine exactly what heading home with your newborn will mean for you and your family. One thing that you can count on, though, is that your life *will* certainly change—physically, emotionally, and financially. By this we're not just referring to the shedding of pregnancy pounds, the psychological stress of sleep deprivation, and the cost of baby bedding (not to mention college, which is forever looming in the distance), but also your general perspective on life. The phrase "Toto, we're not in Kansas anymore" springs to mind.

Great Expectations

How you deal with the inevitable changes and challenges of parenthood is likely to be colored by your initial expectations of what life with your newborn is going to be like. While we will provide the information to help prepare you for the day-to-day tasks of life with a newborn, in the end it will be up to you to create a positive mental attitude. After all, we firmly believe that an important part of preparing for life with a newborn involves getting into the right mindset.

Rude Awakenings

Fairly often we find that new parents expect too much of their newborns (and themselves). While we've dedicated entire sections of this book to the topics of breastfeeding and sleep, they make for perfect examples of unrealistic expectations. Suffice it to say that although the "textbook" pattern of feeding may be 15 minutes on each breast every 3 hours, a newborn who nurses sporadically and frequently throughout the day and night is much closer to the norm. And if you're expecting a full night's sleep right from the start as opposed to being grateful for a 4-hour stretch—we're sorry to say you're likely to be in for many rude awakenings. We could use any number of similar examples to support our belief that expecting too much inevitably sets parents up to *feel* like they've derailed when in reality they are usually still right on track.

Keeping It Real

Whether you are heading into the homestretch of your pregnancy or are already homeward bound, take a minute to ask yourself how you feel about your parenting abilities. Some people find themselves petrified while others maintain a cool confidence. As you get ready to go from birth to the sudden reality of parenthood, we suggest adopting the mantra "I think I can, I think I can, I think I can…" long before you ever formally become acquainted with *The Little Engine That Could* (much less find yourself reading this timeless children's book aloud for the hundredth time). Whether your expectations of yourself and your newborn simply need some fine-tuning or a major readjustment, we hope you'll head home confident and soon be saying, "I *knew* I could, I *knew* I could, I *knew* I could…."

High Hopes

We have the highest hopes and sincerely believe that you and your baby will settle into a manageable lifestyle. After all, millions of parents before you have had newborn babies and still choose to have second, third, fourth…children. In the short term, we encourage you to set your sights not so much on the day-to-day challenges but on the more intangible aspects of parenthood—the joy, pride, and sense of awe and accomplishment that is the essence of parenthood. These should be your great expectations. We can all but guarantee that the joy will outweigh the fatigue, and your overall sense of accomplishment will erase many of the doubts you may have.

The Price of Things to Come

Labor and delivery .... Uncomfortable

Furnishing, decorating, and stocking the nursery .... Expensive

Keeping up with your newborn's eating
and (not) sleeping schedule .... Tiring

Forgetting to brush your teeth or shower .... Unhygienic

Being a parent .... Priceless

 BRAVE NEW WORLD

While you have many years ahead to familiarize yourself with the nuances, joys, and responsibilities of raising a happy, healthy child, we want to help make the first baby steps you take up the new-parent learning curve a little less wobbly. We decided that the most logical way to begin this journey is with a look at one of the most unforgettable events of parenthood—when new parents like you pack up their things at the hospital, take a deep breath, place their precious new babies in carefully installed car seats, and boldly go where they have never been before. We call it heading home with your newborn.

PART I

into the mouths of babes

As the parent of a newborn, you'll undoubtedly be spending a good deal of time paying attention to what goes into your baby's mouth. Whether by breast or by bottle, the frequent task of feeding a newborn has the potential to raise a whole host of questions ranging from how to know if your breast milk has come in or how to prepare your baby's formula to the facts about sucking and whether it's OK to use pacifiers.

Before we really dive in, let us first point out that infancy isn't referred to as the oral stage for nothing. At the risk of sounding like an academic textbook, it's nevertheless worth acknowledging what professionals as far back as Freud himself once proposed: What goes into your baby's mouth during this stage of the game is going to be a big part of her life experience (not to mention yours). Not only will eating and growing be one of her biggest and most important responsibilities for many months to come, but her mouth will also play a valuable role in allowing her to comfort herself and discover the world around her long before she learns to use her hands and other senses to explore.

With that mouthful in mind, you may find that you look at your baby's cute little lips with new respect and awe. The rest of this chapter is dedicated to taking a hands-on look at the reality of feeding your newborn—not only as a nutritional necessity, but a wonderful opportunity for you to bond with your baby. Our ultimate goal is to help you settle into a comfortable routine and give you a clear idea of what you can expect as well as what to look out for.

Now to turn our attention to the substance of the matter at hand—breast milk and/or formula: For the sake of convenience, we have tried to separate breastfeeding from formula feeding—a well-defined separation in print that is not always so clear-cut in real life. That's because quite a few parents ultimately find themselves relying on some combination of the two. Once you've finished the part that applies to you—whether it's breast, formula, or both—we encourage you to keep reading because later in this section we address subjects that are likely to be of interest to all of you. They include pacifiers, feeding schedules (or the lack thereof), and supplemental vitamins. And you'll be able to brush up on the basics of bottle-feeding—from supplies to technique and cleanup—in a section meant to be useful to anyone who plans to use a bottle, regardless of what you choose to put in it.

 DOLLARS AND SENSE

If the decision about whether to breastfeed or formula feed were based solely (or even partly) on finances, breastfeeding would win hands down. The added expense of breastfeeding includes the cost of a few extra calories a day for mom (somewhere around 25% more) and the cost of nursing bras, breast pumps, breast pads, or any of a multitude of other optional supplies you happen to pick up along the way. With formula feeding, on the other hand, most of the inherent costs are not optional. As you may have already discovered, formula tends to be quite costly. Based on current prices, the average cost of formula can range anywhere from $1,300 to $3,000 a year, depending on the type used (more on the actual types later in Chapter 2).

breastfeeding

In our humble opinion, the most significant contribution we stand to make to your breastfeeding success is to start you off with realistic expectations. To do that, we have taken the time to address many of the common breastfeeding myths and misconceptions that tend to weigh new parents down. We have found it particularly helpful for new and expectant parents to remind themselves of 2 reassuring facts.

1. Millions of mothers before you have been able to breastfeed their babies successfully.
2. The first couple weeks of breastfeeding are by no means representative of what your entire breastfeeding experience will be like.

While a handful of fortunate new moms do ease into breastfeeding as if they were born to do so and are quickly rewarded with an overwhelming sense of accomplishment, in reality there is usually a period of self-education and on-the-breast training. Consider this time to be one of trial and error—a "get acquainted with and accustomed to the process" phase in which breastfeeding your baby may take a bit more time, thought, and effort than it will in your not-so-distant breastfeeding future. With a few safety precautions and an eye on the prize, you will likely be able to dodge many common obstacles—both perceived and real. And if you're coming to us already frustrated and all but resigned to giving up any hope of breastfeeding altogether, we hope to offer you a new lease on your breastfeeding life.

A Comment on "Breast Is Best"

As you enter the world of parenthood, you will undoubtedly encounter the phrase "breast is best." That's because it has become an almost universal slogan that graces the pages of parenting magazines, Web sites, medical textbooks, and formula advertisements alike. Given that breast milk is impossible to duplicate and the health benefits it offers invaluable, we wholeheartedly support the American Academy of Pediatrics recommendation to feed your baby breast milk as long as possible—ideally 1 year or even longer. With that as a backdrop, what we have to say about your decision to breastfeed may therefore come as a bit of a surprise—especially from 2 pediatrician-moms who are fully aware and in support of the idea that there are great benefits to breastfeeding. We feel the need to mention that we have come across instances in which breastfeeding has not always worked out for the best. Now lest the preceding statement be regarded as a letdown to breastfeeding advocates everywhere, let us explain.

The standard consideration in favor of breast milk is very straightforward. Breast milk is currently unrivaled as the ideal food for infants. Not only is it considered to be a perfect mix of nutrients, including the fatty acids DHA and ARA that are thought to play an important role in brain and eye development, but the infection-fighting antibodies it contains just can't be bottled in even the most expensive of commercial formulas. It has also been shown to reduce a newborn's chance of developing everything from ear infections, allergies, vomiting, and diarrhea to asthma, diabetes, pneumonia, meningitis, and potentially even sudden infant death syndrome. There are also health benefits to nursing mothers. Just about the only caveat we feel compelled to mention is that for some caring and devoted new mothers, when it comes to putting recommendations into practice, sometimes breastfeeding just doesn't work out right. Whether it's a matter of modesty, attitude, medically related issues, or the disappointment of unsuccessful attempts, breastfeeding is a potential source of frustration for some new moms. Worse yet, difficulties with breastfeeding can be the cause of some serious feelings of parental inadequacy—leaving devoted mothers questioning their overall ability as parents. Too many of these new parents are led to believe—either by convincing themselves or by being told by others—that to be a good mother, breastfeeding is an absolute requirement.

We will now say to you what we suggest to every new or expectant mother that comes to us with questions or concerns about the early days of breastfeeding: First decide for yourself whether you are looking for breastfeeding help or secretly hoping someone will tell you that it's OK *not* to breastfeed. If you've already made the *informed* (and by informed we mean not only having all the facts, but also discussing your choice with a qualified health professional) decision that breastfeeding is not for you, then you have our full support in flipping directly to the formula-feeding discussion of our book without experiencing unrelenting pangs of guilt. If, on the other hand, you've never given much thought to breastfeeding, you find yourself questioning your ability to do it successfully, or you have run into a few bumps on the road to what will almost surely be breastfeeding success, we hope you will read on. We want to take a stab at boosting your confidence and make sure your breastfeeding experiences are not only successful, but also enjoyable.

BREASTFEEDING'S BUDDING POPULARITY

The popularity and number of women breastfeeding in the United States has grown over the past several years as compared to some 30 years ago when essentially no new moms in the United States attempted to breastfeed. Now, more than 70% of women at least try their hand (or breast) at it—a significant change for the better, if you consider what we now know about the health benefits of breastfeeding.

How Far We've Come and How We Got Here

Anyone looking at breastfeeding popularity in the United States over the past several decades is sure to notice what we like to call a roller coaster phenomenon—up in the '70s, down in the '80s, and back up again starting in the '90s. And of course, what was considered to be "best," not to mention socially acceptable, has varied considerably not only over time, but also based on many other factors such as what area of the country the parents live in, their age, and their background. While we've certainly come a long way from the days when breastfeeding moms were the exception to the rule and ostracized for their choice, we have not come so far that there aren't still outdated, hard to believe, and even downright comical laws that prohibit public displays of breastfeeding.

BREASTFEEDING WITHIN YOUR LEGAL RIGHTS

There are laws in most states that protect a woman's right to breastfeed. Forty-three states, the District of Columbia, and the US Virgin Islands all make it perfectly clear that it's legal for mothers to breastfeed in public, while 28 states specifically exclude breastfeeding from public indecency laws. Some of the more creative pro-breastfeeding laws we've come across include 12 states that exempt nursing mothers from jury duty or a law in Maryland that exempts any products that help initiate, support, or sustain breastfeeding from being charged sales tax. If we've piqued your interest and you somehow manage to find yourself some spare time, you can check out the La Leche League Web site at www.lalecheleague.org to brush up on breastfeeding rights and regulations in your own state.

Getting Started

What's "Natural" Doesn't Always Come Naturally

Yes, the act of breastfeeding is "natural," but the truth of the matter is that it doesn't always come naturally. All too often, new parents expect to be handed a newborn who gracefully latches on, nurses no more than 15 minutes on each breast every 3 hours, and delights in a plentiful supply of breast milk within a few short days. While we can only wish this scenario on all of you, clinging to this idealistic picture of breastfeeding bliss is all but guaranteed to set most of you up for perceived failure. If, however, you prepare yourself for the distinct possibility that your newborn may lack interest or sucking stamina, that each feeding may be different, and your nipples may be a little worse for wear early on, well then you only stand to be pleasantly surprised. The most likely scenario: Breastfeeding may be natural, but expect it to be a learning process for you and your baby. Some babies are quick learners, while others take their own sweet time.

Advice Abounds

As you try to educate yourself or start your on-the-job training, you're almost certain to find that anyone who has ever breastfed (or been remotely involved in breastfeeding) considers themselves a full-fledged expert. Some of the advice you get will undoubtedly prove to be very helpful, but be aware that you'll probably get your fair share of unsolicited suggestions and contradictory, confusing, or just plain wrong advice—even when it comes from moms who have nursed a virtual litter of children, are highly intelligent, and have the best of intentions. Just keep in mind that at the end of the day, there are only a few universally accepted facts about breastfeeding. The rest of what you do and how you do it will be a matter of establishing your own personal breastfeeding style.

Sending Out an SOS (in Search of Support)

Breastfeeding really does have its rewards, but it also can be a very demanding and tiring 24-hour-a-day job. If you find yourself experiencing feelings of frustration, isolation, or even feelings of entrapment, one of the worst things you can do is try to cope alone. Of course it's not any better to find yourself in the company of a well-meaning grandmother who is just waiting for the opportunity to tell you how easy formula feeding would be in contrast. Please take a moment and tell yourself that you are absolutely not alone and don't need to be figuring out the tricks of the trade the hard way! We strongly suggest that if what you really need is a supportive shoulder to lean on, put down this book and find one (or several). It may seem like yet one more thing you don't have time for, but finding that you don't have to learn to breastfeed alone can make all the difference in the world.

- La Leche League International has local chapters throughout the world. You can either check your phone book or go to their Web site (www.lalecheleague.org) to find area leaders and meeting places and times.
- Get help from your hospital. Labor and delivery staff, nurses on the mother-baby unit, and hospital lactation specialists are a great place to start exploring what types of support are available in your community before, during, and after you deliver.

- Turn to your pediatrician for advice and/or assistance. As pediatricians, we routinely observe newborns breastfeeding in our offices and are very accustomed to providing practical advice and troubleshooting tips. Be sure to ask your pediatrician for advice, or for a referral to a lactation consultant or other breastfeeding resources in your area.
- Don't be afraid to enlist your spouse, partner, friends, family members, or neighbors—anyone you think might be able to lend a hand and/or offer emotional support. Even though no one else can breastfeed for you, we've never met a new mother who couldn't use a little help with cleaning, cooking, laundry, or watching the baby for a bit so she can get a break every now and then.
- In the wired world we now live in, virtual breastfeeding support groups abound; you can find them by doing a search or through different parenting Web sites. As with any Internet activity, you should of course be careful about any private information you might divulge and look for credible sources of information.

A BREAST A DAY KEEPS THE DOCTOR AWAY

Based on many studies done in the United States and elsewhere around the world, we know that breastfeeding is not only nutritionally sound and decreases the risk of sudden infant death syndrome (see "The Reality of SIDS" on page 91), but can translate into fewer colds, allergies, infections, hospitalizations, and visits to the doctor's office. That's because protective proteins called antibodies, along with other infection-fighting cells found in breast milk, are continually transferred from you to your baby for as long as you breastfeed. This added level of defense against bacteria and viruses is particularly beneficial during the first several months of your baby's life when his immune system isn't yet functioning at full speed.

My Baby, My Breasts, and I

Becoming a new breastfeeding mother really does involve a fundamental shift in one's view of the world—a shift that is lifelong in the sense of awe you get from nurturing a child of your own, but more immediately in a practical, concrete way. That is, you are suddenly thrust from a world primarily focused on "me, myself, and I" (or perhaps "me, my spouse, and I") to one that inevitably is structured around "my baby, my breasts, and I." As you set out to master the fine art of breastfeeding, you are likely to look on your breasts in a whole new way, and most likely give them far more consideration than ever before (regardless of how significant they were to you in your pre-breastfeeding past). In fact, we are of the strong belief that if your baby's health provider doesn't ask you how you, your baby, *and* your breasts are doing in your early days of breastfeeding, he or she has, for lack of a more tactful description, completely missed the boat.

First Attempts

Assuming that all goes well with the birth of your baby and both of you are doing well in the minutes and hours immediately following delivery, then the best time to attempt your first breastfeeding is as soon as possible. While this may seem obvious, it's easy to find yourself feeling like you have no say or control in what takes place during your hospital stay, much less in your own delivery room. If you wait for someone to tell you what to do and when, then whether you are encouraged to breastfeed right away will depend on your hospital's attitudes toward breastfeeding.

Helping Hands at the Hospital

Your goal for breastfeeding in the delivery room (and throughout your stay at the hospital) should be to make sure you and your baby work out the concept of latching on correctly. At some hospitals it is standard for labor and delivery nurses to not only bring mothers their newborns within minutes of delivery, but to offer plenty of breastfeeding instruction and encouragement. At other hospitals, however, it is still routine for newborns to be taken off to the nursery to be cleaned up and even given a bottle while their mothers get some rest. If you want to get breastfeeding off to a good start, don't be afraid to take things into your own hands and give it a try while you're still in the delivery room. Many babies tend to be temporarily wide awake right after delivery. After all, they've just been through a pretty eye-opening experience right along with you. If and when you get the chance, take advantage of your baby's temporary state of alertness (which we liken to a honeymoon period). Within a matter of hours you may well find you have a very sleepy baby on your chest.

ROOMING IN

Depending on the hospital where you deliver, your baby will either
be allowed to room in with you for most of your hospital stay, or will be
kept in a centralized nursery and brought into your room on occasion.
If you're planning to breastfeed, we strongly recommend exploring your
options and, if available, choosing a so-called baby-friendly hospital that
actively promotes breastfeeding and will accommodate your desire to
stay close to your baby and nurse frequently.

Getting Comfortable

Given that just about all new moms are prone to focusing their attention
on their breasts (and their babies) when they first sit or lie down to nurse,
we also want to remind you to take a moment and make yourself comfortable. Supporting yourself with extra pillows, making sure you have
on convenient and comfortable clothing, and having anything you might
want or need within arm's reach (a glass of water, a book, the phone, or the
TV remote control) *before* getting down to business can definitely make
the experience more enjoyable. When it comes to the actual position you
try, the choice is really up to you. In case you aren't aware of them, we will
briefly describe several of the most popular options.

- **Cradle hold.** This is the position most novice breastfeeders start with,
  and the one that many new moms prefer. The most common exceptions are new moms who have just had cesarean sections and find, for
  obvious reasons, that they want to avoid having their newborns pressing
  on their bellies. While sitting up (preferably with lots of comfy pillows
  and good back support in place), you simply lay your baby across your
  lap sideways so that she is facing you with her head in line with your
  breast. In the typical cradle hold, you will use your right arm to support
  your baby's head and body while she nurses on your right breast (her
  head resting in the crook of your right arm with your hand supporting
  her bottom), and then your left arm for support while she is nursing
  on your left breast. To help ease the strain on your back, shoulders, and
  neck, try putting a regular or specially designed breastfeeding pillow or
  two across your lap to help raise your baby up to the level of your breast.
  And while you may be content with cradling your baby in your arm(s)

as she nurses, trust us when we tell you that a few well-positioned pillows placed under your arms can work wonders and spare you some unnecessary aches and pains. As you get into the finer points of positioning, you also can try what is referred to by breastfeeding experts as the cross-cradle hold. With your baby lying across your lap ready to nurse on your left breast, you can use your right arm instead of your left, as in the typical cradle hold, to support your baby's head and body. For either type of cradle hold, whichever arm you are not using to support your baby's head and body is free to help position your baby's mouth onto your nipple.

- **Football hold.** To position yourself for breastfeeding using the so-called football hold, some parenting books suggest you picture a football player holding a football under his arm as he runs downfield. We're willing to bet that conjuring up this mental image just won't be enough to help many of you avoid some unnecessary roughness or fumbling. As you sit down and try to replicate the position with your baby, here's an explanation we hope you will find more practical. Unlike the cradle hold, where your baby lies across your lap, the football hold involves laying your baby to one side of you or the other. If you're going to start nursing on your right breast, position your baby so that her face is level with your breast while her body rests against your right side. You can then use your right arm to support her body. Well-placed pillows under your baby—this time placed along your side instead of across your lap as in the cradle hold— can really take a lot of strain off your supporting arm, shoulder, and neck. Quite honestly, we're not sure how many moms actually prefer this hold. We ourselves never had much success scoring touchdowns with it, but for your purposes all that really matters is that it works well for some moms and not so well for others, so feel free to try it out for yourself.

- **Side-by-side or lying down.** In this position, you and your baby lie down facing each other, with your baby's mouth in line with your breast. You'll probably find yourself using your lower arm to support your own head, leaving your upper arm to help adjust your baby (and/or breast) as needed. While most women seem to prefer nursing from their lower breast (ie, when lying on the right side, they offer their right breast), there are no hard-and-fast rules. If you find yourself recovering from a cesarean section, or even if you're just plain exhausted and don't feel like sitting up, you may decide this is a great way to nurse with less effort— especially once you get the hang of it.

Breathing Room

Regardless of what breastfeeding hold works best for you, a couple of simple "rules" apply to all positions. Once you've brought your baby to your breast, make a point of allowing him to move his head as needed instead of holding it firmly against your breast. Yes, his head needs support, but you can relax your hold (and yourself) a bit once your baby has latched on and is nursing, allowing him to adjust himself whenever necessary. You can also help make sure he has adequate room to breathe at all times by making sure at least one nostril is visible and not completely covered by your breast.

 WHAT'S FOR DINNER

Your breasts are likely to start producing colostrum even before your baby is born—as early as the second trimester. Colostrum provides most newborns with everything they need for the first several days of life. By the end of the first week, if not sooner, your body should begin to make a larger volume of milk that is less yellow and more watery—known as "transitional" milk. This milk is definitely more likely to satisfy your baby's hunger and help him settle into somewhat of a more predictable pattern of feeding. How you choose to approach the waiting period until its arrival is up to you, but we suggest you put a positive slant on things and view your colostrum-producing breasts as half full, rather than half empty.

Catching On to Latching On

Anyone who's ever breastfed can tell you that there's a big difference between getting babies to latch on and getting them to latch on *correctly*. For nursing mothers everywhere this can mean the difference between smooth sailing and choppy waters, as defined by sore, cracked, or even blistered nipples. For babies it can mean the difference between actually getting some milk in return for their efforts and the equivalent of sucking on the closed end of a straw. To nurse effectively, babies need to use their tongues to essentially lap or massage milk out of the breast. This requires that the tongue be positioned under the breast in such a way that the baby can draw the nipple *and* the darker colored area around it (the areola) into her mouth as she sucks. If your baby starts out nursing by simply pursing her lips around your nipple and sucking away, you'll very quickly realize 2 important facts: The harder she sucks the less likely she is to get anything, and the more likely your nipples are to suffer the consequences.

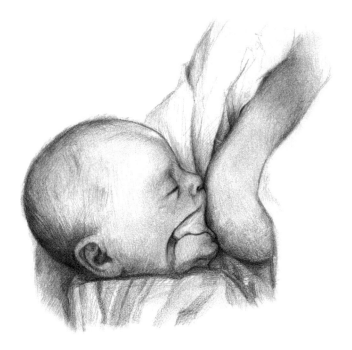

Lending a Helping Hand

With any luck you will find that there is at least one nurse or other health professional present in the delivery room or available on the mother-baby floor of your hospital who is skilled at assisting new mothers with getting newborns to latch on correctly. Even if there's not, you can play an active role and facilitate.

- **Expressing interest.** Gently expressing a few drops of breast milk onto and around your nipple can help your baby hone in on his intended target.
- **Rooting for success.** If your baby still doesn't seem interested in opening his mouth, try lightly stroking his cheek just to the side of his mouth to stimulate what's known as the rooting reflex—a reflex that should cause him to open his mouth in search of your nipple.

- **Open wide.** If he doesn't open his mouth wide enough, you can gently help him open it further by pushing down on his chin.
- **If at first you don't succeed.** By all means, if he doesn't get it right the first time, don't be fooled into thinking that any latching on is better than none. If it seems that your baby's mouth didn't open wide enough to assume the necessary position on your breast, he seems to have only gotten your nipple in his mouth, or it continues to hurt when he sucks, then don't hesitate to take him off and encourage him to try again.
- **Don't get tongue-tied.** Be aware that some babies are born with their tongues a bit tethered. This is caused when the piece of tissue under the tongue limits the tongue's ability to stick out and move around freely (a condition known as ankyloglossia). Given that the tongue plays a very important role in latching on and breastfeeding, be sure to double-check that your baby isn't a bit tongue-tied if he continues to have difficulty, since a simple procedure to release the tethered tongue can sometimes make a difference in breastfeeding success (see "Tongue Tied" on page 287).

 GOING FOR THE GUSTO

Newborns have been shown to have an amazing and inborn drive to nurse. In one study, newborns actually demonstrated their impressive ability to inch their way up from their mothers' bellies all the way to their breasts in search of food within mere minutes of being born. Given that this is a book about practicality, however, we don't suggest you sit around waiting for your own newborn to propel herself up to your breasts before offering her the opportunity to breastfeed.

Getting It Right

We are well aware of the fact that telling you to take your baby off your breast and getting him to try again until he gets it right is sometimes easier said than done. For lack of a better analogy, many infants are like leeches when it comes to latching on. Once they're on, they're on tight and holding on for dear life. Getting them to let go by attempting to pull them off is therefore a misguided and potentially painful prospect, but there is a relatively easy solution (that does not involve the use of the salt or matches commonly recommended for leech removal). Before removing your baby from your breast, gently slide one finger into his mouth to break the seal of his lips around your nipple. Once the seal is broken, you'll find it much quicker, easier, and less painful to take him off and have him start over again. You can also use this technique whenever you need to interrupt or end a feeding. While it's true that most babies don't like being taken off the breast in the middle or even the start of a feeding, this can actually work in your favor. If your baby subsequently cries in disapproval, he's all but guaranteed to open his mouth wider, increasing the likelihood that he'll latch on correctly on his next attempt.

 ## NOT ALL NIPPLES OR BREASTS ARE CREATED EQUAL

To get straight to the point, nipples come in all shapes and sizes, as do breasts themselves. That said, new and expectant moms often wonder whether flat or inverted nipples or a past history of breast surgery will impact their ability to breastfeed. The good news: As long as a baby can latch on enough to get a good portion of the breast into his mouth (which may take a little extra assistance and/or consultation), most types of nipples don't inherently interfere with breastfeeding success. As for women who have had any prior breast surgery, the underlying factor is going to be whether the milk ducts and/or major nerves were affected. The best way to find out? Ask the surgeon who performed the surgery.

Breastfeeding Irritations

During the first days and weeks of breastfeeding, it's entirely normal for mothers to experience a certain degree of irritation as their nipples grow accustomed to repeated sucking and stimulation. How then, you might wonder, are you supposed to know the difference between the discomfort associated with starting out anew and the pain and irritation that result when a baby doesn't latch on correctly? Beyond paying close attention to how your baby latches on, try also to figure out whether the irritation tends to subside as your baby gets into a rhythm of sucking. Mild irritation or discomfort that occurs only at the start of each feeding is generally associated with the newness of nursing. As you and your nipples toughen up over the days and weeks to follow, you're likely to find that this type of irritation quickly fades away (thank goodness!). Nipple pain that persists or gets worse as your baby nurses, on the other hand, is more likely to be a sign that she is not latched on correctly, and is often accompanied by cracked or blistered nipples—the thought of which is enough to make anyone (especially breastfeeding moms) cringe.

Nurturing Your Nipples

In the spirit of being honest and preparing you for what may lie ahead, the bad news is that cracked or even blistered nipples can appear after even just one nursing session gone wrong. The good news, however, is that nipples do heal. With the proper care, patience, and a little extra attention, they can get better within a matter of days. Given that this never seems fast enough to those of us who've experienced such nipple insults firsthand, here are some temporizing measures you can try if you happen to find yourself with sore, dry, cracked, or blistered nipples.

- **Hang in there.** Pain and misery is not what breastfeeding is ultimately all about. As the saying goes, "This too shall pass."
- **Latch assessment.** First and foremost, readdress how your baby is latching on. Sometimes, rather than having your baby latch straight onto your nipple like a target, you may find more success by using what's called an "asymmetric" latch, where your baby's mouth centers more on the lower part of your areola.
- **The lesser of 2 evils.** If one breast feels any less sore than the other, then by all means go with the lesser of 2 evils and offer that one to your baby first because babies tend to suck harder when they first start nursing.
- **Smooth things out.** Consider the use of specially designed nontoxic creams such as lanolin (available in most stores that sell baby products) after breastfeeding or even use a little dab of your own breast milk on your breasts, then expose them to open air.
- **Bare yourself if need be.** If the pain doesn't start to resolve despite your best efforts or if you have any questions, you should seek professional help sooner rather than later—as in within a day or so at most—to get things back on the right track. This should be from someone accustomed to offering breastfeeding advice and ideally someone that you are comfortable baring your nipples to, if need be.

- **Options are out there.** It's well worth remembering that there are many more options, techniques, and tricks of the trade available to nursing mothers who find themselves sore, frustrated, and with seemingly uncooperative breasts. They include, but are not limited to, pumping, breast shields, and supplemental nursing systems. In other words, be sure to see your local lactation consultant if you think that any of these additional options might help ensure your breastfeeding success.

WHAT'S BEHIND BURNING NIPPLES

If you happen to experience nipple irritation that is better described as a tingling, burning sensation, then a yeast infection may be to blame. Yes, yeast like moist areas and don't discriminate between your baby's mouth (see "Thrush Attack" on page 286), rear end (see "Diaper Rashes" on page 130), and your nipples. Letting your nipples air-dry before stuffing them back in your bra or under moist breast pads can help lessen your chances, but once yeast have taken up residence on your nipple(s), you'll want to discuss appropriate yeast-fighting measures with your doctor. Sometimes all it takes is a little appropriately applied medication—on your nipples and in your baby's mouth—to clear things up and get your nipples on the fast track to full recovery.

Cramping

While you may have heard plenty of tales of sore breasts and nipples from others who have ventured to breastfeed before you, they may have forgotten to forewarn you about the associated cramping (of the uterus) that some new mothers experience during the early days of breastfeeding. By this point in the chapter you may be asking yourself if the fun ever stops, but trust us when we say that breastfeeding isn't all about enduring pain. It's just that when you sit down to breastfeed, your uterus is likely to cramp (described by some as resembling a contraction) in response because the signal that is known to cause contractions is the same one responsible for triggering the milk let-down reflex (see page 23). So while the cramping itself isn't exactly pleasant, you can look at it in a different light and consider it a good sign that your baby is latching on correctly and sending your body all the right signals. In fact, this dual response also plays a significant role in helping your body recover more quickly from pregnancy and childbirth—decreasing the likelihood of uterine bleeding and shortening the amount of time it takes your uterus to shrink back down to its normal size.

Going With the Flow

A Simple Matter of Supply and Demand

Once the latching-on part of breastfeeding is squared away, many parents find themselves worrying about whether their newborn babies are getting enough to eat. If you want to know the truth, in many ways the answer is no. Now let us clarify. Yes, your baby will be getting enough to live on until your full volume of milk comes in, but what he is getting is a relatively small volume of a milky, yellowish-white substance called *colostrum*. While colostrum is rich in protein, it is lacking in fats, sugar, and overall calories, as well as sheer volume. The fact that a new mother's body comes equipped with colostrum makes perfect sense in the grand scheme of things. Nature has made it so that newborns get just enough nutrients to get them through the first few days, but at the same time leaves them hungry soon after each feeding. This causes them to want to nurse more frequently, thus helping to ensure that their mothers' milk production will increase in response. During your first few days of breastfeeding—and for as long as you continue to nurse your baby—the more he nurses, the more your body will sense his increased demand and respond by stepping up the milk production, thus increasing your supply of breast milk accordingly.

 SIZE MATTERS

You may be relieved to know that breast size doesn't really matter when it comes to milk production, as it is not proportional to breast size. While everyone's bustline tends to expand during pregnancy in preparation for breastfeeding, rest assured that when it comes to breastfeeding success, mothers who barely fill their A-cups can rival their D-cup colleagues.

The Turning Point: How Will I Know When My Milk Comes In?

You may think that knowing when your milk has "come in" is another one of those "you can't relate until you experience it yourself" scenarios, but chances are good that when your breasts have gotten the message and respond by making larger volumes of milk, it probably won't be an occurrence that goes unnoticed. We can think of no clearer way to describe it than how my (Laura's) husband put it the day my milk came in. He matter-of-factly said, "Wow! You definitely did not have those when I married you." In other words, one's milk coming in is more often than not accompanied by a not so subtle change in breast size.

Some new mothers find that the change from producing colostrum to transitional milk takes place over a couple of hours. For others, the course of change is spread out over a day or two. In either case, most moms experience a noticeable increase in breast size accompanied by a feeling of fullness. That said, new moms can sometimes be deceived into thinking that they're producing enough milk before their breasts actually get the hang of it. If you don't experience a reassuringly noticeable change, or if there is even any question in your mind as to whether your milk has started to flow and your newborn is getting enough—especially during these early days and weeks—take your questions or concerns to your baby's doctor without delay.

Progressive Production

The changeover from colostrum to transitional and then mature milk is an important one. It gives you and your baby's doctor reassurance that all is going well. Because the actual transition is not always so clear-cut, as some women notice very little change in their breasts as their milk supply increases, it is useful to be aware of several other clues that can help you figure out that everything is moving ahead as planned. They include

- Your breast milk is white instead of yellow in color and appears thinner or clearer.
- Your baby makes more obvious gulping and swallowing noises when nursing.
- Your baby begins to pee and poop much more frequently (see "What Goes In Must Come Out" on page 61).

- Your baby no longer is losing weight or just holding steady, but instead has begun to gain weight relatively noticeably both on and off the scale (see "Weighing In" on page 30).

The Let-Down Tingle

While the sensation that typically accompanies let-down isn't exactly the same for everyone, and for that matter isn't present at all for some breast-feeding moms, most women do experience what is often described as a tingling, a prickling, or even an electrical-like feeling in their breasts. Such sensations at the start of a feeding are helpful but not necessary in signifying that your milk has started to flow. As an aside, you may find (if you haven't already) that there are plenty of other potential triggers of milk let-down besides just a latched-on baby at your breast—including but not limited to the sound of a crying baby (yours or someone else's), a breast pump, nipple stimulation, sexual arousal, a warm shower or, on occasion, nothing at all.

 GETTING THE GOOD TIMES TO ROLL

New mothers who breastfeed typically experience a clear increase in milk production, commonly referred to as having their milk come in, anywhere from 2 to 5 days after the birth of their babies (usually on the later side for moms who've had a c-section). How well you keep up with your fluid intake, your baby's ability to latch on correctly, how often you are able to nurse in the first few days, and many other factors can all play a role in the timing of this much anticipated turning point. This is a major reason why your pediatrician will want you to come in for a follow-up new-baby check within 24 to 48 hours after you leave the hospital. If your milk supply hasn't come in yet or you're unsure as to whether it has, your doctor will be able to evaluate your baby and offer reassurance or additional assistance to get your milk supply going.

Alleviating the Discomfort of Engorgement

For some of you, "fullness from breast milk" will be a purely euphemistic way of describing engorgement, a word familiar to many new breastfeeding moms and defined as being filled to the often painful point of capacity or congestion. Yes, your body may well have some work to do in the first days and weeks of breastfeeding before your breasts learn to control how much milk they make and spare you the discomfort of over-distension. Until your milk production matches your baby's needs—your breasts making as much as she needs, when she needs it, without going overboard—you may find yourself in some uncomfortable positions. Fortunately, there are things you can do about engorgement.

The 2 mainstays of managing engorgement are to wear a supportive bra (as sort of a "push-back" measure to decrease milk production) and to express a little milk whenever necessary to relieve the pain. When it comes to the latter, be sure to think about the concept of supply and demand we mentioned earlier before expressing a lot of milk; you'll find that there's a fine line between expressing enough breast milk to relieve the pain and expressing so much that you give your body the unintended message to produce even more. Using a warm compress or taking a warm shower and then expressing a little milk, as well as feeding your baby a bit more frequently, all may help relieve your symptoms.

 MASTITIS

If you are a breastfeeding mom, it's going to be well worth your time to be on the lookout for mastitis. In mastitis, bacteria infect the breast ducts that store milk, resulting in painful, red, swollen breasts. Be forewarned that mastitis has a way of sneaking up on nursing mothers. That's because the more obvious signs of breast infection may not be obvious until a day or two after you start to feel achy, sick, and/or feverish. As long as you're familiar with mastitis, you stand a fighting chance of noticing it early on, getting the necessary medical advice, and getting treated with antibiotics sooner rather than later.

It's Not Worth Crying Over Spilt Milk

Having also experienced leaky breasts firsthand, we readily admit that they all too often come with the territory as your body adapts to breastfeeding. While they may represent a mild nuisance for some, they can be a source of considerable frustration and great embarrassment to others. It's not clear why some women's bodies seem to have better control of their milk flow than others—experiencing only minimal leakage limited to the few days after milk comes in instead of a more pervasive problem that can last for weeks (or even months) into the course of breastfeeding. If nothing else, we can offer you some words of advice and encouragement that we hope will help you take this potential fact of breastfeeding life in stride.

- **The power of perspective.** You may hear an occasional account of someone whose breasts never quite contained themselves and proceeded to leak the entire time she breastfed. Statistically speaking, your own chances of "recovery" are actually quite good. Any leakage you may experience at the outset will most likely subside or even resolve completely over time. And just because you leak a lot with your first baby doesn't mean that you are destined to leak a lot with every subsequent child. OK, so it may not be that much of a consolation this time around, but at least there's light at the end of the next tunnel!

- **Breast pads.** Breast pads are a very useful invention. Feel free to try out the thin cotton disposable ones if you have only minimal leakage, but head straight for the washable reusable (and generally more absorbent) type if the disposable ones don't do the trick. And for those of you whose breasts just haven't gotten the hang of holding on to the milk until your baby requests it, you wouldn't be the first to decide to stuff a burp cloth, hand towel, or even a clean cloth diaper in your bra to keep things under control while sleeping or lounging around in the privacy of your own home.

- **Provide back-pressure.** Back-pressure helps. If you start to leak (or are blessed with some advanced warning of impending leakage in the form of a let-down tingle), put pressure on your breasts to slow or stop the flow. When in public, you can subtly fold your arms across your chest and squeeze firmly. This gives new meaning to assuming an arms-crossed power pose.

- **Contain yourself.** Taking extra measures to contain yourself, so to speak, such as wearing a supportive bra during the time when you are nursing, is not only said to decrease your odds of being left with saggy breasts after your breastfeeding days are over, but doing so can also help to decrease the likelihood of engorgement and leakage. While it may not be a common topic of public discussion, believe us when we tell you that plenty of new moms (particularly those who are prone to leakage and/

or engorgement) take up the habit of wearing a bra 24/7 for as long as it takes for the flow to ebb.

If the Bra Fits...

As a general rule—even before pregnancy and breastfeeding are factored in—we firmly believe that splurging on comfortable bras and underwear is well worth whatever it costs you. You've probably already discovered that pregnancy is often responsible for increasing one's bust size, as is breast-feeding. By how much varies, but it's relatively safe to say that the bras that once fit you in your pre-pregnancy days are not going to be of much use for a while. With that in mind and the task of bra shopping at hand, we suggest you

- **Consider comfort and convenience.** Above all else, look for bras that offer comfort *and* convenience. After all, you'll be breastfeeding as many as 12 times a day, and this is a garment that you may well find yourself wearing 24 hours a day! You'll have enough going on with your breasts that the last thing you'll need is to add another potential source of discomfort or irritation.

- **Expect expansion.** Expect that you'll keep expanding until your milk supply comes in. While you may have already invested in some new, bigger bras during your pregnancy, you may find that your cup size "runneth over" as you start breastfeeding, thus requiring yet larger bras to accommodate.

- **Evaluate for ease of use.** Nursing bras nowadays come with all sorts of modern-day conveniences—not the least of which are flaps that can be opened on each cup to allow easy and more discreet access. Be sure to try on a couple to see not only if they are comfortable and fit well, but also if the flaps are easy to fasten and unfasten.

- **Go with what works.** Regular bras are also an option. Some women find that wearing a regular bra and simply pulling the shoulder strap (and therefore the cup) down or partially opening a front-fastening bra is as easy as wearing a true nursing bra, not to mention less expensive and in some cases more comfortable.

BIG GIRLS _DO_ CRY

On a more serious note, many a new mother has cried over spilt milk, as well as the absence of milk, an inadequate milk supply, or just about anything else to do with breastfeeding or new parenthood. The fact of the matter is that "the baby blues" and postpartum depression are very real (and can, in fact, affect both new mothers _and_ fathers). While it's perfectly OK for "big girls" to cry too, if you find yourself frequently frustrated; more teary than usual; or feeling persistently sad, anxious, overwhelmed, or more moody, be sure to talk to your doctor about your feelings right away.

How Much Is Enough? How Much Is Too Much?

Unlike their formula-feeding counterparts who are able to rely on the ounce-by-ounce markings displayed on the sides of their babies' bottles, breastfeeding parents typically have questions and concerns about exactly how much breast milk their newborns are getting, and whether it is enough.

To address this understandable but often unnecessary concern, it's helpful to first distinguish between the several days _before_ your milk comes in and the period _after_ this turning point. As we've already discussed, the 2- to 5-day period preceding your milk coming in is inherently going to be a different breastfeeding experience—for you and your baby—than what you should expect as soon as the tide has come in, so to speak. By breastfeeding as often as you can during the first few days, without letting yourself become _too_ irritated or sore, you can help ensure that your baby doesn't become dehydrated before your body reaches full milk production. Practically speaking, we recommend that you nurse more frequently during the day (at least every 2–3 hours, but more often if your baby is ready, willing, and able), while letting up a little at night (set your alarm for every 4–5 hours at the most if your baby will sleep that long). If your baby is jaundiced (see "Seeing Yellow: Jaundice" on page 313) or you suspect he may be getting dehydrated, you'll definitely want to have him checked out, as well as discuss specific feeding recommendations and expectations with your baby's doctor.

Settling Into a Routine

Once your milk supply comes in, be prepared to enter into a new phase of nursing that more closely resembles the mental image many new parents have about breastfeeding—one that includes frequent feedings accompanied by lots of wet diapers and soft if not outright liquidy poop (more on that subject in "What Goes In Must Come Out" on page 61). What you should not expect, however, is that you and your baby will gracefully fall into a predictable routine defined by a set feeding schedule. Even after the first week or two, you may still find that there are days when your baby wants to nurse every hour or two—a pattern that often signals a growth spurt (see "Growth Spurts" on page 55). At other times she may sleep her way through 4 or more hours and still show no signs of waking up to eat. These considerations are what make the strictly defined patterns of feeding touted in some parenting books so unrealistic. That said, a somewhat predictable feeding schedule would not be misguided unless you try to get your baby to adhere to it without exception from day 1. Overall, it is reasonable to expect to feed your baby at least every 2 to 3 hours as a baseline, with the goal of one longer stretch of 4 or more hours (preferably at night) within a few weeks. Remember that this is a work in progress over the next several weeks or possibly months.

Breastfeeding on the Go

While a handful of new moms seem to be as comfortable baring all on a bench in the middle of a mall, in the center seat on an airplane, or at the home of a friend as she is in the privacy of her own home, there's nothing wrong or prudish about you if you aren't ready to tackle breastfeeding in public—now or ever. It's all about your own comfort level. There's certainly a sense of liberation that comes with learning some of the tricks of the trade that will ultimately allow you to breastfeed discreetly in public places (some of which we will be sharing with you elsewhere in this book), but unless you're ready, don't worry about mastering it now. For many mothers, this is but one of the many differences between the first and subsequent children.

EXTREME BREASTFEEDING

As a point of interest and caution, there are occasionally those women who give the phrase "breastfeeding on the go" new meaning— such as the woman who once made national news for breastfeeding her 7-month-old while driving more than 60 mph on the Ohio turnpike. Even if there is apparently no shortage of loopholes in the law when it comes to extreme breastfeeding, we certainly hope that those of you who are already comfortable with the whole "baring your breast for the sake of breastfeeding" routine don't decide to engage in such risky acts in the name of good nutrition.

Breastfeeding by Numbers

The following are some handy definitions and rules of thumb to use when establishing your own approach to a breastfeeding routine:

- **Feeding intervals.** If you haven't started breastfeeding yet, it's probably hard to imagine how this can be a source of confusion. The issue at hand has to do with the starting point—whether to use the *start* of a feeding or the time at which your baby actually *finishes* the meal to determine when it's time to feed again. The pokier your newborn is at nursing— with some babies taking upwards of an hour to actually complete a feeding—the more this subject will apply to you. The standard convention is to use the time from the start of the first feeding to the start of the next. And yes, this may well mean starting a second feeding within an hour or two of finishing the previous one. What this means in real life: If you are attempting to make sure your baby eats at least every 2 to 3 hours and he starts nursing at 10:00 am, has to be woken up several times along the way, "requests" a diaper change at 10:30 am, and requires your active encouragement to latch back on to the second breast before finishing at around 11:00 am, you may still be looking at sitting down for another feeding no later than noon or 1:00 pm. While there are certainly new moms who have confided in us that this schedule can feel like a life sentence, you can take great comfort in knowing that it is likely to last no more than the first few weeks of your breastfeeding experience.

- **Breastfeeding frequency.** The most commonly recommended schedule for newborn breastfeeding is every 2 to 3 hours, which translates into a minimum of 8 to 12 feedings during any given 24-hour period. The reason it's so important for you to focus on fitting in this many feedings a day is to make sure that your baby is getting enough to eat to avoid dehydration and gain weight. Newborns who are still waiting for their mothers' milk supply to come in or those who are slow to catch on, latch on, or nurse even after milk is made abundantly available to them may end up having less energy and becoming increasingly more interested in sleeping. When newborns start to go longer periods between feedings—especially when they have yet to establish themselves as good eaters and regain their birth weight—they run the risk of getting even less to eat, becoming even more fatigued, and a vicious cycle can ensue. It is this cycle that you should be aware of, and which you are working so tirelessly to avoid with all of your round-the-clock feedings.

 SKIPPING MEALS

Conventional wisdom tells us it's not a nutritionally great idea for us to skip meals. When a newborn decides to do so 2 or more "meals" in a row for any reason—whether out of disinterest, lethargy, or difficulty feeding—you need to take heed and consult your baby's doctor without hesitation to find out why.

- **Weighing in.** You will find that just about everyone tends to focus on how much babies weigh in the days and weeks after they are born. That's because it gives us a measurable, objective way of determining if babies are getting enough to eat. Newborns are expected to lose 7% to 10% of their birth weight in the week or two after birth (mostly in the form of water weight). A useful rough rule of thumb is that they should gain it back and at least return to their birth weight by 2 weeks of age. With that in mind, if you find that your baby goes in for his 2-week checkup and comes out weighing well over his birth weight, then you can take it as a reassurance that breastfeeding is going well. On the other hand, if you have concerns that your newborn isn't gaining weight or is continuing to lose weight, don't wait for the routine 2-week check to consult with your pediatrician. It is absolutely no reflection on you or your success at your first attempts at parenthood if you end up on the phone with your doctor's office several times in the first week or two of your parenting journey. After all, that's what they're there for!

One Breast or Two

The often-debated question of whether it is better to breastfeed a baby on one or both breasts at each feeding does not, in fact, have a single right answer. Some experts in the field recommend one—allowing babies to drain the breast fully and therefore get to the "dessert equivalent" of breast milk (known as hind milk), which has been shown to be richer in the fat babies need to grow and develop. Others recommend the double-breasted approach—noting that 15 minutes of nursing on each side typically drains most of a breast's total milk volume and offers the more practical benefit of preventing women from becoming "lopsided" after each feeding. Some women choose to drain the first breast fully to be sure their baby gets the hind milk and then nurse as long as possible on the second. From a practical standpoint, we've found that it is reasonable to go either way.

- If your baby is a poky eater who can hardly be woken up to tackle the second breast after nursing from the first—especially if she happens to have a hard time latching on, is finicky, or rebels whenever you attempt to take her off the first and switch her to the second—well then the "one breast per feeding" approach may better suit your needs. Just remember to keep track of which side your baby last nursed on and then alternate breasts at each feeding. This routine may require you to actually write down which breast your baby fed from last, because many a new mother has found that her memory isn't quite what it used to be before being in a chronic state of sleep deprivation. Or simply put an extra breast pad on the side you need to nurse on first or a bracelet on your wrist as an easy reminder of which side to start on the next time.

- If, however, you find that your baby is content to switch from one side to the other during the course of a feeding, or if you find that your "neglected" breast becomes uncomfortably engorged when you alternate—then you may decide to settle into the 2-breast routine. Depending on how your baby acts at any given time of day, you may just want to follow her lead and try to keep each side as even as possible. As we mentioned earlier, this is more of a consideration when it comes to engorgement, leaking, and milk production in the first couple weeks of breastfeeding than it is down the road.

When all is said and done, your body will learn to accommodate whatever pattern you and your baby settle into, and you will have more flexibility in deviating from your standard routine.

Falling Into Bad Habits?

Even though you may be a relative newcomer to the world of parenthood, you've nonetheless probably already been warned not to let your baby use your breasts as a pacifier or a snack bar, not to let him fall asleep while nursing lest he become dependent on doing so for months if not years to come, and to try to get him onto a set feeding schedule as soon as you can. Well, here's news that will make your life easier: These warnings and recommendations don't apply to you during the first several weeks of your baby's life. Spoiling is not and should not be a concern at this stage. In fact, resisting the urge to follow the scheduled approach to feeding, especially early on, and instead offering your baby the opportunity to nurse frequently now can actually help establish breastfeeding in such a way as to ensure future success. Once you and your baby have gotten comfortable and settled into the whole breastfeeding routine, you can more appropriately consider your options when it comes to feeding schedules and nursing as a pacifier substitute if you so choose. And let us just add, for those of you who may have already read other parenting books, that trying to keep a *newborn* from falling asleep while nursing is, in our experience, nothing short of an exercise in futility. All of these things will come in time, but you don't need to worry about them for several weeks.

The Confusion About Nipple Confusion

A good deal of attention seems to be paid to the notion that babies who are in the process of learning to breastfeed can sometimes be led astray by the introduction of any sort of artificial sucking device—whether it's in the form of a nipple on a bottle or a pacifier. Again, even the experts seem to be divided when it comes to supplementing with a bottle or offering pacifiers to breastfed babies. We have found that it is entirely feasible to do either or both without sabotaging your chances for breastfeeding success if you understand a few simple concepts and follow a few basic rules.

As we said before, your baby's mouth is and will continue to be the center of her universe. Quite simply, babies naturally want to suck—and some more than others. In the first days and weeks of life, this urge to suck certainly can work to everyone's advantage in speeding up a nursing mother's milk production, but once the milk is in and breastfeeding is well established, some new mothers find themselves in the challenging and sometimes uncomfortable position of having a baby who *constantly* wants to suck (or so it seems). That's because for some babies, sucking is not just about getting fed. This additional interest is referred to as nonnutritive sucking and is the reason why pacifiers (or fingers) can and often do come in handy in consoling a fussy baby. While there's nothing inherently wrong with letting your young infant nurse long after your breasts are drained and in between feedings (unless it is causing you undue pain), it is perfectly acceptable to use a pacifier instead (see also "Practical Pacifier Principles" on page 58). It may help to limit the pacifier use to those times when your baby really wants it and when she's falling asleep instead of offering it to her all the time. Be sure to talk to your baby's doctor if you have more questions about the use of pacifiers.

Nipple Confusion Defined

The problem that some experts have with artificial nipples is that they have the potential to confuse a baby who is being breastfed. During the time when a baby is learning to breastfeed, sucking on the nipple of a bottle to get milk is thought to be considerably easier than the effort required to effectively lap milk out of a breast. The concern, therefore, is that babies not yet fully accomplished at breastfeeding may opt for the "easy way out," or become confused about the necessary way to suck when returning from bottle to breast. Although pacifiers aren't responsible for supplying an alternate source of milk, they too require a baby to suck differently than he would on his mother's breast. That said, we have found that most breastfed babies do just fine with the introduction of a bottle and/or pacifier if their parents wait long enough to introduce it. How long is long enough? The practical answer is: long enough to let your baby get the gist of breastfeeding first, but not so long that he will accept no substitute. There's definitely a fine line between long enough and too long. While the exact timing is debated, somewhere in the vicinity of 2 to 6 weeks is generally accepted as a perfectly reasonable time to introduce an artificial nipple onto the sucking scene. If your baby is latching on, nursing, peeing, pooping, and gaining weight well, then we have found that many babies can successfully take a pacifier even within the first week without it interfering.

Supplementing Scenarios

The decision to give a breastfed baby additional breast milk or formula from a bottle—better known as supplementing—may be strictly a matter of choice and convenience for some mothers, but born out of nutritional necessity for others. In reality, something as simple as needing to get a single stretch of sleep longer than 3 hours in the course of several tiring weeks motivates some exhausted new and experienced moms to supplement. Other motivating circumstances typically include babies who have latching and/or feeding problems and are getting dehydrated and/or jaundiced, and mothers who are struggling to increase their milk supply or have physical/medical limitations or work responsibilities that impact their ability to breastfeed. In any of the previous scenarios, supplementing is an acceptable option. Tempting though it may be, we do want to make sure that those of you who are struggling to breastfeed and beginning to question your abilities don't find yourself reaching for a bottle for lack of perceived alternatives. Instead, we urge you to enlist the help of your pediatrician or a local lactation consultant and explore all of your breastfeeding options first.

Into the Mouths of Moms

In addition to potentially finding yourself thirstier and with an increased appetite once you enter the milk production business, you may also find yourself the recipient of a whole lot of advice about exactly what you should and shouldn't be eating and drinking—all given in the best interest of your milk. We've found that most moms who are new to breastfeeding, however, benefit a great deal from a little practical perspective on this subject.

- **The scoop on eating for 2.** Some breastfeeding moms figure they can eat just about anything they want. Others become overly focused on quickly regaining their figures and set out to diet. As a breastfeed-

PUMP IT UP

With only occasional exception, it's technically never too soon to start pumping your milk and building up a stockpile for present or future use. Pumping can help stimulate a new mom's milk supply to come in, increase her milk production, or relieve engorgement once the supply has been established. That said, adding pumping into the already rigorous newborn feeding schedule can be quite challenging and a whole lot of extra work. Unless you are eager to get started, used to pumping, or need to pump out of necessity, we suggest waiting until you are comfortable with nursing and your milk supply is well established. If you plan to pump infrequently, you may get by with a manual pump (or even manual expression). For anything more frequent, we highly recommend an electric version. Let us also mention that there are some women (Jennifer included) who have little luck with pumping (much less manual expression) and are perfectly content to supplement their nursing with a bottle of formula when deemed necessary and/or convenient. For all of you who are met with pumping success, you'll want to make note of the following breast milk storage recommendations:

- Breast milk can remain in room temperature for up to 6 hours, the refrigerator for 3 to 5 days, and in the freezer for about 3 months.
- Frozen breast milk that is thawed in the refrigerator is safe to use for up to 24 hours, whereas breast milk thawed in warm water should be used within 4 hours.
- Once thawed, stored breast milk should not be refrozen.

ing mother, you are certainly entitled to take advantage of eating for 2. However, just as in pregnancy, breastfeeding should not serve as an open invitation to let your cravings run wild. Rather than doubling how much you eat and overindulging in desserts and empty calories with little nutritional value, it is perhaps more prudent to increase your daily caloric intake by 25% (in some cases even more) and try to eat a relatively well-rounded diet while nursing.

- **The good, the bad, and the spicy.** Given that much of what a nursing mother eats or drinks has the potential to ultimately end up in her breast milk, you might be convinced that you are in for many months of a bland diet. You may be relieved to know then that most breastfed babies happily tolerate a lot more variety than you'd think—even if your favorite foods include garlic, onions, cabbage, broccoli, or the like. Unless you have a strong family history of certain food allergies or can pinpoint a particular food that seems to upset your baby, there's no need to take the spice out of your life—or your food.

- **Staying well hydrated.** While there is no truth to the old wives' tale that you need to drink milk to make milk, drinking plenty of liquids and staying well hydrated can definitely help keep things flowing. Some moms actually experience strong pangs of thirst associated with milk let-down each time they breastfeed—conveniently ensuring that they remember to take time to drink. Even if you don't, use your nursing times as reminders to make sure you take time to drink and stay well hydrated.

Medications

Regardless of whether you are going to be taking herbal remedies or prescription, over-the-counter, or homeopathic medicine(s), it's safest to assume that any medication you take may affect your breast milk and harm your baby (or decrease your milk supply), so always check with your doctor first. In reality, some medications don't find their way into the breast milk at all and some do but are perfectly safe and have little or no effect on nursing babies.

INDULGENCES AND VICES

Caffeine. If you didn't already quit caffeine cold turkey when you were pregnant—or you did but now can't wait to welcome caffeine back into your life—you may be relieved to know that breastfeeding and enjoying a little caffeine every now and then aren't mutually exclusive. In fact, La Leche League International reports that up to 3 cups of caffeine-containing beverages per day pose no inherent harm to nursing mothers or babies. That said, if you notice your baby is irritable or fussy, you might want to try decreasing or gradually eliminating your caffeine intake.

Cigarettes. If you were able to quit smoking during your pregnancy, then congratulations—now is most definitely not a good time to restart. And if you didn't attempt or manage to quit before—now is as good a time as any (if not better) to succeed, for your baby's health and your own. While you undoubtedly know that smoking cigarettes isn't good for you to begin with, it may still come as a surprise to some of you that doing so while breastfeeding allows chemicals to pass into breast milk and cause dangerous side effects. Secondhand smoke increases your baby's risk of infections, asthma, and sudden infant death syndrome. If you do choose to smoke, the American Academy of Pediatrics (AAP) recommends only doing so right after you finish nursing your baby, limiting yourself to a few cigarettes per day, and never smoking around your baby or even in your house or car.

Alcohol. Breastfeeding legend suggests that drinking alcohol increases a nursing mother's milk supply. According to the AAP *New Mother's Guide to Breastfeeding* book, "Contrary to popular myth, drinking beer does not increase your milk supply." What we do know for sure is that alcohol, if consumed in large amounts by pregnant or breastfeeding mothers, can harm babies, not to mention significantly impair their mothers' ability to care for them. If you choose to have an occasional drink of alcohol, it is best to do so right after you finish breastfeeding, knowing that it will show up in your breast milk soon thereafter (within 30–90 minutes) and will likely be cleared within 2 hours. You can either wait the 2 hours it typically takes for alcohol levels in breast milk to drop before starting the next feeding, or decide to take the more purist approach and "pump and dump" the next feeding's worth of breast milk.

CHAPTER 2

formula for success

We admit it. In many ways, feeding your baby formula may seem much easier than breastfeeding, especially in the beginning weeks. After all, you don't have to worry about having enough of a supply, it's rather painless (if you don't count the sleep deprivation that comes with round-the-clock feeding), and it's easy to monitor your baby's intake. Granted, formula can be costly, you have to wash your supplies, and on occasion a baby will be finicky about which nipple and formula she is willing to accept, but at some point during their child's first year, most of today's parents end up using formula. With that in mind, we intend to give you a practical approach to formula, buying and cleaning bottles and nipples, and troubleshooting for newborns who don't seem to play by the rules.

Sifting Through the Formula Facts

In this day and age, all it takes is a casual glance down the formula aisle at the grocery store or baby super center to become overwhelmed by the number of customized formula options available to you and your baby—a little "ultra lipid powder" here, some "lactose-free concentrate" there—all marketed in the name of formula feeding without fussiness, gas, colic, spitting up, or causing other unwanted problems…. We therefore thought it might be useful to simplify the world of formula a bit and give you a quick overview. It's easiest to start by categorizing formula into the 3 most commonly used types: those that are cow's milk-based, those that are soy-based, and those that are specialized (such as lactose-free) or are partially or extensively hydrolyzed (sometimes called gentle, sensitive, or hypoallergenic and meaning that their components are broken down to be more easily digestible). Some parents choose soy formulas due to personal preference (such as to maintain a vegetarian-based diet for their infant).

A VERY BRIEF HISTORY OF FORMULA AS WE KNOW IT

In addition to being a prominent mainstay of modern-day parenthood, formula is very big business. Despite the many options that make their way to the grocery store shelves, there are only a handful of major manufacturers in the United States, all of whom must meet the same well-defined standards established by the US Food and Drug Administration. As you might imagine, a quick look back tells us that this was not always the case.

Mid-1800s: Most attempts to create a substitute for human milk before this time were met with disastrous results. Almost everyone stuck to breastfeeding.

1867: In the mid-19th century, researchers began to analyze breast milk in an attempt to create a reasonable substitute, and the first in today's formula lineage was introduced. A liquid containing wheat and malt flour was mixed with cow's milk, cooked with bicarbonate of potash, and billed as the "perfect infant food." We're not exactly sure what potash is or if this primitive formula was met with open mouths, but by the late 1800s, the foundation of modern-day formula had been laid and the marketing of artificial infant formula had begun.

1951: The first non-powder infant formula hit the shelves and rapidly became the most popular product available on the infant formula market.

1950s: The developed world fully embraced artificial infant formula, and it soon became the feeding method of choice.

There is no proof, however, that using a soy-based formula instead of a cow's milk one will prevent allergies or colic. While you may have heard a lot of talk about babies needing to be switched from one formula to the next, a majority of babies are started on cow's milk–based formulas and do just fine. In fact, most babies spend their entire formula-consuming careers drinking the same formula they were given on day 1. The fact that most babies do well with cow's milk– and soy-based formulas is financially fortunate because while these 2 types of formula tend to be comparable in price (with soy typically costing only pennies more per ounce, if that), the hydrolyzed formulas may be significantly more expensive (as in nearly twice as much). Thankfully, this category of formulas is generally reserved for babies who have significant reactions to cow's milk– or soy-based products (see "Tales of the Truly Intolerant" on page 42) and better tolerate the broken down easier-to-digest proteins found in hydrolyzed formulas.

 ## SWEET ON ORGANIC FORMULA?

With the word "organic" often perceived as synonymous with healthier, it came as no real surprise that organic baby formula was well received by many American parents after its introduction in 2006. What did come as a surprise to many health-conscious parents and pediatricians alike was the 2008 *New York Times* article that suggested the reason babies seemed to be so sweet on their organic fare was due to the leading brand of organic formula's use of cane sugar (sucrose), which is significantly sweeter than sugars used in other formulas.

Formula Intolerance

Some babies have a clear preference for one type or even brand of formula over another. Some prefer the smoothness of ready-to-feed formula to the consistency of prepared powder formula. Others demonstrate a penchant for cow's milk–based formula over soy-based (or vice versa). In many instances, preferences are subtle. For a handful of babies, however, the word "preference" can prove to be a bit of an understatement. In search of a formula cure for a lot of extra fussiness, gas, spitting up, or any number of other ways that babies reject certain types and voice their opinion, parents are prone to a fair bit of formula trial and error. The good news is that most newborns do quite well with whatever form, brand, or type of formula they are given. While many even tolerate being switched back and forth without any problems, we want to caution you that this is generally not recommended by health professionals. If, however, you find yourself with a finicky eater on your hands, we suggest that you talk to your baby's doctor to discuss a reasonable approach to formula switching and determine if your baby happens to be one of the few infants who might truly benefit from any of the assorted "specialty" formulas.

TALES OF THE TRULY INTOLERANT

An estimated 5% to 10% of all babies are truly intolerant of milk- or soy-based formulas—a condition sometimes referred to as *milk soy protein intolerance* (MSPI) where the intestinal tract is irritated by the proteins found in both of these types of infant formulas. Babies with MSPI typically aren't happy. They fuss and tend to react soon after eating. They often spit up a lot, become gassy (sometimes to the point of pain), or have problems with pooping (either constipation or diarrhea). If you suspect that your baby may have a formula intolerance, be sure to discuss your suspicion with your pediatrician. By running a quick test on your baby's poop and looking for traces of blood and other incriminating substances, he or she can help determine if your newborn's intestinal tract is reacting to the formula. If your baby is truly intolerant, your baby's doctor will recommend an alternative formula and discuss with you the game plan for future feeding. Fortunately, babies often outgrow their intolerances after several months.

The Importance of Being Iron-Fortified

It is very important that your baby gets enough iron, especially during the many months before he starts eating iron-rich foods. The reason we considered this particularly important to mention is because in years past, it was very easy to find low-iron infant formulas. Based on the common misconception that the iron in regular formula was to blame for everything from constipation and stomach pain to colic and reflux, low-iron formulas seemed like a reasonable solution. While this assumption is understandable, especially coming from any woman who has ever suffered uncomfortable side effects while taking prenatal iron supplements, the fact of the matter is that the amount of iron in regular infant formula is necessary for normal growth and development and is actually very well tolerated. Ten years after the recommendation was made to either discontinue the manufacture of low-iron formulas altogether or label them as "potentially nutritionally inadequate," you are now unlikely to find any on the store shelves. If you do, avoid them.

CHEWING THE FATTY ACIDS (DHA AND ARA)

Two fatty acids known as DHA (docosahexaenoic acid) and ARA (arachidonic acid) have become a mainstay in infant formulas. In their naturally occurring form, these fatty acids are thought to be crucial for a baby's development—especially of the eyes and brain. According to the government agency that oversees the production of infant formula (the US Food and Drug Administration), the addition of fatty acids is known to be safe. In fact, given the potential benefits and lack of any known drawbacks, the American Dietetic Association recommended in 2007 that "all infants who are not breastfed be fed a formula containing both ARA and DHA through at least the first year." Given their growing popularity, you're sure to be able to find these fatty acids on your next stroll down the formula aisle—either by reading the ingredient list; references on labels such as "immune support," "immunity protection," and "brain and eye health"; or simply looking for prominently displayed words such as "lipids" or just plain "DHA and ARA."

Formula Form and Function:
Powders, Concentrates, and Ready-to-Feed

Infant formulas generally come as ready-to-feed liquid, concentrated liquid, and powder. Which type is going to work best for you is likely to depend on how much formula you plan to use, where you plan to use it (ready-to-feed is definitely very convenient when you're out and about), and how much you want to spend.

Just as pregnancy taught most of you to think in weeks instead of months, bottle-feeding your baby will require you to think in ounces and adopt it as your standard unit of measurement. To prepare you accordingly, we'll first clarify the basic measures you'll need for formula success.

1 ounce = 30 cc (cubic centimeters) = 30 mL (milliliters)

8 fluid ounces = 1 cup

32 fluid ounces = 1 quart

Now that you have some frame of reference, we'll move on to the actual substance of formula preparation.

2 scoops + 4 fluid ounces water = just over 4 fluid ounces of mixed formula

- **Powder.** The simple concept here is that you add powder to pre-measured water and shake a lot. In what we can only assume was an enlightened attempt to eliminate room for mixing errors, most powdered formula is mixed according to the same recipe: 1 scoop of powder to every 2 fluid ounces of water. Powdered formula comes in cans containing enough powder to make anywhere from 90 ounces to more than 200 ounces of prepared formula. It is certainly your most economical choice, and quite frankly works perfectly well for most babies. You can decide whether to mix it up as you go or prepare a full day's worth at a time and refrigerate it.

2 fluid ounces concentrated formula + 2 fluid ounces water =
4 fluid ounces of mixed formula

- **Liquid concentrate.** This is the "just add water as directed and shake" formula option. Mixing and measuring is again quite straightforward, because all brands of concentrate call for equal amounts of water and concentrate. If you intend to end up with a total of 4 fluid ounces of prepared formula, you'll need to mix 2 fluid ounces of concentrate with 2 fluid ounces of water. Of course many people choose to mix an entire can of concentrate (13 fluid ounces) with an equal amount of water. The resulting 26 fluid ounces of now-ready-to-feed formula can be covered and put in the refrigerator to be used over the next 48 hours. While some parents find concentrate to be easier, neater, and/or more convenient than powder, it is a convenience for which you will pay more.
- **Ready-to-feed.** This is your no-mixing, no-measuring, no-mess option. Typically sold in 2-, 6- or 8-fluid-ounce containers (with anywhere from 4 to 24 to a pack) or 1-quart (32-fluid-ounce) containers/cans, the use of ready-to-feed formula is hopefully self-explanatory—what you see is what you give. While the fairly small "Ready-to-Feed" caption isn't always prominently displayed on the label, you'd be hard pressed to miss the distinguishing price tag (see "Comparing Ounces to Ounces" on page 47). While buying ready-to-feed formula inevitably costs the most, it leaves almost no room for error (assuming that you don't mistake it for concentrate and dilute it with water). It also happens to be the easiest way to limit your newborn's exposure to too much fluoride (see pages 46–48). Unopened cans can be conveniently stored at room temperature. Once opened, unused portions can be covered and then refrigerated for up to 48 hours.

Pour 4 fluid ounces of ready-to-feed into a 4-fluid-ounce bottle.

Formula Buying Tips

Buying formula is a significant expense of parenthood. If you are so inclined, we've put together a little list of ways you might save a bit along the way.

- **Do the math.** We realize that it's not always easy, fun, or feasible, but it can be quite worthwhile to take the time and figure out how much you're paying per ounce (see "Comparing Ounces to Ounces" on page 47). You may be surprised by what you find by comparing prices between brands as well as by comparing types and sizes. Once you've looked at the label and figured out how many total prepared ounces you'll be getting in any given can or container, divide the price by the total number of prepared ounces. Depending on the retailer, the price per ounce may already be calculated and listed for your convenience right next to the total price posted on the display shelf.

- **Stock up.** To do this, you'll first want to make sure that your baby is perfectly content with the formula he's getting. Then take advantage of any sales and coupons you may spot along the way. You'll want to remember to check the expiration date printed on the cans before stocking up. While many will have expiration dates well in excess of a year, you won't want to get stuck with a bunch of cans whose time will be up before you can use them.

- **Save receipts.** Early on it's more difficult to know for sure that the formula you buy now is going to be the formula you buy forever after (ie, through the end of the first year). While you're still settling in over the next several weeks, we suggest tucking your receipts—for formula and all of your other new-baby purchases—away somewhere for safekeeping and easy retrieval.

Mixing It Up

Be sure to read the instructions carefully when preparing formula. Any incorrectly prepared formula, whether it's too concentrated or too dilute, has the potential to cause serious problems. While ready-to-feed formula is just that—you can pour the room-temperature contents directly into a bottle, screw on the nipple, and have your baby feed away—the others require accurate preparation. As for the water you use, you'll want to pay attention to fluoride concentration. Because too much fluoride can have a

COMPARING OUNCES TO OUNCES (FOR WHAT IT'S WORTH)

Based on a recent check of prices at the local retailer, we thought it would be helpful to give you a general idea of how the different types of formula stack up ounce for ounce at the checkout counter. To do so, we compared one particular type and brand of formula, and did not factor in sale prices (which can unquestionably save you a lot of money). Also keep in mind that the ounces we are comparing—and that you can easily compare for yourself—are the ounces of *prepared* formula once it is ready to feed to your baby.

Type	Size	Price Per Prepared Ounce
Ready-to-feed	Four 8-fluid-ounce cans	28 cents
Ready-to-feed	1 quart	20 cents
Concentrate	13-fluid-ounce can	16 cents
Powder	Small can	15 cents
Powder	Large can	14 cents

To compare ounces to ounces for yourself, first look at the formula container and figure out how many ounces you'll be able to make from it once it is properly prepared. Then simply divide the price by the number of prepared ounces and you're guaranteed to be a better-informed formula-buying consumer in no time!

negative effect on your baby's developing teeth, it is recommended that you use water that is either fluoride-free or contains low levels of fluoride when preparing liquid concentrate or powdered infant formula. The best way to find out how much fluoride your tap water contains (since it can vary considerably) is to contact your local water utility. If you find that you want (or need) to limit your baby's fluoride exposure, most grocery stores sell low/no-fluoride bottled water typically labeled as purified, demineralized, deionized, or distilled. You can also remove fluoride from tap water with a reverse osmosis filter.

While new parents sometimes choose to use boiled water, at least in the first month or two, the fact of the matter is that for most normal healthy babies, regular tap water with fluoride levels below 2 mg per liter (sometimes listed as 2 ppm) is perfectly acceptable. Check with your pediatrician or water department before using well water (which can contain dangerous nitrates), or if you have any concerns about the purity of your tap supply. If you have any questions about mixing your formula, don't hesitate to contact your baby's doctor for recommendations. Although rare, mixing mistakes can, in fact, cause very serious problems for infants in a period of only days.

 ## FOCUSING ON FOOD SAFETY

Wash your hands thoroughly with soap and water and dry them well before preparing formula for your baby. Because babies can get very sick otherwise, it is important to carefully follow the instructions on the product label for preparation, use, and storage. Do not use prepared formula if it has been left unrefrigerated for more than 2 hours. Once you have fed your baby from a bottle, do not refrigerate the bottle in hopes of using it again later; bacteria from your baby's mouth can multiply, even in the refrigerator. Be sure to discard any formula remaining in the bottle after 1 hour from the start of your baby's feeding.

CHAPTER 3

bottles and nipples

Whether you plan on bottle-feeding your newborn with formula or pumped breast milk, you will obviously need to properly equip yourself with a supply of bottles and nipples. Nowadays, you can choose from lightweight plastic bottles; glass bottles; collapsible (disposable) plastic bottle bags; angled bottles; colored bottles; contoured bottles; and count-less shapes, sizes, and consistencies of nipples. Although we're certain that many of you would like to have all your bottles in a row in anticipation of your baby's arrival and most babies really could not care less, there's just no good way to know ahead of time if your baby will agree with your initial choices. That's because when it comes to nipples, and even the bottles you choose, be forewarned that one size does not always suit all. If your baby happens to be less than tolerant of the type/brand you've so carefully selected, you may be faced with a trial period as you test out the different shapes, sizes, colors, and brands of bottles and nipples in an attempt to find a good match. We therefore recommend starting off with the basics and waiting to buy in bulk until you find a keeper. If you are set on stocking up on a particular type of bottle in advance, simply hang on to your receipts. Once a sample bottle and nipple has been met with your baby's approval, you'll be all set.

The Model Bottle

We've found that in reality, most babies go along with their parents' taste in bottles and there really isn't such a thing as a single "model bottle"—one that outshines all the rest. Nevertheless, we have found the following con-siderations to serve bottle-buying parents well:

- In general, a transparent (ie, not colored) 4-ounce bottle is the most practical choice for newborns.

- Larger (6- or 8-ounce) bottles are fine if you don't mind using them half-full until your baby is bigger.
- Angled bottles and those with disposable nurser bags, built-in vents, or flow and control systems are said to help decrease the amount of air your baby swallows (although regular bottles held at the proper angle will also).
- Disposable bags have the added benefit of, well, being disposable; you only have to wash the nipples after each feeding.

 A BIT ABOUT BPA

BPA (bisphenol A) is a chemical used in many hard plastic products, including some baby bottles, and the plastic lining used in cans of ready-to-feed formula. What's the concern? Studies have shown that this potentially toxic chemical can leach out into food and pose a potential health risk—especially to infants and young children. The likelihood of BPA contamination is thought to be greatest when BPA-containing plastics are scratched or heated, contain warm liquids or food, or are washed with harsh detergents. While the use of BPA is not yet banned in the United States, several cities and states are considering or have already prohibited its use.

The advice we have for parents? Minimize your baby's exposure to BPA by purchasing baby bottles that are labelled "BPA-free" and consider avoiding plastics with a #3 or #7 recycling symbol on the bottom (since these recycling categories may sometimes include BPA-containing plastics). And lastly, check for labels that state "dishwasher safe" or "microwave safe" before placing plastic containers in the dishwasher or microwave.

CHAPTER 4

going with the flow

One of the most useful things to consider when choosing a nipple
is finding one that allows the right amount of milk flow for your baby.
Because different babies can handle different flows at different ages and
stages of development, you'll find that nipples come in many different sizes.
They are typically marketed based on a baby's age, with the preemie and
0- to 3-month nipples allowing for slower flows than those nipples designed for use by 6- or 9-month-olds. Voracious newborns, however, may
do perfectly well with a faster-flow nipple, while others may take months
before being able to drink from the age-appropriate nipple without having
large volumes of milk streaming down the sides of their mouths. As for the
openings—not only will you find yourself with a choice of 1-hole, 2-hole,
and 3-hole nipples, but also nipples that are cross-cut and who knows what
else. For practical purposes, all you really need to pay attention to is how
fast the milk flows—too fast, too slow, or just right.

While neither of us had to spend much time in search of a suitable
nipple for our babies, it is worth mentioning that nipples also come in
many shapes and sizes, from regular to orthodontic and beyond. If your
baby is finicky, then you'll want to pay more attention to the vast array of
nipples and choose whichever shape your baby decides to accept. We will
add that most experts we've asked don't believe that the orthodontic shape
adds much, if any, benefit.

Heating Things Up

While there is no inherent medical, nutritional, or even comfort-related
need to warm your newborn's bottles, if you're like a good many parents
these days, you'll be spending the next several months heating formula or
expressed breast milk for your baby. The recommended way to do this is to

put a bottle of breast milk or formula into a bottle warmer or saucepan of warm water until the milk is warm. You can also hold a bottle under running warm water for a few minutes. Despite these convenient options, you would not be the first parent tempted by the microwave. Before you succumb to temptation, however, let us point out that microwaves are known to heat unevenly, creating potentially dangerous hot spots in the middle of the liquid, not to mention destroying the protective antibodies found in breast milk. In addition, potentially toxic chemicals may leach out of plastic bottles when heated in the microwave (see "A Bit About BPA" on 50). For these reasons, we recommend that you avoid the use of the micro-wave altogether for the purpose of warming bottles. If you're still deter-mined to use the microwave, we strongly suggest you do so only with formula (not breast milk), for no more than a few seconds at a time, and that you make absolutely sure to take extra precautions to mix the formula well and make sure it's not too hot before giving it to your baby.

 ## WHAT WILL THEY THINK OF NEXT

Many of the bottle-warming and bottle-cooling products now fall into parenthood's "what will they think of next?" category. These include travel baby bottle warmers you can plug into your car's power port as well as the all-in-one bottle-cooler-heater-alarm clock that you can plug in next to your bed at night. There are mini-coolers, compact refrigerators, and insulated baby "lunch" bags that come equipped with ice packs.

We think you will see a pattern here. It's always refreshing to know that people are looking out for ways to make life easier for parents these days!

To be perfectly honest, if it's ease of use you're looking for, we suggest a trial run of unwarmed formula or breast milk before you convince yourself that you and your baby can't live without the latest in milk-warming tech-nology. You might be pleasantly surprised to find that your baby takes to bottles straight out of the refrigerator. After all, that's what you'll offer without a second thought when your baby switches to drinking regular milk at a year of age!

Finally—The Feeding Part

Once you've found a good bottle-nipple combination and have formula or breast milk on hand, you are ready to bottle-feed your baby. One of the most helpful things to remember when bottle-feeding is to angle the bottle. By holding the bottle fairly upright in your baby's mouth instead of horizontally, you will avoid feeding your baby air and make sure she is getting only the milk. To do so,

- Lean her back at a slight recline while supporting the back of her head and neck.
- If she isn't already open-mouthed in eager anticipation, you may find it helpful to stroke the side of her mouth or cheek with the nipple to get her to open her mouth (see "Rooting for Success" on page 16).
- Then insert the nipple into her mouth and hold the bottle with the end tilted up enough that the milk completely fills the nipple as your baby drinks.
- As the bottle empties, you may find you need to hold the bottle almost upright.

Bottle-feeding by Numbers

You've probably read enough by now to know that we have no way of telling you exactly how many ounces your newborn will take. As you get a feel for feeding your baby (and the associated peeing and pooping that should accompany it), here are a few numbers for you to use as general guidelines.

- **First feedings.** Newborns typically take anywhere from ½ to 1½ ounces at each of the first few feedings.
- **Daily totals.** After the first several days, most newborns drink between 12 and 24 ounces during the course of each 24-hour day.
- **Feeding frequency.** On average, formula-fed babies drink every 3 to 4 hours, while those given bottles of breast milk still tend to eat every 2 to 3 hours. Regardless of feeding frequency, any newborn who refuses feedings 2 or more times in a row should be brought to the immediate attention of his doctor.
- **Weighing in.** The true test of whether your baby is drinking enough is if he is gaining weight as expected. This holds true for breastfed and formula-fed infants (see "Weighing In" on page 30).

DOUBLE-SIPPING

We recommend filling each bottle with only as much as you think your baby will take—with a little extra for good measure in case she happens to be particularly hungry. That way you can minimize the amount you end up having to discard at the end of each feeding. The party line is that it's OK to hang on to leftover formula or breast milk for a little while in hopes that your baby decides to finish it off—especially if you've got a grazer on your hands or your baby decides to drink less than you expected. However, plan on keeping leftovers around no longer than about an hour before throwing them away, because bacteria from a baby's mouth are known to multiply fairly rapidly in milk (or just about any other food or drink that's been subjected to double-dipping or double-sipping).

Cleaning Up

Sample nipples obtained from the hospital or doctor's office conveniently come in sterilized packages for the earliest feedings and are meant to be disposed of after a single use. Aside from that, the standard recommendation is that all feeding supplies and pacifiers should be washed and, whenever possible, sterilized prior to first use.

- You can easily sterilize your supplies by placing them in boiling water for about 5 minutes. Commercial sterilizers are also available for this purpose.
- In general, many parents are content to hand wash bottles and nipples in hot, sudsy water and rinse right after feedings to keep the remaining contents of the bottle from sticking/drying to the sides, nooks, and crannies.
- Bottle and nipple brushes are inexpensive and invaluable for cleaning even the hard-to-reach places.
- You can either re-sterilize your bottles and nipples between uses or wash them in a very hot dishwasher.
- There are plenty of dishwasher-safe plastic baskets on the market specially designed to serve the sole purpose of holding all of the small items involved in bottle-feeding—the nipples, lids, and other baby accessories that will likely take up a sizable chunk of your dishwasher's upper rack. A small mesh laundry bag can also serve this function.

Schedules and Routines

Setting a Schedule or Going With the Flow

Getting babies to follow some semblance of a feeding schedule is a subject of great interest to many parents of newborns—ranking right up there with longing for predictable sleep schedules (see "Sleeping Like a Baby" on page 89). You should know that it is also a topic that inspires great debate. You'll find many differing opinions depending on whom you ask, what you read, and where you look. While we certainly don't presume to have the one and only answer to the eternal question of whether one should feed on demand or follow a set schedule, we can certainly give you the background you'll need to choose a practical and safe approach to the whole issue of when and how much to feed your baby.

Schedules Gone Awry

As you might have already gathered, we are not advocates of strict feeding schedules—at least not in the true sense of the phrase. That's because more often than not babies aren't either. While there are some general feeding rules of thumb, babies aren't exactly aware of them and often choose not to play by the rules. Following are several of the more common and normal variations in newborn feeding habits that are all too often perceived as schedules gone awry.

Day-to-Day Variability

We feel compelled to point out that nobody (with rare/eccentric exception) eats the same thing, in the same amount, at the same time, every day, day in and day out. Babies are no exception, so prepare yourself for a reasonable amount of variation in the amount your baby drinks on any given day. Focus your attention instead on making sure that your newborn is waking up every few hours to feed, getting enough to drink, and growing as expected.

Growth Spurts

Until we had our own children, growth spurts were merely a concept we learned about as pediatricians. They sounded logical enough—involving intermittent brief periods of rapid growth accompanied by increased hunger—but they didn't seem to us to have that much bearing on reality.

And then reality set in (as it does for most new parents). Your first introduction to a growth spurt will probably come when your baby is 2 or 3 weeks old. Everything will seem to be going just fine, you'll have just started to feel like you have control of things (and of your milk supply if you are breastfeeding), and then out of nowhere your baby will let you know otherwise. Almost overnight he's likely to be less easily satisfied, more frequently fussy, and seemingly hungry all the time. While formula-feeding parents can certainly be thrown for a loop by growth spurts, adding an extra ounce or two to their babies' bottles and/or feeding more frequently can quickly settle everyone back into a comfortable new routine. For breastfeeding moms, accommodating growth spurts can take a little more time and flexibility. During the several days it may take for your breasts to adjust to your baby's increased needs and demands, try not to question your breastfeeding abilities. Instead of letting growth spurts shake your confidence, remind yourself that it is only natural for newborns to be fussy and to seem like they're temporarily not getting enough milk. Based on the concept of supply and demand as it applies to breastfeeding, this is the only way your baby will be able to tell you to increase the amount of milk you are producing to meet his growing needs.

Cluster Feeding

Cluster feeding is just as it sounds—when a baby decides to eat several times in a relatively short period of time, in seeming defiance of those who dare to suggest feeding no more often than every 3 hours. This pattern is sometimes referred to as grazing—especially when a baby is a frequent feeder with seemingly little stamina and seems to be taking the snack-bar approach to breastfeeding in general. In your newborn's first days and weeks we strongly recommend you follow your baby's lead—whether that means feedings that are evenly spaced or clustered together, long sessions or short. Even after your baby's feeding patterns become relatively predictable, it's worth mentioning that a good many babies still choose to cluster feed—most commonly in the evening before bedtime. Without scientific data to support it, let us just say that some parents swear by cluster feeding in the evening as a way to "top off the tank" in the hopes of buying everyone involved a longer stretch of nighttime sleep before hunger strikes again.

Routine Considerations

The Merits of an All-Liquid Diet

For the next several months, your baby will get all the nutrition he needs from breast milk and/or formula. While we are well aware of the fact that babies of generations past were given rice cereal as young as a few weeks of age, giving any form of solid food to babies before 4 to 6 months is no longer recommended (except under certain circumstances such as significant reflux). Doing so is thought to increase a baby's risk of developing allergies, constipation, and even choking. Even if you find yourself pressured by well-meaning grandparents or friends who swear by it, we suggest you suppress the urge to give your baby any type of solid food until 4 to 6 months of age, or until you discuss it with your pediatrician and get the go-ahead.

Where Does Water Fit In?

In response to a question many parents ask: Yes, water is a liquid, but no, your newborn baby does not need any. It's fine to give her a sip or two on occasion, for example if she has the hiccups and they're bothering you (because babies don't tend to care), but giving a young infant more than that runs the risk of filling her up and leaving her less room for the more nutritious breast milk or formula she needs to grow. In addition, too much water can even make your baby very ill.

No Milk (for Now)

Until your baby reaches 1 year of age, you should continue to reach for the breast milk or formula instead of regular cow's milk. This recommendation is based on the fact that cow's milk is less easily digested, contains higher concentrations of certain proteins and minerals, offers inadequate amounts of vitamins and iron, and has the potential to place unrealistic demands on your baby's kidneys and intestinal tract.

Sucking Sense and Sensibility

It's a rare parent who doesn't find the classic "baby sucking thumb in utero" ultrasound picture worthy of framing—or at least showing off to friends or around the office. But the ability to suck is more than just cute. It's important for other reasons as well. While babies are sometimes caught on ultrasound sucking their thumbs as early as 18 weeks or less, the sucking and

VITAMIN D FOR NEWBORNS

With only a few exceptions, most healthy full-term newborns get all the vitamins they need from breast milk and/or formula. One of the most notable exceptions is vitamin D—an important nutrient that helps prevent rickets and is thought to help strengthen the immune system and decrease the risk of diabetes and other chronic diseases, as well as some types of cancer. As of 2008, the American Academy of Pediatrics recommends that all exclusively breastfed newborns receive vitamin D drops (400 IU per day) beginning soon after birth. As for formula-fed babies, those who are not getting at least 32 ounces of formula a day should also take extra vitamin D.

swallowing efforts necessary to drink from breast or bottle don't become coordinated until closer to 34 weeks. Not only do babies perfect their sucking skills once they are born in the name of good growth and nutrition, but most of them rely on sucking to soothe themselves—some relying on it more heavily than others. The fact that babies don't have enough control over their fingers and hands to reliably get them to their mouths and suck on them for many weeks after they are born naturally leads many parents (and us) into a discussion of pacifiers.

Practical Pacifier Principles

Pacifiers have proven themselves to be yet one more source of parenting controversy. Breastfeeding purists say stick to your guns and keep them out of your newborn's mouth (see "The Confusion About Nipple Confusion" and "Nipple Confusion Defined" on pages 32 and 33)—even when your baby is not yet able to use his own fingers as an alternative. (We would note that if and when your baby is able to find his own fingers, it's OK to let him continue using them as natural pacifiers.) Others forewarn that pacifiers are simply a bad habit waiting to happen. Well fear not, as long as you understand a few practical pacifier principles and pitfalls. In fact, pacifiers have, in recent years, earned the status of a valuable ally in the fight against sudden infant death syndrome (see "The Reality of SIDS" page 91). Whether you choose to breastfeed or bottle-feed, or a combination of both, here are some tips for if and when you decide to give your baby a pacifier.

- **Soothing through sucking.** Pacifiers can be invaluable in soothing babies as well as satisfying those who want to suck all the time. You need not worry about your baby developing a lifelong dependency on them. Just be very careful not to offer your newborn a pacifier at times when he really should be fed instead because pacifiers can inappropriately pacify hungry babies as well as those who are looking for comfort.
- **Picking out the perfect pacifier.** These days, picking the perfect pacifier may seem like a considerable task, given all of the various brands and styles on the market. To the best of our knowledge, there's no correlation between price or marketing strategy and effectiveness, so we simply recommend trying one out and seeing if your baby likes it.
- **If at first you don't succeed.** When you first offer your baby a pacifier, don't be surprised if he seems uninterested, gets downright angry, or spits it out even when you know he's not hungry and just wants comfort. For breastfed babies, sucking on a pacifier inherently requires a different technique, and one that may take a few tries. For breastfed and bottle-fed babies alike, a nipple that does not provide milk may not be quickly welcomed. As you offer your baby a pacifier, try lightly stroking just to the side of his mouth and then gently holding the pacifier in his mouth for a moment as he starts sucking to keep it from popping right back out.
- **A practical pacifier substitute.** The cheap, easy, and ever-present pacifier substitute: your pinky finger. If you find yourself in the position of wanting to soothe your baby by giving him something to suck on other than your breast, you can always use your (clean) little finger. Simply turn your hand palm-side up and let your baby suck on your pinky finger, allowing it to rest gently in the roof of his mouth. As a word of caution for anyone with longer fingernails than ours—you may want to rethink how much you value your long nails, or at least the one on your little finger. You may find that it's a small sacrifice to make to clip it shorter for the sake of having a contented baby. Some babies will learn to find their own fingers to suck on earlier than others, so do your best to be prepared by making sure those fingers are clean (and have clipped nails too!).

- **Passing on pacifiers.** If your baby just isn't that much of a "sucker," he may not need to be soothed by sucking on a pacifier at all. Just be thankful that there's one less thing to keep track of during the day, and just consider offering one as he is falling asleep.

PART II

what goes in must come out

This section is devoted to a subject that, if nothing else, will help you realize just how far you're about to come—from your days as an expectant parent to master of bodily fluids and functions. A very basic understanding of how your baby's body works—combined with some reflection on a few of your own life experiences—should be more than enough to tell you that a good deal of what goes into your baby's mouth will eventually come out in one form or another. Granted your baby will be putting a significant portion of whatever is going into her mouth toward her growth and development, but all the indigestible, unnecessary, or undesirable stuff—be it solid, liquid, or gas—is all but guaranteed to make its way out on a very regular basis. First and foremost, pee and poop will soon be in abundant supply—at least after you've made it past the first few days when your baby's system is still gearing up for "bigger and better" things. Don't be surprised if these and other previously less than tasteful subjects indiscriminately make their way into your casual (and not-so-casual) conversations. In fact, we consider the contemplation and shared discussion of such topics to be a defining feature of parenthood.

Looking Into What Comes Out

In this section, we will take a close look at the inner workings of newborns and what's behind all of the peeing and pooping, not to mention the gas, hiccups, burps, spit-up, and vomit that comes along with having a baby. Your personal day-to-day experiences will certainly leave some of you scratching your heads in wonder, confusion, or amazement. Don't worry if it doesn't all sink in right away. Trust us when we say that it soon will (refer to "Stain Removal" on page 153).

Peeing and Pooping

If we were attempting to write a medical textbook, we would now be turning our focus to the topics of urine, stool, and bowel movements. The fact of the matter is that (1) this is not in any way meant to resemble a medical textbook and (2) once you've been buried in a sea of diapers over the first days, weeks, and years of parenthood, there's just nothing academic about it. Given that most parents we've talked to over the years simply refer to it as good old pee and poop, we will too. With our choice of words thus briefly explained, let's get to the real substance at hand. To give you some context, the reason why pediatricians seem to care so much about whether a baby is peeing and pooping normally is because it is one of the easiest and most reassuring ways we have to determine if a baby is getting enough to eat, all systems are in good working order, and he is generally healthy.

As you settle into your own daily feeding "routine" (a term we use loosely, as explained in "Into the Mouths of Babes" on page 1) and attempt to gauge if your own baby is getting enough to eat, drink, and be merry, you'll find that pee and poop play a leading role. First, to figure out whether your baby's plumbing is working normally, you'll need a good understanding of just what is meant by the word "normal."

CHAPTER 5

to pee or not to pee

How Wet Is Wet Enough?

The answer to this question depends on how you're feeding your baby (breast or bottle) and how old your baby is, because the first few days can be far fewer than the by-the-book 8- to 10-plus wet diapers a day. For formula-fed newborns who are taking well to the bottle, it's perfectly reasonable to expect a good 5 or more wet diapers a day within the first day or two. Breastfed newborns, however, can be a little trickier to assess during the first several days while their mothers' milk supply has yet to come in (see "Breastfeeding" on page 5). While breastfed babies get their necessary calories from the early milk (colostrum), this first form of breast milk comes in a much smaller volume. It therefore stands to reason that breast-fed newborns pee less frequently—sometimes only 2 or 3 times a day—and in much smaller amounts until their mothers' full-volume milk supply comes in (anywhere from 2–5 days after delivery). Once you reach this breastfeeding milestone of milk production, *then* you can expect your baby to catch up to her formula-fed colleagues and have at least 5 (if not 8 or 10) wet diapers in any 24-hour period. When everyone's drinking and peeing are up to full capacity, then the standard 8 to 10 wet diapers a day applies. If at any time you are concerned that your baby is not peeing as much as she should, this is as good a reason as any to enlist the help and expertise of your pediatrician.

IN SEARCH OF A LITTLE PEE
IN A BIG DIAPER

Detecting small amounts of pee in a newborn's super-absorbent disposable diaper can at times be likened to finding a needle in a haystack. If
you're having difficulty determining whether your newborn's diaper is wet,
some diapers make your job a little easier by including moisture sensing
strips that change color when wet. You can also try putting a cotton ball or
folded tissue inside of a regular diaper—toward the front of the diaper near
the penis for baby boys and lower in the crotch area for baby girls. Then
be patient. Any subsequent pee will now be much easier to detect and the
challenge of detecting it most likely short-lived. It shouldn't be more than a
few short days before you find yourself faced instead with the problem of
overly soaked diapers and laughing at the thought of cotton balls and tissue. For additional information on difficult to identify diaper contents, see
"UDOs: Unidentified Diaper Objects" on page 129.

CHAPTER 6

poop happens

When it comes to newborn poop, it helps to be aware that there is a normal and expected poop progression that takes place over the first week or so. Most doctors expect newborns to demonstrate their pooping ability before sending them home from the hospital. And most newborns happily oblige—doing so without much difficulty or delay. The very first newborn poops you'll see, usually in the first 24 hours or so, are typically thick, tarry, and black. This lovely, gooey mess is simply the poop that accumulated before your baby was born and is referred to as meconium.

The Scoop on Poop

As breast milk or formula begins to make its way through your baby's system over the next few days, you can expect your baby's poop to become more of a pasty brown color (the so-called transitional stool) and then ultimately become the standard mustardy yellow and seedy poop typical of breastfed babies, or the more pasty/formed and variably colored poop of formula-fed babies. For all babies, but especially for those who are breastfed, the establishment of frequent poop that has gone through this predictable change in color and consistency is a good indication that they are getting enough to eat. For the breastfed baby, it also suggests that the eagerly anticipated full-volume milk supply has arrived.

The Many Colors of Poop

Long after adjusting to parenthood and your role as principal poop watcher and wiper, you may still find yourself fretting over changes in the color of your baby's poop. In reality, once your baby has pooped enough to get rid of the tarry meconium, all the varying shades of yellow, brown, and even green are considered perfectly acceptable. Mustardy yellow is

PRECOCIOUS POOPING

In some instances, babies actually poop before they are born—allowing meconium to mix into the amniotic fluid. While this is a reassuring sign that all's well in the poop department, such babies may require closer observation in the period immediately after being born to make sure that the meconium hasn't made its way into the lungs.

the color of choice for most breastfed babies, and yellow-tan with hints of green for those who are formula-fed. Being presented with a changing palette of colors is not uncommon, however, particularly later on down the road when your baby is introduced to such things as solid foods and snotty nose colds, both of which can add new shades and substance to the mix.

Black, White, and Shades of Red

There are a few colors of baby poop that, should you see them, always warrant discussion with your baby's doctor.

- **Red.** Seeing red can mean blood, especially in the newborn period when your baby isn't eating or drinking anything red-colored that could be mistaken for blood when it comes out the other end. Blood should not signal you to panic immediately, but you should bring it to the attention of your pediatrician, who will be able to help you sort out the cause. It is possible for babies to swallow some blood during delivery that presents itself shortly thereafter—either in the baby's spit-up or poop—but, nevertheless, any amount of bloody poop should be evaluated because it can also be a sign of a problem.
- **Black.** Black-colored poop sometimes represents old blood because blood is known to turn from red to black over time in the intestinal tract. Remember that this black color alert does not apply to your baby's first few meconium bowel movements, which you can fully expect to be black and tarry looking.
- **White.** White poop is quite rare, but needs to be brought to the attention of a doctor ASAP because it can be caused by an underlying liver problem. The earlier it is addressed, the better—either for peace of mind or medical management.

The Eating-Pooping Connection

You'll find that for many young babies, a little thing called the gastro-colic reflex (*gastro* referring to the stomach and *colic* referring to the colon—the end of the road in the intestinal tract) is responsible for making eating and pooping occur nearly simultaneously. In fact, many newborns have such a strong gastro-colic reflex that they poop just about every time they eat— sometimes even in anticipation of being fed before any milk has graced their lips. If you stop and think about it, you may find that you're already quite familiar with this particular reflex because it is not unique to infancy. While generally less exaggerated and hopefully less immediate, a good many adults never fully outgrow this gastro-colic reflex. Unlike newborns, however, most adults are able to control the urge long enough to finish their meals before needing to excuse themselves to the bathroom to take care of business.

 FULL SPEED BEHIND

Once your baby has gotten the hang of eating—especially if you have chosen to breastfeed and your milk is fully in—don't be surprised to find yourself faced with poop that can be described as nothing less than ex- plosive. In fact, it brings to mind the problems Southern Californians once had with paintball shooting sprees. Wayward teenagers drove around with paintball guns terrorizing neighborhoods by firing off blobs of paint at high speeds, targeting whomever and whatever happened to cross their paths. That's the best analogy we've come up with to date to convey the potential forcefulness (and subsequent mess) that can result when a breastfed baby's intestinal tract is fully up to speed. Having now been fore- warned, we suggest you review our diapering chapter to make sure you're comfortable with your diapering technique. And remember to keep your baby's back end securely contained whenever possible—or be prepared to take cover and suffer the consequences!

Consistency: A Word About Diarrhea and Constipation

Many parents are concerned (usually unnecessarily) that their new babies have diarrhea. And with the definition of diarrhea typically involving the words "frequent" and "watery," it's certainly not hard to understand why. In fact, most young babies simply have well-functioning gastro-colic reflexes and everything that goes in one end comes flying out the other. That said, if you are concerned or simply want a reality check that what you're seeing in your baby's diaper is normal, then go right ahead and grab a poopy diaper (if you have one available to submit as evidence), stick it in a plastic bag, and head on over to check things out with your pediatrician.

 ## TRULY INTOLERANT POOP

On occasion—somewhere on the order of 5 to 10 out of every 100 babies to be exact—a baby's intestinal tract doesn't react well to formula and/or breast milk. This type of intolerance is worth being aware of, as it is caused by a milk and/or soy protein intolerance (sometimes called milk soy protein intolerance, or MSPI for short). Babies with MSPI typically make their intolerance known by acting quite uncomfortable, fussy, or colicky; vomiting; and/or having diarrhea—especially after or while being fed. Every now and then, blood turns up in their poop. As a parent, it is admittedly not always easy to pick apart MSPI from your more run-of-the-mill crying, fussy, spitty baby who poops a lot. And you shouldn't feel as though you have to. If you have questions about whether the formula or breast milk you are feeding your baby is not being well received by his intestinal tract, pack up your baby and a recent poop sample, if you can, and head on into your pediatrician's office.

Pooping by Numbers

Once babies have proven themselves capable of clearing out their meconium and have moved on to dishing out the "real thing," you can be relatively assured that their plumbing is in good working order and can turn your attention to the so-called normal pooping patterns of infancy. What's considered normal at this stage of the game (and for months to come) ranges anywhere from one poop every several days to several poops every day. Some are like the sprinters of the pooping world—fast and furious—while others are more like distance runners—slow and steady. In general, breastfed babies poop more than formula-fed ones, and younger babies poop more than older ones. Newborn babies and young infants also tend to have several tiny poops in succession, so as a point of practicality we recommend waiting a few minutes until your newborn is convincingly finished rather than jumping into diaper-changing action after the first signs of activity. From your pediatrician's perspective, the actual number of poops is likely to be less important than the fact that everything is generally moving along.

 ENOUGH IS ENOUGH?

In the spirit of helping you distinguish between the healthy but fast and furious pooper and those newborns pooping beyond the limits of acceptability, experts in the field of newborn care suggest the following rule of thumb: Any time a newborn's poop becomes progressively more watery or outpaces feeding frequency, it's time to seek medical advice.

When the Pooping Gets Tough

On the flip side of loose or watery poop, many parents have questions about constipation as soon as their babies begin to grunt, strain, or get red in the face while trying to poop, or the first time they go several days without a poopy diaper. Fortunately, true constipation—as defined by hard, difficult to pass, or infrequent poop—isn't a big issue for most young infants. Believe it or not, going as many as 5 to 7 days between poops is not inherently going to be a problem for babies who have already proven themselves fully capable of pooping during their first couple of weeks and are now eating and growing well. As long as your baby's poop is fairly soft and comes out easily when it does appear, you can breathe with relative ease despite the exaggerated degree of discomfort your baby seems to display. Even if your baby occasionally seems to have difficulty getting the poop out, remind yourself that pooping while lying flat on one's back isn't exactly natural. Given that your baby won't have many options for a while, you can try to facilitate by pushing your baby's knees up toward her chest while she's lying on her back to give her some resistance against which to strain. If, however, your baby consistently seems to have problems pooping—she does so infrequently or with apparent pain, or you notice blood or poop that just doesn't seem right to you—be sure to check in with your baby's doctor about what (if anything) you should do to remedy the situation.

📦 **IRONING OUT ANY** 🔍
MISUNDERSTANDINGS

The iron found in formula is often given undue blame, despite its unquestionable benefit. Given that iron supplements are well known to wreak havoc on adult regularity (a side effect with which some of you may have had recent firsthand experience), it's no wonder that parents are quick to blame the high iron content in their infant's formula for perceived problems with constipation. In reality, we know that the iron in infant formula is rarely, if ever, responsible for causing constipation. In fact, iron in infant formula is not absorbed all that well, and the seemingly large amount that you see listed on the label is actually necessary to ensure that your baby ends up getting the iron he needs (see also "The Importance of Being Iron-Fortified" on page 42).

Persistent Problematic Pooping (Hirschsprung Disease)

When all of a baby's parts are in working order, poop makes its way southward and comes to rest in the last part of the digestive tract—called the large intestine or colon. It accumulates there while awaiting its release from the anus. Every now and then, the nerve cells that control the anus (and sometimes those in the lower part of the colon) don't develop properly. As a result, the muscles responsible for letting the poop out can't relax. This condition is known as Hirschsprung disease. Only about 1 out of every 5,000 babies will have it. In extreme instances, the anus is unable to open at all—in which case pooping is noticeably absent from birth. Many babies with Hirschsprung disease, however, lack only some of the nerve cells and are still able to relax enough to let some poop out, just not as easily or as often as expected. This milder form of Hirschsprung disease can result in constipation, as characterized by infrequent or difficult poops, and may not signal a problem until the parents or pediatrician begins to notice a chronic pattern over time. While we've only taken the time to give you the quick and dirty explanation, it should be enough to give you some sense of what to keep in the back of your mind if you find yourself concerned about your newborn's pooping practices.

CHAPTER 7

other unmentionables and inconveniences

In addition to peeing and pooping, parents of newborns seem to encounter a disproportionate number of other "unmentionables and inconveniences"—namely gas, burping, spitting up, and vomiting. The following 2 chapters will help you sort through what's considered normal, what's considered a nuisance, and what should not be ignored.

Full of Hot Air

With all the gulping some babies do during feedings and crying, it's no surprise that they swallow quite a bit of air. Once air makes its way in, there are only 2 logical ways for it to escape—up and out as a burp or down and out as gas. Air that is destined to be passed as gas must travel through many feet of intestines—a process that invariably takes longer and is often believed to cause more fussing and discomfort than if that same air manages to come back out in the form of a burp. While we can't honestly say that this theory has been proven, it doesn't usually take a lot of convincing to believe that gassy babies tend to be uncomfortable babies. For this reason alone, it's worth taking some simple steps to minimize the amount of air your baby swallows.

- **Feed early and often.** Whenever possible, feed your baby *before* she is screaming her demands at you. The more she cries before a feeding, the more likely she is to fill up with air.
- **Rise to the challenge.** When feeding your baby, keep her body at somewhat of an upright angle—at least so that her head is a little higher than her stomach. Try to do this even if you have already figured out how to nurse lying down. This position theoretically allows the liquid to sink to

the bottom of a baby's stomach while the air stays on top—thus making it easier (and less messy) to burp out. Any air bubbles trapped below the milk will be burped up with liquid (spit-up) or have to pass through the intestinal tract.

- **Bottoms up.** When bottle-feeding your baby, hold the bottle at an angle so that there is always milk filling the entire nipple. This helps keep babies from sucking air.

- **Let things settle.** During and/or after each feeding, keep your baby upright for a few minutes to let things settle and then try to burp her.

Burping

Babies and parents alike seem to get significant relief from getting out whatever gas happens to make its way in—and the sooner the better. The next best thing to helping your baby avoid sucking in a lot of air in the first place is to get any resulting air bubbles to come out in one big satisfying burp (or two) shortly afterward. That said, some babies really seem not to be bothered by the presence of stomach gas—in which case you don't need to exert too much effort in the following burping endeavors.

The Technique

Given the amount of attention paid in parenting books, in magazines, and on Web sites to the topic of burping babies, you might be led to believe that nothing short of a class on the subject could properly prepare you. Well, in hopes of bursting your bubble, let us stress that burping is not rocket science by any stretch of the imagination. Burping is actually a relatively natural process that you simply stand to help along. If anything, most parents just benefit from a little guidance on if, when, and how vigorously to do it. We've seen many a parent frantically trying to elicit a burp every few minutes during and after each feeding. The fact of the matter is that some babies just don't swallow as much air or need to burp as much as others, and if your baby is going to burp, he will probably do so within a few minutes of having his back patted. Ideally, you simply want to decrease your baby's chances of discomfort by coaxing out whatever air has found its way into his stomach. That said, here are some basic burping techniques.

- **Positioning.** The classic burping technique (and often the most popular) involves holding up your baby facing you against your chest with his head resting just over your shoulder. You can also sit your baby upright on your lap, supporting his trunk by putting one hand across his chest and under his armpits while patting his back with the other. Or you can lay your baby on his belly across your lap or on the floor to help compress his stomach and press the air out.
- **Patting.** Pat or rub your baby's back for a couple of minutes after he drinks. Your patting should be less forceful than an all-out clapping motion, but harder than a soft touch. Many parents either burp a little too delicately or—on occasion—with a little too much enthusiasm.
- **Postponing.** If your baby hasn't burped after a couple minutes of coaxing, you can stop trying to elicit the elusive burp and simply lay your baby down for several minutes. If necessary, simply try again later if he seems uncomfortable. Sometimes allowing the air bubbles to settle will make it easier. Quite honestly, however, when left alone for a few minutes many babies are able to muster a burp all on their own. If you find your baby is very spitty, swallows a lot of air, or is uncomfortable during feedings, you can certainly try stopping and burping him in the middle of each feeding. Just be forewarned that in our combined experience, babies hate to be interrupted while eating without good cause.
- **Patience.** Accept the fact that some babies do not need to burp (or be burped) with every feeding—especially when they don't swallow much air, aren't prone to spitting up, or just plain don't tend to burp much. It's definitely not worth losing sleep over if you're unable to elicit a burp.

Pumping Gas

Despite your best efforts, some air will inevitably make its way past the stomach and into your baby's intestines. If you find that your baby seems uncomfortable as a direct result of gas, try laying her on her back and "bicycling" her legs to help work the air bubbles out. You can also try gently putting her face down along your arm, her legs straddling either side with your hand palm up under her belly, chest, and chin. If you're now wondering how to go about coordinating this whole one-arm thing—which hand, and facing which direction?—then you can opt to do what we do and rest your baby belly down on top of a flat surface. Lifting up slightly on her belly, use your fingertips to lightly massage or squeeze her tummy area for a few minutes. These motions seem to help break up gas bubbles— or at least help make gassy babies and their parents more comfortable with their predicament. Although it is not always the case, some babies reportedly respond well to over-the-counter anti-gas drops containing simethicone—the key ingredient found in Mylicon, Gerber Gas Drops, Phazyme, and certain colic drops. You'll notice we say "reportedly respond" because to tell the truth, we can't find definitive evidence to show that the effort and expense of anti-gas drops always pay off. If, however, you feel your baby may benefit, there's usually no harm in trying them as long as you consult with your pediatrician first—just as we hope you would before using any medication. Be sure to hang on to your receipt because should you find them to be ineffective, we've been told that some companies will reimburse your money.

Hiccups

The good news about hiccups is that they're not dangerous and they are almost always more bothersome to parents than they are to babies. At best, your baby won't get any at all, or only have an occasional cute little run-in with them. At worst, they'll make their presence known at all hours of the day and night and effectively disrupt what may already be a delicate balance in your baby's stomach—giving your baby yet one more excuse to wake up and/or spit up. The fact of the matter is that newborns have a lot of very active reflexes, and hiccupping can be one of them—sometimes even popping up before birth. Hiccups are thought to occur when a baby's diaphragm is "tickled" for any reason—by sudden swallowing or irregular breathing—or for no apparent reason at all. It is our understanding that any form of breath-holding (which, for a newborn, is pretty much limited to sucking or crying) effectively helps to stop them. If you're convinced that your baby is uncomfortable you can try offering a pacifier or, if you just can't resist trying it out, you can experiment by giving a little "sip" of breast milk, formula, or water to see if it stops the process. If you ask us, however, breath-holding doesn't seem to work so well—often even for adults—and you might be just as well off ignoring the hiccups, knowing that they're harmless and likely to be short-lived.

CHAPTER 8

spitting up and vomiting

We have found that many baby books describe spitting up as a harmless nuisance that goes away over time, while at the same time cautioning parents that vomiting—sometimes described as projectile— is to be taken seriously. They then proceed to offer up such definitions of spitting up and vomiting as follows:

- **A typical definition of spitting up:** The easy flow of stomach contents through the mouth that may or may not accompany a burp.
- **A typical definition of vomiting:** The forceful flow of stomach contents through the mouth.

Now for a little reality check: Does anyone else besides us happen to think the definitions seem somewhat similar? Well that's because in real life, spitting up and vomiting can be somewhat difficult to distinguish— especially for those who have never had to give it much thought before. If you've already discovered you've got a spitter on your hands, you may be wondering just how forceful is "forceful" and just how projectile do stomach contents have to be and over what distance do they have to travel before qualifying for the upgraded status of vomiting. Don't beat yourself up if you discover you were born without the innate ability to distinguish between the two. The distinction between happy spitters and those with bigger issues has been known to elude doctors at times too. We will do our best to prepare you for the run-of-the-mill spit-up challenge, while at the same time familiarize you with warning signs that can signify something more serious. Take the following descriptions for what they're worth, do what you can to distinguish between easy and forceful flow, and then go with your own gut instinct as to whether you need to involve your pediatrician.

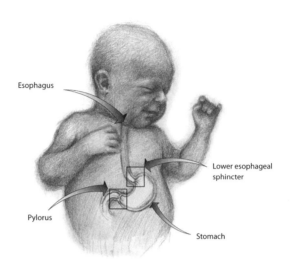

Esophagus

Lower esophageal
sphincter

Pylorus

Stomach

Spitting Up

If you are fortunate, you will be blessed with a baby who, from birth, has
the ability to politely keep whatever he drinks to himself and realizes that
spitting up does not count as sharing. The information that follows will not
be as relevant to you as it will be to those new parents who quickly become
conditioned to expect that some part of every feeding will inevitably come
back up and out. If you happen to already be sitting with a spit rag over
your shoulder(s) and protective coverings over most of your furniture, then
you'll undoubtedly be able to relate to this part of the chapter—the part we
like to think of as the "what you've worked so hard to put in always seems
to come out, even when you don't want it to, despite all your best efforts to
keep it in" section.

For most babies, spitting up is simply the result of a not yet fully
developed muscle that is supposed to serve as a gatekeeper at the top of the
stomach—in general allowing food (drink, in this case) into the stomach
and then *keeping* it there. For those of you who are dying to know the name
of the muscle most likely to blame for your spit-up woes, it is called the
lower esophageal sphincter, or LES for short. For a clearer picture, take a
minute to visualize your baby's stomach as an upright water balloon with a
narrow opening at the top—in the case of a spitty baby, a water balloon left
a little too loosely secured. It's not hard to imagine how any amount of

applied pressure—a poke or squeeze on the side—or a change in position could cause its contents to overflow, especially at times when the balloon is relatively full. For some newborns, a simple gas bubble or a press on the belly is often quite enough to overpower a novice sphincter muscle and allow spit-up to happen. Fortunately, most of the time, spitting up doesn't bother babies. For the parents of these so-called happy spitters, a loose sphincter simply means being more diligent about burping, stockpiling a larger supply of burp cloths or spit rags, and investing in a bottle (or three) of stain remover.

 THE SHAPE OF THINGS TO COME (UP)

No matter how curdled or "spoiled" your baby's spit-up appears, you can reassure yourself that it doesn't really matter. The curdled appearance just reveals that your baby's stomach had already started processing the milk before it managed to escape, and nothing more.

Remedies for Spitty Babies

Burping and spitting up often go hand in hand for newborns. The air in a baby's stomach decides to come up, and the stomach contents often opt to tag along for the ride—a tendency that serves to explain why you'll find a fair bit of overlap between burp prevention and spit-up avoidance techniques. If you find that your newborn tends to spit up quite a bit, there are several things you can try to remedy the situation.

- Position your baby's head higher than the rest of her body when she's eating.
- Step up your burping efforts. You can either just put a little more effort into eliciting a good burp after each feeding, or even try burping more frequently during the feeding—after every 5 minutes of breastfeeding or every ounce or so from a bottle. Only you and your baby can decide whether the interruption in feeding is worth the results.
- Feeding your baby smaller amounts more frequently may help reduce spitting.
- Also try holding or positioning her relatively upright for a good 20 to 30 minutes after meals.

- While some parents find that simply switching brands of formula (see "Formula Intolerance" on page 41) or eliminating certain foods in a breastfeeding mother's diet can help decrease the amount of spitting up, it's always worth checking with your doctor before considering such changes (see "Into the Mouths of Moms" on page 34). While on occasion a change might help, for many newborns and their parents it's an unnecessary inconvenience.

 THE PATH OF LEAST RESISTANCE

Many parents get alarmed when liquid comes spewing out of their baby's nose, but let us reassure you that this is an anatomically normal (albeit potentially surprising and/or unpleasant) occurrence. In case you haven't already discovered it for yourself, we all have a direct connection between the backs of our throats and our noses. Stomach contents expelled by spitting up or vomiting usually follow the path of least resistance, so depending on the circumstances—your baby's positioning and the force of the eruption to name a couple—the exit route may be his mouth and/or his nose.

Assessing Your Losses

Only rarely do babies spit up enough that it becomes more than a matter of inconvenience and affects their overall nutrition and weight gain. That's not to say that the amount an otherwise healthy baby spits up doesn't seem impressive from a parent's-eye view. When looking at the spit-up stains on your baby's clothes (or your own), it is very easy to overestimate the amount of lunch actually being tossed. If you don't want to just take our word for it and are determined to get a better idea of the true volume, you can try pouring some milk or water in measured increments onto a clean towel or cloth diaper. You'll see that the liquid will spread out quite a bit on the dry fabric. Compare the size of a spot made by 1 teaspoon, 1 table-spoon, or 1 ounce of fluid to the spot made by your baby's spit-up or vomit and you may be reassured that all has not been lost. The bottom line: A spitty baby who continues to eat well and gain weight well does not gener-ally need much, if any, intervention. On the other hand, any newborn who isn't eating well, isn't gaining weight as expected, or is increasingly spitting up larger amounts more frequently and/or more forcefully needs to be seen by a doctor.

GERD

GERD is simply the acronym for gastroesophageal reflux disease. In simpler terms, you can think of it as the baby equivalent of heartburn—the result of stomach contents making their way back up into the esophagus, sometimes causing discomfort and on rare occasion resulting in more significant intestinal or breathing problems. It is often the diagnosis given to babies who spit up enough to warrant a discussion, evaluation, and potentially even medical treatment by their doctors. This is not something a book can (or should) diagnose for you—only make you aware of its existence. If in doubt, get it checked out.

Vomiting

More often than not, new parents worry about vomiting when what is coming out of their babies' mouths more closely fits the admittedly vague definition of spitting up. Although less common, newborns can and do vomit for a variety of reasons. Your baby may occasionally vomit if, for example, she has a particularly sensitive gag reflex and/or you have a particularly forceful milk let-down when breastfeeding, or if she's a little overly eager and happens to overfeed. Some babies who seem to have more persistent vomiting may be intolerant of whatever it is they are being given to drink, have an underlying infection, or have a problem in their digestive tract that doesn't allow things to flow through as directed—all instances that should be discussed with and evaluated by a doctor. That said, if you suspect true vomiting, you should be on the lookout for fever or any other signs of being sick. You can also keep an eye out for blood in the poop, diarrhea, or excessive fussiness and gassiness. These sorts of symptoms can indicate intolerance to formula or breast milk and are therefore helpful to report to your pediatrician. Because vomiting can cause dehydration and electrolyte imbalances much more quickly in newborns than in older children and adults, don't wait until your baby seems truly lethargic or dehydrated (as signaled by less pee, a dry mouth, doughy skin, sunken eyes and fontanelle, and weight loss) to contact your pediatrician—just do it right away.

THE TRUE MEANING OF PROJECTILE

Projectile is a word that is often used in the context of spitting up and vomiting. Some parents graphically describe their baby's vomiting as "shooting across the room." While moderately forceful spitting up or vomiting can cause liquid to "jump" or "gush" out a few inches from your baby's mouth, truly projectile eruptions—more force, longer distances, etc— especially when they occur on a regular basis, may indicate more serious problems. For more information, read on.

How Much Is Too Much? When to Consider Pyloric Stenosis

At the point when vomiting seems to be getting progressively worse and becoming more and more out of hand, you and/or your pediatrician may suspect a condition called pyloric stenosis. The pyloric sphincter is simply the muscle at the far end of the stomach that serves as gatekeeper—allowing food to pass into the intestinal tract (see diagram on page 78). In contrast to its often too lax counterpart at the top of the stomach, this sphincter muscle can sometimes become a bit too thick and strong for its own best interest (or anyone else's) and consequently does too good of a job regulating what can get out of the stomach into the intestinal tract. Stenosis simply refers to any type of narrowing; in the case of pyloric stenosis, the opening at the bottom of the stomach becomes progressively narrower than it should be. The more difficult it becomes for stomach contents to go down and out through this narrow region, the more they head up and out instead.

Pyloric stenosis is a condition that occurs in about 3 of every 1,000 babies and is much more common in first-born boys and those with a family history of the condition. It typically causes babies to start spitting up in the first few weeks—usually around 1 month. Unlike the frequent but happy spitters or even the intermittently impressive vomiters, however, babies with pyloric stenosis vomit with increasing force and frequency— most often building up to the full-fledged projectile vomiting by 6 to 8 weeks. If your baby's spitting up or vomiting is persistent and seems to be progressing, it's worth contacting your physician sooner rather than later. If your baby does, in fact, happen to be diagnosed with pyloric stenosis, there is a sure-fire remedy to stop the vomiting; babies with pyloric stenosis require an operation to widen the pylorus muscle's opening at the bottom of the stomach. Babies usually recover quickly and begin feeding normally within a couple of days following surgery.

 ## DOUBLE TROUBLE

If an infant vomits most or all of a feeding for 2 or more feedings in a row, it should be taken as a warning sign of something potentially more serious, and prompt medical evaluation is needed.

Gagging and Sputtering

Some babies tend to have more sensitive gag reflexes than others, which on the one hand is a very good thing because it is the gag reflex that is responsible for keeping food (or in your newborn's case, breast milk or formula) from "going down the wrong way" and getting into the lungs. On the other hand, a gagging or sputtering baby can admittedly be very scary for parents. If your baby starts gagging or having trouble breathing while feeding, you can promptly sit him upright, pat his back, turn his head to the side or slightly face down to let any milk or saliva run out of his mouth, and let him catch his breath. In almost all cases, babies quickly recover from such episodes on their own. If your baby has frequent gagging episodes, or especially if he ever stops breathing even briefly or turns blue for a moment during a gagging or coughing spell, you should seek immediate medical attention.

 ## FOR SAFETY'S SAKE

For safety and peace of mind, we recommend that you and any of your baby's potential caregivers find the time to take a CPR course in case any emergencies arise regarding your baby. You can start by contacting your pediatrician, local Red Cross, or local hospital for class information.

activities of daily living

INTRODUCTION

Included in the following chapters are many of the newborn topics we consider to be the bread and butter of parenting. In them, you will find answers to the most commonly asked questions new parents typically have about the activities you are likely to be partaking in day in and day out once all the baby showers have passed, the waiting and wondering is over, and you've finally checked out of the hospital and headed for home. Sandwiched between the ins and outs discussed in the preceding sections and looking ahead toward heading out and about (to be addressed in the section to follow), we now focus our efforts and your attention on those important aspects of everyday life with a newborn that will initially dominate your thoughts and occupy much of your time, but will soon become second nature: the topics of newborn sleep, crying, diapering, bathing, and clothing.

CHAPTER 9

sleeping like a baby

It is for good reason that sleep (and a new parent's relative lack
thereof) always seems to top the list of popular parenting topics. There's
no doubt about it, heading home with a newborn is quite an eye-opening
experience, both literally and figuratively speaking. Even the years we spent
on call as pediatric residents didn't prepare us for the interrupted sleep
schedule that typically characterizes life with a newborn. It's safe to say that
few things will change more dramatically than your sleep habits, at least
for the foreseeable future when you suddenly switch roles from expectant parent to new parent. Beyond the basic questions of when, where,
and how much to expect your baby (and you) to get, you may also find
yourself wondering what to do about your newborn's blatant disregard for
the "rules" of sleep—including but not limited to the sanctity of nighttime
sleep, the importance of "beauty" sleep, and just plain letting everyone in
the household get enough. As you head into the first few weeks of what
is all but guaranteed to be relative sleep deprivation, we suggest that you
remind yourself of one thing: This too shall pass.

What a Difference a Day (or Two) Can Make

During the first day or two after you have your baby, you might find
yourself impressed with and thankful for how much your baby is sleeping. Many a mother of a newborn gets her best rest in the hospital, only to
come to the conclusion she is destined to be one of the lucky few whose
baby is destined to sleep through the night from day 1. Although we really
don't enjoy bursting anyone's bubble, we feel obliged to give you a heads-
up on what changes are likely to be right around the corner: These first
couple of days are most likely just a honeymoon phase in the grand scheme
of newborn sleep patterns. Many newborns spend their earliest days on

the outside catching up on sleep after the exhausting effort it took to get them there. It's almost as if they are briefly too tired to realize they are now out in the real world where there is so much to see and so much fun to be had. But once they wake up to the fact that they have at their disposal new scenery; parents to "play" with; and a lot of eating, peeing, and pooping to do—not to mention that they are no longer being lulled to sleep in the cozy confines of a uterus complete with soothing background noise—well then all bets are off and the games typically begin. As you first set out to learn the rules of this "can you survive your newborn's sleep habits?" game, you'll find that there are, in fact, very few rules. And even for the few rules there are, your baby may not be much for following them. With time (a few weeks), patience, and a bit of endurance mixed in, you and your baby will catch on and adjust.

Back to Sleep

Chances are good you were raised as a "belly baby"—spending all of your non-waking hours (as well as many of those when you were awake) lying comfortably on your belly. Yes, we acknowledge the fact that parents in generations before us did the best they knew how and all of you reading this book obviously managed to make it to the point where you are trying out parenthood for yourself. Since those days when we were so tenderly laid belly down to rest, new information has come to light about the potential role sleep position plays in sudden infant death syndrome (SIDS)—an occurrence that is admittedly rare but nonetheless terrifying to think about. Based on an ever-increasing amount of evidence linking belly sleeping to an increased risk of SIDS, the American Academy of Pediatrics (AAP) first recommended back sleeping in 1992 and then partnered with several national organizations to launch the official Back to Sleep campaign in 1995. After more than a decade of education aimed squarely at getting parents and caregivers to place infants to sleep on their backs instead of their tummies, the percentage of back-sleeping babies increased accordingly while the SIDS rates decreased impressively. If you're interested in the actual numbers, we are happy to oblige: As of 2008, more than 85% of babies were estimated to sleep on their backs, in contrast to 25% in 1992. Over this same period, there was a dramatic decline in the number of SIDS deaths—by some estimates as much as 58%. However, in the past few years,

THE REALITY OF SIDS: CREATING A SAFE SLEEP ENVIRONMENT

Sudden infant death syndrome (SIDS), sometimes called crib death, is the sudden, unexplained death of an otherwise healthy baby during the first year. It is certainly not a topic we, as parents or pediatricians, enjoy bringing up with excited new parents, but one that we are committed to raising in the hopes of saving babies' lives. While SIDS is always a tragedy for the roughly 2,500 babies and families it affects each year in the United States, the odds of it happening to your child are very low and it is well within your power to minimize the risk. Although SIDS rarely occurs during the first month of life (the risk is greatest from 2 to 4 months), there are simple things you can do to create a safer sleep environment for your newborn right from the start.

- **Be safe.** Play it safe by making sure that you and anyone else who cares for your baby always puts him down to sleep on his back.

- **Be firm.** This means making sure your baby always sleeps on a firm surface. Make sure your crib meets all safety standards, and that the crib mattress fits securely in the crib. Being firm also means keeping all soft items out of your baby's crib—including such tempting but potentially dangerous items as fluffy blankets, stuffed animals, and soft or pillow-like bumpers.

- **Stay cool.** Overheating increases the risk for SIDS. Dress your baby in lightweight sleep clothing. Consider using a wearable blanket in lieu of a regular one, and simply keep the temperature in the room where your baby sleeps set at what would be comfortable for a lightly clothed adult.

- **Clear the air.** Keep the air your baby breathes smoke-free, both to reduce the risk of SIDS but also for your baby's overall health! This includes your home, car, and any place your baby spends time both awake and asleep.

- **Provide a pacifier.** During your baby's first year, consider offering him a pacifier when he is falling asleep. If you are breastfeeding, we recommend waiting until nursing is going well (about 1 month) before introducing the pacifier.

- **Share a room.** The AAP recommends sleeping in the same room but not the same bed as your baby for at least the first 6 months. This can make breastfeeding easier while at the same time help protect your baby from SIDS.

there has been no further increase in back sleeping. The SIDS rate has also not gone down.

Putting Back-Sleeping Concerns to Rest

We're willing to bet that this isn't the first time you've been introduced to the benefits of raising a back-sleeping baby. Most new parents today are well informed when it comes to SIDS and why back sleeping is so strongly recommended. We'd be missing the boat, however, if we didn't acknowledge the fact that you may find yourself with some practical concerns when faced with putting principle into practice. For the most part, the following concerns cause parents to worry unnecessarily:

- **Spitting up and vomiting.** The most common concern we hear is the understandable but unfounded fear that babies will spit up and choke while on their backs. Fortunately, several reassuring studies as well as the test of time have demonstrated that healthy babies put to sleep on their backs are not only able to turn their heads and/or protect their airways if and when they spit up, but are no more likely to have breathing or digestive-related problems than their belly-sleeping counterparts of years past.

- **Flat heads.** It is true that the shape of your newborn's head is not yet set in stone, and that there has been an increase in the number of babies "walking" around with flat heads since back sleeping came into vogue. The fact of the matter is that it's really not that much of a problem for most back-sleeping babies. In large part, that's because you have a good deal of control over the situation. All you need to do is alternate the direction your baby faces each time she lies on her back—both while she is asleep and also when awake. By offering your newborn plenty of tummy time and time spent in positions other than flat on her back while she is awake, you can also help decrease the likelihood of a flat or misshapen head. For more on newborn heads, see "The Shape of Things to Come" on page 276.

- **Delayed milestones.** Some of you will undoubtedly hear or read that back sleeping has been associated with delayed motor development. In addressing the question of delayed milestones—or more specifically, a delay in the time when back-sleeping babies first begin to roll over—rest assured that this all seems to even out in the end. Even if your baby

DON'T TAKE SIDES

In the early days of SIDS prevention, both back and side sleeping were considered to be acceptably safe sleep options for babies. However, subsequent concerns about the safety of side sleeping led to the current recommendation for exclusive back sleeping. That said, some parents have turned to wedge-like cushions, often referred to as sleep positioners. Whether this is because they have unwarranted concerns about spitting up, are worried about flat heads, or simply think side sleeping is safe, the fact of the matter is that devices designed to maintain sleep position have not been sufficiently tested for their safety or effectiveness. Additionally, they are often made of soft material or memory foam, both of which have no place inside a baby's crib (and more specifically, nowhere near a baby's face).

doesn't take to rolling quite as early as her belly-sleeping counterparts of generations past and present, to our knowledge no college application has ever asked applicants how early they mastered the ability to roll over (or, for future reference, sit, crawl, walk, or toilet train). When it comes to strengthening the muscles your baby needs to roll and, at the same time, decreasing your baby's chances of ending up with a flat head, just be aware that both can be easily accomplished by allowing your baby plenty of time on her belly when she's awake.

Good Night, Sleep Tight

We'll be the first to admit that going belly up doesn't always seem to agree with all babies. While not true of all babies, we've found that quite a few are prone to startling themselves awake from peaceful slumber. That's because all babies are at the whim of their own reflexes—which, by definition, they cannot control—and are born with one particularly inconvenient reflex (the startle, or Moro, reflex). This reflex causes infants to jerk suddenly, flail their arms and legs, and even cry out in response to being startled—hence the name (see "Reflexes" on page 301). And yes, even when you've gone to great lengths to create a startle-free environment for your sleeping baby, he may just take matters into his own hands (and feet), startle himself awake, and then proceed to flail around like a bug stuck on his back until someone comes to his rescue. But don't give up on uninterrupted sleep just yet, because there is something quick and easy you can do: a handy little technique we call the "burrito wrap."

The Burrito Wrap

In other words, we suggest you wrap your baby up as snug as a bug in a baby blanket before putting him down to sleep. Hands down, the most talented people we've ever seen at this sleep-saving technique are the nurses in the newborn nursery. These baby-bundling experts take uncomfortably free and exposed newborns and almost effortlessly have them bundled in blissful, no-flailing-allowed slumber in the blink of an eye. If you have an opportunity, we highly recommend watching these professionals in action. For those of you who are already home and either missed out on the hospital demonstration or could use a little refresher course, we've laid out the details for you as best we can without actually being there to demonstrate in person.

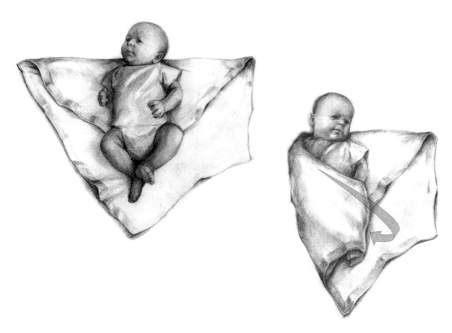

1. Lay a thin baby blanket out like a diamond in front of you.
2. Fold the top corner of the blanket down a bit so that the folded corner almost reaches the middle of the blanket.

3. Place your infant on his back, centered on the blanket with his arms at his sides and his head just above the folded edge and his shoulders just below it.

4. Take one of the side corners of the blanket and fold it over your baby's shoulder and across his body, making sure to tuck the corner underneath him on the opposite side.

5. Then take the bottom corner of the blanket (below your baby's feet) and fold it up over your baby. If the blanket is large enough that the bottom corner reaches up to (or over) your baby's face, you can simply fold it back down until his face is no longer covered or bring it over either shoulder and tuck it under him.

6. Finally, take the only remaining corner and pull it over your baby's other shoulder and across his body. Again, tuck this corner snugly under your baby's opposite side.

Once you have the general idea, remember that variations are perfectly acceptable. Feel free to play around with what works best for you and your baby. While the exact details and the order in which you do them may not matter too much in the end, we will point out that there is a good reason why we recommend folding the bottom of the blanket up *before* flipping the last corner across (ie, step 5 always before step 6) and always tucking corners under your baby: Doing so helps to keep your handiwork from coming undone quite as easily.

Hands-free Bundling

Some of our esteemed parenting colleagues suggest doing whatever it takes (with regard to bundling, that is) to ensure that your baby's arms and legs stay snugly secured in the blanket. Other equally convincing and respectable experts recommend never restricting your baby's arms—focusing your bundling attention on just your baby's legs while allowing her arms free rein. We personally have tried bundling both ways with good results. If you find that your baby seems unhappy having her arms "pinned down" by her sides instead of up next to her head, then just go ahead and burrito wrap her without placing her arms inside. One thing most child health experts do agree on, however, is that a baby's hips should not be bundled too tightly. Instead, they should be allowed to relax in their natural frog-leg positions to allow for proper growth and joint development.

 ## A NEWBORN'S PERSPECTIVE ON THE COMFORTS OF HOME

In addition to being at the mercy of their own reflexes, babies also tend to take a while to adapt to their new and often less appealing living (and sleeping) quarters. Keeping in mind that your newborn has just spent almost a year inside a continuously warm, dark, snug, and soothing environment, it becomes easier to understand how the sudden transition to lying sprawled out flat on one's back can seem like nothing short of a rude awakening—one that your newborn may take some time adjusting to.

Sleeping by the Book

"Sleeping like a baby" can mean different things to different people—usually depending on whether they've ever had or taken care of one before. For just about all newborns it fairly predictably means having the ability to sleep at any time and in any place, while at the same time being completely unwilling to entertain any "suggestions" as to how, when, or where to put such talent into practice. You may come across those who have ventured down the path of parenthood before you who simply shake their heads sympathetically and wish you luck in getting your newborn to wake up when you want/need him to, and even better luck getting him to go to sleep when you want. Because we're committed to helping you set appropriate expectations for yourself and your baby, we're going to approach the whole subject of sleep by first helping you get into the right frame of mind. We decided to start out by providing you with some basic sleep-related milestones.

- **Daily sleep.** The average newborn spends at least 16 hours a day sleeping, but there can be big differences from one newborn to the next. The total amount of sleep babies need in any given 24-hour day gradually decreases over time, but still totals just over 14 hours at 6 months of age and just under 14 hours at 1 year.

- **Naps.** Sure, many newborns nap in 1- to 2-hour spurts, but before you go planning your schedule around any preconceived idea of nap time, let us add that the length of most newborns' naps is also very variable and they tend to be scattered throughout the day (and night) in a completely random and therefore unpredictable manner. The 3-nap-a-day schedule with which you may be familiar should be considered a sleep pattern you should aspire to down the road, because most newborns don't settle into this type of nap routine for at least a month or two. Even then, it can take a few additional weeks or months before you can count on a morning, early afternoon, and early evening nap.

- **Night versus day.** During the first few days and weeks of parenthood, you are likely to find that there's not going to be a whole lot that distinguishes your days from your nights. More often than not, they just seem to blend together into one big sleep-deprived blur. That's because it will be almost completely up to your newborn when he chooses to be awake and when he chooses to sleep. Most newborns spend equal amounts of time sleeping during the day and night—a tendency that can be quite challenging for those of us accustomed to more of an awake-by-day, asleep-by-night approach. By the end of their first month, most newborns do manage to figure out how to consolidate their sleep into longer stretches and start to get at least one extended stretch of sleep during each 24-hour day. So with any luck, you'll be blessed with a baby who decides to choose nighttime as the right time to do so. And for the real light at the end of the tunnel: By 3 months of age, many babies get approximately two-thirds of their total daily sleep during the night.

Reversing Day-Night Reversal

Some babies, however, settle into the newborn sleep routine dreaded by many expectant parents—the so-called day-night reversal. As the description implies, newborns are known on occasion to mix up their days and nights. These temporarily backward-sleeping babies often begin to increase the amount of sleep they get each time they go to sleep according to plan, but simply do so more during the day, while demanding to be fed, changed, *and* entertained throughout the night. As painfully exhausting as this upside-down approach to sleep may be for those of us accustomed to getting most if not all of our sleep at night, the assurance that this too shall pass once again comes to mind. We can all but guarantee you that hope is not far away. In most instances, the fact that your newborn is learning to replace lots of short little catnaps with longer stretches of sleep—whether they happen to fall during the day or at night—bodes well for a more "civilized" sleep routine in your not too distant future.

Lights On, Lights Off

If your baby seems determined to "play" during the night and sleep during the day there's really no quick fix, but there are some easy things you can do early on to set the stage for more acceptable sleep habits in the future. During your first few weeks at home with your baby, try to establish an atmosphere that clearly differentiates night from day. A good night's rest may not result overnight, but this approach can help get you there sooner.

- **Allow for active sleep.** During the day, have your baby sleep in more active areas of the house—in rooms with the lights on, or perhaps even in the car seat or stroller when you determine that you are ready to make your way out of the house.
- **Consistent contrast.** Don't spend much time worrying about background noises such as talking, telephones, or music during daylight hours. In contrast, try to make your nighttime interactions calm and quiet.

- **Maintain focus.** Whenever possible, take a more focused approach to your nighttime interactions—limiting them to feeding, burping, changing, and gentle soothing when necessary.
7. **Soft-spoken approach.** Get in the habit of taking the aforementioned measures in a dark room using a soft voice whenever you want to signal to your newborn that it would be a fine time to sleep.

Learning to Sleep, Drink, and Be Merry

Before lying down, closing your eyes, and simply considering yourself lucky that you have a baby who has precociously caught on to sleeping long stretches at a time, you'll want to first consider whether prolonged periods of sleep could get her into trouble. That's because some babies—especially those who are born small, who have not yet mastered breastfeeding, or who are just a bit too sleepy for their own good—can be drowsy enough that they don't remember to wake up and eat. Just how long should you let your newborn sleep at any one time and how often should you feed her? The answer will depend on a variety of factors, not the least of which will be based on your pediatrician's assessment and subsequent recommendation.

Let Sleeping Newborns Lie?

Some pediatricians buy into the idea that full-term, healthy babies do not need to be woken up to eat during the night as long as they are eating and gaining weight well. Others feel very strongly that all young infants—at least for the first several weeks—should not be allowed to sleep for more than 4 or 5 hours at a time (at most) without being woken up to eat. Our opinion on the matter: Wait at least until you are sure your newborn has fully mastered breastfeeding or bottle-feeding, proven himself capable of taking a regular interest in eating, and regained his birth weight according to plan within the first 2 weeks after being born before kicking back and enjoying the luxury of 4 or more hours of uninterrupted sleep. Whatever you do, be sure you discuss any sleep habits that seem too good to be true (and may, in fact, be falsely reassuring) with your baby's health care provider before reveling in the thought of a good night's sleep.

Waking Up Is (Sometimes) Hard to Do

Now is as good a time as any to discuss briefly the age-old adage "never wake a sleeping baby." Many expectant parents take this advice to heart and prepare themselves and their homes accordingly. In anticipation, they begin by locating the ringer on/off switches on their phones and making signs to tape over their doorbells that read, "Please knock quietly—baby sleeping." After bringing home a newborn of your own, however, you're far more likely to discover that most young infants (older babies are a different story) can sleep through just about anything—vacuums, doorbells, and the ringing of telephones included. Instead of figuring out ways to ensure peaceful slumber, many new parents find themselves wondering if, in fact, their babies would awaken to the sound of a freight train going by or the house being hit by a tornado. You'll find that as your baby gets older she will probably become a lighter sleeper, but for the time being you can feel free to relax a little on the noise control, unless of course you need it so you can sleep.

How to Wake a Sleeping Baby

As we mentioned at the outset, newborns have an impressive ability to ignore the world around them when they see fit to sleep. If you find yourself in the position of needing to wake up your baby, here are some simple techniques that sometimes (notice we said "sometimes") work.

- **The kinder, gentler approach.** You might as well start out with the kinder, gentler approach to baby waking and see what kind of response you get. This can include such basic measures as talking, singing, and gentle stimulation. Pick your baby up, talk to him, move his arms and legs around, even tickle the bottom of his feet or rub his cheek—whatever works to rouse him.
- **Dressing down.** Whether it's the physical stimulation or the increased exposure to cool air that does it, many newborns absolutely hate to be undressed. Your newborn may find it well worth the time and effort it takes to awaken and voice his opinion.
- **Double-duty diapering.** Even if your baby doesn't technically require one, going through the motions (even reusing the same diaper) may help if undressing alone doesn't do the trick. This works especially well for those babies who have a tendency to fall asleep before finishing their meals. We think of it as dual-purpose diapering because not only do diaper changes tend to wake up sleeping babies, but this also tends to be

a time when newborns are more likely to actually need to be changed (see "The Eating-Pooping Connection" on page 69).

- **Cleanliness is next to wakefulness.** Giving sleepy babies a bath certainly takes things a step beyond undressing and changing diapers, but has been known to work when all else fails. While we certainly don't approve of cruel and unusual punishment in any way, shape, or form, there may be times when some of you simply have no other choice than to resort to a bath to get your baby to wake up. This more "drastic" measure is most appropriately used sparingly, such as in the event that a newborn is long overdue to eat, and can be modified to accommodate your baby's umbilical cord as needed (see "Baby Bath Basics" on page 133).

The approaches we have described to you are obviously based on the assumption that your newborn is healthy. While it is true that newborns are known to be challenging to wake up at times, you should also be aware that babies who are not arousable or responsive despite their parents' best efforts need medical attention. Do not wait to discuss any questions or concerns you might have about your baby's sleepiness with your baby's doctor: Seek medical help immediately if your newborn seems increasingly sleepy, unresponsive, or hard to arouse.

Now I Lay Me Down to Sleep

Many new-baby books matter-of-factly lay out the merits of teaching babies to fall asleep on their own without parental assistance. You know: no rocking, no nursing, and no driving circles around the neighborhood in search of sleep. If you have taken heed, you may be wondering to yourself exactly how you are supposed to go about getting your newborn to fall asleep independently without guaranteed screams of protest. The reality is that babies should (and can) learn to fall asleep all on their own within the first 4 months. In the early days, however, we suggest you avoid losing sleep over whether you are doing yourself and your newborn a great disservice by occasionally allowing her to start drifting off to sleep cradled in your arms or snuggled up on your chest before putting her in her crib. That said, we do suggest taking any opportunity you get right from the start to promote healthy lifelong habits—and that most certainly includes the very important life skill of falling asleep without assistance.

TO SLEEP, PERCHANCE TO DREAM

Even though they have shorter sleep cycles than adults, overall the average newborn spends far more time in what is known as active (REM) sleep. Not only is this the stage of sleep where dreaming takes place, but also where there is likely to be a lot more sucking, kicking, grunting, and moving going on. This is also a good time to catch a few first smiles.

Suitable Sleep Sites

At first, we figured we ought to allot a good bit of time to addressing the various sleep-site options available to you—starting predictably with the crib and then running through everything from bassinets, cradles, cosleepers, and playpens to car seats and dresser drawers. Then it occurred to us that most parents we talk to seem to handle this part of new parenthood pretty well on their own, and either don't care too much or already have their hearts set on one or the other (or several) of the options. Given that there are plenty of informative baby product books like *Baby Bargains* and Consumer Reports' *Best Baby Products* around, we decided not to take up too much of your time on the subject. Instead, we are going to lay out for you what we consider to be the practical considerations and safety tips most useful in deciding where to lay your baby down to rest.

Sleeping Solo or Filling the Family Bed

Probably since the beginning of time, babies and parents around the world have slept together in what has come to be commonly referred to as "the family bed." In recent years, particularly in industrialized nations including the United States, the trend has been to have children sleep separately starting from infancy. We suggest you let common sense and a strong commitment to safety prevail.

- **The family bed.** Whether due to space limitations, cultural norms, or a strong belief that bed sharing is an integral part of parenting, parents have slept with their babies for thousands of years. In many parts of the world and in a good 60% of US households, many babies still do sleep in bed with their parents at least on occasion, despite increasing concerns about the associated risks. Followers of attachment parenting seem to

THE CONVENIENCE OF COSLEEPERS

For those of you who find the convenience of having your baby nearby at night appealing but find the concerns about having him in bed with you concerning, then a cosleeper may be just the right answer for you. If you ask us, these specially designed baby beds are ingenious. They are somewhat like playpens, generally rest at the same height as a standard adult bed, have a drop-down (or absent) rail on the side that fits next to the bed, and can therefore be placed right alongside it for easy access. Not only do they fit the bill when it comes to the AAP SIDS prevention recommendation to have your baby sleep in the same room but not the same bed, but they also facilitate safe and successful breastfeeding.

feel quite strongly that parents and babies benefit most from bonding whenever possible, including during sleep. Proponents also feel that bed sharing makes breastfeeding easier.

- **Sleeping solo.** In the United States, there has been a definite shift toward putting babies to sleep independently, whether in a crib, cradle, or bassinet. Our country's movement toward independent sleep may well be, in part, attributable to recent concerns that bed sharing may increase the risk of sleep-related infant deaths (see "The Reality of SIDS" on page 91). Other practical reasons why parents opt for solo sleeping: They find it to be safer, sounder (for the baby and her parents), and less intrusive on their "adult" time.

Bed-Sharing Safety Concerns

Many new parents are tempted to take their newborn into bed with them—often out of fatigue and convenience, as well as for cultural and philosophical reasons. Whether bed sharing is safe, however, has been the subject of much debate. Recent studies suggest that bed sharing may significantly increase the risk of infant suffocation, so you'll find that many experts now strongly advise against it and instead suggest the very practical and safer alternative of sharing the same room, but not the same bed. If you do choose to sleep with your baby in your bed, even if only infrequently, here are some extremely important safety considerations.

- Bed sharing and the use of tobacco, alcohol, or drugs (including over-the-counter or prescription medicines) simply don't mix. These substances may cause excessive drowsiness—making you potentially less aware of your baby.
- The heavy blankets, comforters, pillows, and other accessories that are typically found on adult beds can suffocate or smother a baby and therefore have no place being in the same location where newborns sleep. While we're on the subject of simple yet potentially life-saving measures, we also strongly recommend removing any and all such items that may have already found their way into your baby's crib.
- Bed-sharing babies are at risk from falls or the possibility of being trapped between the mattress and the wall, headboard, or other furniture.

Crib Safety Considerations

Whether you decide to set up a crib for your baby as soon as your pregnancy test turns positive or months after your newborn's much-anticipated arrival, there are a few general safety principles that you'll want to follow to ensure your baby's safety. Some may not seem particularly relevant during your baby's first few months, but given that cribs tend to be big-ticket items and the one you invest in is going to be put to the test for years to come as your baby learns to roll, sit, stand, and climb in it, it's well worth considering present and future safety concerns.

- **Crib slats.** The slats should be no more than 2⅜ inches apart. All new cribs must meet this standard, but older cribs may not.
- **Posts and cutouts.** Steer clear of bedposts taller than 1/16 of an inch and/or cutouts in the headboard (or any other parts of the crib) where a baby's or toddler's body parts could get stuck.
- **Crib toys.** They may seem harmless, entertaining, cute, and cuddly, but it's considered wise to keep all stuffed animals (and most toys) out of your newborn's crib because they can pose a small but nevertheless real safety risk. The exceptions are the types of toys that strap securely to the side of the crib. Some babies like mirrors or toys with parts they can play with (such as spinners, rattles, and music), but your newborn probably won't be terribly interested in them for at least a few weeks.

- **Mobiles.** Mobiles are special hanging toys designed to entertain your baby and can be attached to the crib, ceiling, or wall. Some are even adorned with lights or play music. They are fun but definitely optional. If you do choose to use mobiles, make sure they do not hang low enough to entangle your baby, especially once she begins to roll. In fact, once your baby is able to sit up, it will definitely be time for her mobile to come down.

- **Crib placement.** Unless you don't mind a bit of redecorating and rearranging when your baby starts to get around, we suggest you place your crib well away from any windows and no less than an arm's reach away from any nearby dressers or table-tops. Knowing that it won't be long before anything and everything within reach will be fair game, we also recommend limiting your over-the-crib wall decorations to painted walls and wallpaper. Picture frames and mirrors over cribs are often an accident waiting to happen. Be forewarned that even paper borders placed within reach of the crib, while safe, don't often stand up well to prying fingers.

- **Firm-fitting mattress/fitted sheet.** While they seem to be mostly standardized, cribs and mattresses can and do come in more than one size, so be sure to double-check measurements and read labels to make sure you end up with a mattress that fits snugly into your chosen crib. Any extra space between the mattress and crib frame has the potential to trap a baby's arm, leg, or head. Also make sure your fitted sheets are tight enough that they don't slip off easily, thus posing a serious safety hazard. See the following sections for more on bedding for your baby's crib.

- **Tooth-resistant rails.** Some railings are covered by a special plastic to prevent teething babies from gnawing on the paint or wood.

- **Adjustable mattress height.** Many cribs have adjustable heights so you can lower the mattress as your baby gets taller, making it more difficult for him to climb out. You will likely want to keep it at the highest level while your newborn is relatively immobile and you are coming and going frequently because it will allow you to save a good deal of strain on your back. Remember that by the time your baby is able to sit or stand up, you'll want to lower the level of the crib mattress accordingly.

RAISING CONCERNS ABOUT
DROP-SIDE CRIBS

In recent years, crib railings have almost always been adjustable—
meaning you can raise and lower one or both side railings. While
this feature has long been appealing to parents as a convenience
factor, it has now become one of significant concern. That's because
numerous injuries from crib side-rails resulted in the largest crib recall in
history (2.1 million cribs!) in 2009. As a result, the organization that sets
voluntary industry safety standards required that going forward,
all full-sized cribs be manufactured with 4 immovable sides. In other
words, drop-side cribs may soon become a thing of the past. The
take-home message for all parents: Always be sure to check out the
latest safety information on the Consumer Product Safety Commission
Web site (www.cpsc.gov) before dropping your guard.

Baby Bedding, Bumpers, and Blankets

If you come to find that the excitement you feel about having a new baby is
wrapped up in the buying of a fancy baby bedding set complete with bumper and quilted blanket, then don't let us stop you. After all, we couldn't
resist the parental urge to splurge either—at least not the first time around.
For those of you who are interested in taking a more minimalist approach,
now is the time for us to point out that as cute as it may be to walk into the
nursery and see the lamp match the wallpaper border match the blanket
match the diaper holder…you get the picture, you really don't need any of
it. For safety's sake, those big crib quilts should be kept out of your baby's
sleeping environment, and you should avoid bumper padding or remove it
as soon as your baby starts moving around to make sure she doesn't stand
a chance of getting tangled in it. The receiving blanket(s) and/or pajamas
you use to wrap your baby in should be enough for warmth. If you're really
set on using a baby blanket, we suggest using a small, thin, lightweight one
instead of anything thick or fluffy.

Feet to Foot

For those of you who choose to cover your sleeping babies with blankets,
the AAP recommends using the "feet to foot" method as an easy and effective way to keep them from getting tangled up. Simply place your baby's

feet at the foot of the mattress, cover him with a blanket, and tuck the ends of the blanket into the sides and foot of the crib.

Monitoring the Situation

Modern parents now have the option of using baby monitors to listen to or even watch their babies from afar. Many parents find that monitors buy them peace of mind—allowing them to roam freely around the house while still keeping close tabs on their babies. If you choose to use a monitor, you may want to keep the following considerations in mind:

- **Range.** Baby monitors are only as good as their technological limitations, so we suggest you take a look at what kind of "listening" range they each offer.
- **It works both ways.** In more densely populated neighborhoods, apartments, or townhouses you may pick up interference from other baby monitors. Not only do you run the risk of eavesdropping on neighboring households, but your monitor-owning neighbors stand an equally good chance of hearing what's going on in the monitored room(s) in your house as well.
- **Disrupting the peace.** Some of you may find that leaving the monitor on at night significantly disturbs whatever limited sleep you stand to get—causing you to be wide awake in response to your slumbering baby's every twitch or snort.
- **Channel surfing.** In this age of modern electronics there's more than enough to interfere with your monitor, including cordless phones, cell phones, radio stations, and other monitors. Try to find a monitor with good reception and more than one channel to decrease the likelihood of interference. We also suggest holding onto your receipt in case you run into any unforeseen technological conflicts that become apparent only once you put the monitor to use at home.
- **Bells and whistles.** Give some thought to which bells and whistles you really want and which simply serve to raise the price. Some of the available added features include a portable receiver with a belt clip, 2-way walkie-talkie radio capability, a receiver that vibrates or flashes lights so you can leave the sound turned off, and the possibility of purchasing multiple portable receivers that can accompany a single base station.

- **Nothing beats the real thing.** Never let your baby monitor substitute for taking sensible safety measures. There is no evidence that using a monitor will decrease the chance of SIDS.

Parental Sleep Priorities

We couldn't end a chapter on newborn sleep without addressing what you can do to get yourself some much-needed rest too. Typically offered by those who've been in the trenches before you, the often-repeated advice to sleep whenever your baby is sleeping actually makes very good sense—regardless of whether you considered yourself the type of person to take naps in your pre-parenting days. After all, if you don't take any and every opportunity that comes your way, we're pretty sure you'll come up quite short when trying to squeeze in your own REM cycles. We encourage you to put sleep high on your own priority list and either delegate or let other activities take a back seat for the first few weeks or months. As a point of practicality, let us also mention that trying to accomplish routine but complex tasks such as balancing your checkbook, preparing elaborate meals, entertaining, or operating heavy machinery in a sleep-deprived state is best avoided whenever possible (more on this in "Taking Care of Yourself" on page 157). And in all seriousness, don't try to drive when you're extremely exhausted. Finally, take people up on their offers to help out around the house so you can get some much-needed rest. They wouldn't offer if they didn't mean it, right?

CHAPTER 10

crying

A Welcome Cry

All newborns are supposed to cry—and most of them do a very good job of it. In fact, most newborns tackle this important rite of babyhood immediately after being delivered. A newborn's first cries actually serve a very important purpose. By helping to fill the lungs with air, crying helps newborns make the momentous shift from being dependent on the oxygen carried to him in his mother's blood before birth to breathing it in on his own as soon as he enters the outside world. Even without an explanation of fetal and newborn circulation, you probably don't need us to tell you that delivery room cries are worthy of eager anticipation; generally represent the arrival of a happy, healthy baby; and are almost universally met with tears of joy and relief. What cries may come in the days that follow can vary considerably from baby to baby—but more likely than not you'll find yourself with a relatively sleepy baby (see "Sleeping Like a Baby" on page 89) who only cries to be fed (see "Into the Mouths of Babes" on page 1).

Why Cry?

Once newborns have slept off the excitement of delivery and opened their eyes to the brave new world that lies before them, you can bet that they all inevitably and intermittently start crying. That said, one of the first and most helpful lessons to teach yourself is that babies don't always cry for the same reasons as adults. After all, most of us cry when we are either (a) hurt or (b) upset. We assume it is for this reason that many parents become distressed at the sound of their baby's cry and feel like absolute failures if they can't stop their baby's presumed cries for help, much less stop them immediately. Babies, on the other hand, have the uncanny ability to burst into tears (minus the tears, of course, which don't tend to show up in any noticeable amount for the first month or so—see "Loud and Tearless" below) if they're startled, hungry, cold or hot, tired, wet, bored, annoyed, have gas…you get the picture. The way we look at it, babies are justified in crying a lot if for no other reason than that they really don't have many other ways of communicating their feelings. If you remind yourself that crying isn't always synonymous with pain or being upset, you'll be much less likely to find yourself on the verge of tears in the months to come.

 LOUD AND TEARLESS

Most babies typically don't seem to shed tears in the first month or so—not for a lack of trying but as we understand it, simply because their tear glands don't make enough to be very noticeable. While you may not exactly treasure your baby's cries (at least after the first one in the delivery room) you may actually find yourself a little misty when your newborn reaches the teardrop milestone and her cries are accompanied for the first time by overflowing tears.

Tales of a Telltale Cry

Most books will tell you that your parenting instincts will quickly take over and you'll be able to identify the reason for each of your baby's unique cries. We definitely don't want to minimize the importance of taking crying seriously and we wholeheartedly agree that you should try to understand the underlying meaning of each of your baby's cries, but in our experience this is often easier said than done. When you're not quite sure why your baby is crying, look first for the "obvious" causes—hungry, poopy, wet, tired—as well as reassure yourself that it's not because of the potentially more serious causes—fever and illness, poking pins, an eyelash or scratch in the eye, or wayward hairs or strings wrapped around fingers or toes (2 universally listed causes we felt obliged to include although they are, in reality, pretty rare). But for those of you who in the end still can't pinpoint why your newborn is or was crying and feel hopelessly incompetent as a result, we hope we can convince you to be less critical of yourself by telling you that we did not always find cry identification to be a simple task with our own newborns either. We did what we could, and we gave it our all (although sometimes our "all" was a bit limited due to sheer sleep deprivation). If our children could remember their infancies and were allowed to publicly discuss our own parental "inadequacies" we're sure they would tell us they were fed when they were wet, put to bed when they were hungry, and over-stimulated when they were tired. Sure, there will be times when your baby's needs are obvious, but it's worth keeping in mind that there will also be times when you're just not sure about anything except, perhaps, wanting to pull your hair out.

 CALCULATED CRYING

In your first weeks and months, remind yourself that it is absolutely normal for babies to cry. A typical newborn will increase the amount he cries during any given day from about 2 hours a day at 2 weeks of age to a peak of up to 3 hours by 6 weeks. Light at the end of the tunnel: After the first couple of months, the amount of daily crying that babies do gradually decreases and the reason(s) for their crying is usually much easier to figure out as time goes on.

Is It Colic?

Pick up any baby book and you're sure to find mention of what many parents refer to as the dreaded "C word." Even though the rule of thumb for colic is that it doesn't usually settle in until 3 weeks or so, we've included it front and center in our crying section because without any frame of reference, quite a few parents start worrying about it even before their babies are born, and then worry that every cry or fussy spell is only one step shy of all-out colic (or might signify the start of it). Quite simply, colic is defined as persistent crying in an otherwise healthy infant. For practical purposes, we like to think of colic as a spectrum ranging from crying episodes that last just a few minutes to those that go on for hours at a time. Only time will tell if your newborn will prove to be a "colicky" baby—one who has regular crying spells that present themselves usually in the evening and for no apparent reason. The good news is that most babies with colic (and even those without) outgrow excessive crying by 3 to 6 months of age.

Controlling Colic

While no one knows the true cause of colic, and many parents and experts continue to attribute the crying to stomach pain and/or something in a baby's diet, the most practical and logical analysis of colic (and what to do about it) was recently laid out for all parents to benefit from in a well-written, practical parenting book and DVD by a fellow pediatrician named Harvey Karp. In *The Happiest Baby on the Block,* Dr Karp takes a close look at previous colic theories and then introduces parents to the 5 Ss (swaddling, side/stomach positioning while awake, shushing, swaying, and sucking) that he—and we—find very effective in calming crying colicky babies during the first few months of life.

 DOES SOOTHING = SPOILING?

You certainly don't need to hold back on responding to your newborn's cries for fear of spoiling her. In fact, for the next several months you can take spoiling off of your list of parenting concerns altogether. Each time you try to respond promptly to your newborn's cries, you simply send your baby a message that you're there to tend to her needs.

Soothing the Savage Beast

How, exactly, can you tell what your newborn's needs are so that you can more successfully soothe him? Well even though we've already told you it's not always simple, you are likely to find that after a few days you notice that every time your baby starts to fall asleep he has a characteristic cry. Or maybe he'll have a certain wail that stops as soon as he is fed. Once you start picking up on these cues and responding accordingly, your baby will take comfort in knowing that he's able to communicate with you, at least some of the time. If you can't identify the cry, consider the last time your baby ate, slept, or had his diaper changed. If it has been a few hours, it may be time again to tend to each of these needs. Here are some other techniques to try if your baby just won't stop crying.

- **Get professional help.** Most books save the worst-case scenarios for the end of the list. Not us. We want you to know right off the bat that if at any point you feel that your baby is simply inconsolable or crying for longer than you're comfortable with, or if he seems sick or has an unusually high-pitched cry, then by all means put down the book(s) and enlist the expertise of your pediatrician without delay—that's what they're there for!

- **Soothe yourself.** OK, we're now going to assume that you've evaluated your situation and don't think it warrants a doctor's intervention. The next step is to take a deep breath and try to relax. Babies can pick up on stress around them and may start to cry if they get negative vibes. Sometimes the best first step you can take is to calm down, even if that means putting your crying baby in a safe place and giving yourself a quick break first.

- **Stay snug and secure.** Try swaddling your baby snugly (as described in "Good Night, Sleep Tight" on page 93). The way we reason it, newborns have all spent 9 months (give or take) accustomed to feeling snug and secure in the very close quarters of the uterus. By simulating this cozy feeling of confinement, the swaddling technique often helps with crying as well as with sleeping.

- **Keep things moving.** Every newborn who's spent any amount of time in utero is simply not going to be born accustomed to sitting still. As a result, you may find that yours takes a while to buy into the notion that the absence of movement and activity can be pleasant and peaceful. In the meantime, you can try the time-tested methods of movement such as carrying, rocking, strolling, or driving to appease your crying or restless newborn. The ever-popular vibrating infant seats and baby swings also serve the purpose of keeping your baby comfortably moving as well. Just keep in mind that you'll want to always secure your baby according to instructions, keep an eye on him while you're using them, and look for features designed to accommodate newborns (additional recline, harnesses that adequately secure small infants, low settings on automatic swings, etc).

- **Supply simple sound effects.** Your baby may also crave the soothing muffled noises similar to amniotic fluid waves or the swishes and pulses of mom's heart and blood vessels. You may find, as many before you undoubtedly have, that the sound of a vacuum cleaner, washing machine, shower running, or human heartbeat (hold him against your chest or play a tape of heart sounds) works wonders. For some of these efforts, you will also have the added bonus of a cleaner house, clothes, or body! Whether you're musical or not, try singing or playing some music. Some parents find that their newborns seem to be particularly soothed by music that was played or sung to them even before they were born!

- **Opposites attract.** Feel your baby's hands and feet. If they are cold, put on another layer of clothing or wrap him in a blanket. If the back of his head and neck are warm or sweaty, remove a layer (and consider checking his temperature as discussed in "Fever: Trial by Fire" on page 303). See if he's interested in a change of scenery—if it's bright, turn off the lights. If it's dark, turn some on. If it's very noisy, turn down the volume. If it's unusually quiet, try out some of the simple sound effects mentioned previously. Too still? Move around. Bottom line: no actual science involved here—more a matter of finding and fine-tuning your own simple calming solutions.

- **Hand off.** If others are around, enlist their help until you're ready to try again yourself.

- **Give it time.** If all else fails, just hold your baby and patiently wait for him to settle down. Crying in and of itself won't hurt your baby, so if you're not in a mindset to handle it, it's OK to let your baby cry for a while. If you're at your wit's end and need a break, don't feel guilty about putting him in a safe place (such as a crib or buckled into a car seat) while you compose yourself.

 WHEN THE CRYING WON'T STOP

Now that we've tried to give you a better feel for why newborns cry, we want to leave you with a general rule about newborns and crying. Even though inconsolable crying does not always mean that there is a serious underlying cause to blame, it always warrants a call to the doctor.

When You Feel Like Crying

While entire books are written on the subject of "baby blues" and postpartum depression, we didn't want to finish off this chapter without telling you that if you don't feel like crying in the first few days or weeks after becoming a parent, then congratulations—you're definitely in the minority. A whopping 70% to 80% of new moms reportedly get some form of the baby blues. For most of you, we suggest you don't spend too much time trying to explain your tears or wondering whether it is the hormonal roller coaster, sleep deprivation, or sheer newness of parenthood to blame. Mild depressive feelings, while common, fortunately tend to go away after a few weeks. For an estimated 15% of new mothers, however, the blues progress to full-blown postpartum depression that can last anywhere from weeks to months and usually requires counseling and treatment. Of note, the same study found that as many of 1 out of 10 new fathers experienced symptoms associated with the diagnosis of postpartum depression as well! If ever you find yourself overwhelmed, frustrated, anxious, persistently teary, or depressed and unable to explain or shake the feeling, please don't suffer in silence or shame. Talk to your doctor right away. Although you may well feel like it, you are not alone.

CHAPTER 11

the art and science of diapering

The Facts About Diapers

It's probably not news to you that becoming a parent will inevitably involve changing a lot of diapers—as many as 8 to 12 a day once you get into the swing of things—but who knew there was a whole art and science to the task? The fact of the matter is that most parents average 6 diaper changes a day and go through nearly 3,000 diapers during their baby's first year alone. With toilet training not often achieved until children are 2 or 3 years old or later in the United States (although it may occur much earlier in other cultures), diapering is an unavoidable part of parenthood. Need we say more? Obviously we think so, because not everyone (ie, almost no one) is born with an innate mastery of this necessary parenting skill.

 DIAPER(LESS) TRIVIA

Did you know that in certain Asian and African cultures babies are not put in diapers? When a baby awakens or the parent notices certain cues, the parent places the baby over a bush or other designated area to pee or poop. Although you may want to adapt this technique when it comes time to potty train, based on social norms in America, we don't recommend you try this with your newborn at home!

The Debate: Cloth Versus Disposable

As newcomers to the world of parenting, some of you may not have heard of the ongoing cloth versus disposable diaper debate, especially because the use of disposable diapers has become so accepted as a modern-day convenience that many parents wouldn't dream of using a substitute. In contrast to 1955 when essentially all American babies wore cloth diapers, an estimated 90% of the turn of the 21st century babies are sporting the latest in disposable fashions. While a simple Internet search on the subject will quickly make it clear to you how strongly some people feel about the cloth versus disposable debate, we have no intention of taking sides. Instead, we figured we'd offer you some facts and practical advice related to the use of each type—with the rest of our information weighted toward disposable use only because it is clearly more applicable to most parents these days.

- **Disposable.** Disposable diapers are very absorbent, which can be good and bad. Using them may mean that your baby's skin has less contact with pee and poop, and may offer the added convenience of less frequent changing. However, it may also be more difficult to monitor exactly how much your baby is peeing—a task that is especially important during the newborn period as well as when you're faced with watching for signs of dehydration (see "Vomiting" on page 81).

  Some cloth diaper advocates argue that babies in disposable diapers have a much higher incidence of diaper rash (presumably due to longer contact with diaper contents resulting from less frequent changing). Interestingly, however, one of the commonly recommended approaches to treating diaper rashes is, in fact, for cloth-diaper users to switch to disposable. Also garnishing a lot of attention is the fact that "disposable" diapers are not biodegradable and an estimated 18 billion a year make their way into landfills. We have been happy to learn that some communities have begun recycling or composting used disposable diapers, and that some of the country's leading diaper-makers are making a con-

---

 DO YOU SEE WHAT I PEE?

Disposable diapers these days are so effective at absorbing whatever pee may come their way, they can actually pose a challenge to parents who are trying to keep close tabs on just how much their newborns are peeing (see also "In Search of a Little Pee in a Big Diaper" on page 66). Fortunately, some diaper brands now come with a colorfully effective solution: a strip on the diaper that changes color when wet—allowing you to more clearly see when your baby pees.

certed effort to be more eco-friendly by improving everything from the materials they use to the amount, transport, and packaging of diapers. We are hopeful that this sustainability-minded approach becomes mainstream in the near future.

- **Cloth.** Cloth diapers are usually made of soft cotton and are supposedly more comfortable than disposable diapers (we say supposedly because neither of us has any personal recollection and we aren't exactly sure how one would otherwise prove such a claim!). Proponents also claim that babies who wear cloth diapers are 5 times less likely to develop diaper rashes than their disposable diaper-clad counterparts. But unlike disposable diapers, cloth diapers are not as absorbent, need to be changed more frequently, and usually need to be worn with an overlying stay-dry cover. These covers typically come in the form of plastic, cotton, or terry cloth. And because cloth diapers (and their covers) require a lot of washing by either the parents or a diaper service and therefore use of a great deal of water and detergent, people in the disposable diaper camp point out that cloth diapers also have a negative impact on the environment.

 AN ENVIRONMENTALLY SUPERIOR DIAPER?

One of the most significant concerns parents have when it comes to the use of diapers these days is the impact they have on the environment—a concern that is well worth paying attention to. What may come as a surprise, however, is that it's in no way clear that disposable diapers have any greater impact than their cloth counterparts. The fact of the matter is that both disposable and cloth diapers do have an impact on the environment—an impact that is determined by taking into account the full "life cycle" of the diaper from start to final use, which includes how much energy, water, and raw materials are used as well as how much atmospheric emissions and waterborne and solid wastes are created. While studies agree that disposable diapers use more raw materials and produce more solid wastes, cloth diapers consume significantly more water and produce more waterborne wastes. The conclusion: When it comes to declaring environmental superiority of cloth versus disposable diapers, it still seems to be a wash.

The Art of Diapering

Yes, believe it or not, there is an art to diapering. After all, who wouldn't be proud of the ability to diaper a moving target, save 5 cents per diaper, always be prepared for a blowout, or simply get the darn tabs to stick when and where we want them to? While as parents we all change a whole lot of diapers, the art of diapering involves doing it better, faster, and cheaper, and with less mess.

Choosing a Diaper

Whether you choose cloth versus disposable, brand name versus generic, or any combination thereof, you and your baby may develop some preferences for the diapers you use. Some babies are "well-contained" using a variety of brands and styles of diapers, whereas others may do best with one certain brand. Some require extra absorbency while others do just fine with the less expensive, less absorbent types. Some babies may be sensitive to particular materials in diapers and may, on occasion, seem more prone to rashes when wearing certain brands. The bottom line: Each baby is different, more expensive brands are not always better but some are worth their absorbency in gold, and finding a suitable diaper for less can clearly be a good way to save a lot of money. So don't be afraid to try something new!

Velcro Versus Adhesive

Deciding on the brand is not the only decision you'll need to make when it comes to choosing a diaper. Disposable diapers now come with a choice of Velcro or tape fasteners. While Velcro may be more expensive, it is easier to reattach—for instance, if you need to check for a wet diaper—especially if you find yourself doing it with water, lotion, Vaseline, or diaper rash cream on your hands. Additionally, the tape fasteners may stick steadfastly to themselves before you get a chance to secure them in the proper position and may also lose their adhesive qualities once detached. Once you become skilled in the fine art of changing diapers, however, it usually doesn't make too much of a difference one way or another under normal circumstances.

Diaper Sizing

The exact numbers vary from brand to brand, but in general, newborn diapers are designed for infants up until they reach about 10 pounds.

Unless your newborn is particularly small (in which case, you might start out with preemie diapers for babies weighing less than 6 pounds), you may find yourself jumping up to size 1 diapers fairly quickly. Given that size 1 diapers are designed to fit infants between approximately 8 and 14 pounds, you may find yourself rounding up and bypassing the newborn diapers altogether.

Diapering Around the Umbilical Cord

Until a newborn's umbilical cord stump fully dries and falls off, it is recommended that you leave it exposed to air as much possible, as well as limit its exposure to pee- or poop-filled diapers (see "The Care and Keeping of the Cord" on page 290). While newborn diapers usually have umbilical cord cutouts, you can also use diapers that don't and simply fold the front of the diaper down below the level of the belly button.

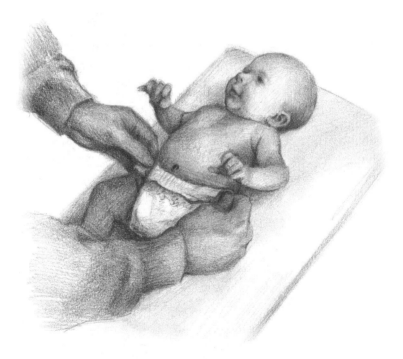

Buying Diapers

At an average of 25 cents per diaper for brand-name disposables and about 3,000 diapers, you can expect to spend around $750 during your first year of diapering—and that's not even factoring in wipes, diaper creams, and all the other diapering paraphernalia. With those figures in mind, we thought it would be useful to point out several potential ways you can save yourself some money in the diapering department.

- **Start small.** Start out buying diapers in smaller quantities. You'll want to make sure you've found a good match, but keep in mind that your newborn will be growing very quickly in the months to come. If at first you happen to settle on a more expensive brand, remember that as your baby gets older (and has less sensitive skin, less leaky poop, and pees less frequently), you may want to experiment with less expensive brands.

- **Divide and conquer.** Calculate your cost per diaper. This may sound obvious, but by simply dividing the cost of a pack of diapers by the number of diapers in the pack, you can figure out if what you're getting is really a good deal, or if it is just being advertised as one. You'll find that mega-jumbo packs aren't always the best bargain, and that one store's sale price doesn't beat the everyday price at another.

- **Cut coupons.** By checking such places as the newspaper and the Web, you can often find enough diaper coupons to make it well worth your while, especially at stores that double manufacturers' coupons or offer buy one, get one free deals.

- **Think big.** When you do find a sale or have coupons, buy extra diapers in advance to spare yourself a middle of the night run to the grocery store because you've used your last one. You might want to consider having your reserve supply be a size up from the one your baby's currently wearing so that you won't wind up with leftover diapers that don't fit.

- **Join the club.** Take note of frequent buyers' clubs. You know you're going to be in the market for diapers for a long time to come, and by simply collecting proofs of purchase (or "diaper points") many companies will reward you with baby clothes, toys, music, and other products.

Similarly, some grocery and drugstore chains now tally up dollars spent on baby items and offer rebates or coupons each time you reach a certain total (eg, get a $10 store coupon every time you spend $100 on baby items at that store).

- **Consider your options.** Consider using cloth diapers and washing them yourself. While some people estimate that using a diaper service only lets you break even compared to paying for disposable diapers, washing cloth diapers yourself can cut your diaper costs by as much as half.

Wipes for Newborns?

It's not uncommon for a new or expectant parent to hear through the parenting rumor mill that wipes are not to be used during the newborn period. Like many parenting recommendations, we're not exactly sure why this one exists. After scouring the pediatric literature (which is not exactly extensive on the subject), it seems most experts believe wipes are safe to use on newborn skin, even if there is a rash or a break in the skin. In general, they are thought to be as mild as using a wet washcloth. In fact, the only report of skin problems we found was in parents with eczema who had skin reactions when their own hands came into contact with wipes (presumably caused by the fragrance or preservatives in the wipes). The best advice we have to give you on the subject is that if they seem to be causing a problem, don't use them. Otherwise, wipe away!

 NOT JUST FOR BABIES

Here's a little trivia that's sure to help you fit right in with the parenting crowd. In researching the subject of wipes, we also happened on an interesting and what we assume to be a little-known fact. There are companies now marketing wipes for adults, and apparently not without reason. A recent study showed that not only do many adults believe that moist wiping after toileting is more effective than using plain toilet paper, but 1 out of 4 adult respondents use moist wipes daily!

A Word on Wipes

Although we haven't officially counted, there have to be about as many brands and types of wipes as there are tennis shoes—environmentally friendly all-natural wipes, scented and unscented, with aloe and without, in round containers, in rectangular refillable containers, and packaged in reusable or disposable travel packs. And while they may only cost a few cents a wipe if you don't go for the top of the line or opt for fancy packaging, the cost can really add up. While the principles discussed in the "Buying Diapers" section generally apply to buying wipes as well, here are a few additional things to consider when buying and using wipes.

- **Packaging.** After one look at the shelves, you won't need us to tell you that when it comes to buying wipes, you pay for packaging. However, doing so is not always a bad thing. For example, someone who clearly had firsthand experience in the use of wipes on the go must have come up with the handy little travel-sized packs, and many parents find the added convenience well worth the extra money. That said, it is useful to hang on to reusable plastic travel containers, as well as full-sized refillable plastic containers. By simply buying large refill packs and restocking them yourself, you can save yourself the extra expense.

- **Don't flush 'em.** Enough said—almost. There are very few wipes on the market that don't have the potential to wreak havoc on your plumbing. Be sure to check package labels before buying if you are determined to find wipes that are flushable, because most of them are not.

- **The overuse of wipes.** Believe it or not, not every diaper change requires the use of wipes. This is not only because pee rarely irritates the skin, but also because today's super-absorbent disposable diapers effectively limit the amount of pee that even comes into contact with the skin. Reserving wipes for cleaning up poop can save you a considerable amount. Also keep in mind that a moist tissue, a wet washcloth, or even a quick rinse in the tub may be used in place of baby wipes when convenient.

Wipe Warmers

Believe it or not, they do make them. Seems that some people are convinced that warm wipes are less shocking to newborns. It sounds reasonable: Given that a baby's body temperature is 98.6°F and regular damp wipes are roughly 60°F or less, we're talking about a 40° difference. By heating up the wipes to just below body temperature, the wipe warmer can lessen the shock, so to speak. When it comes to the question of how hot is too hot, one manufacturer actually set an upper limit on its warmer; the warmer simply shuts off after reaching 105°F. On removal of a wipe from the unit and coming into contact with air, the wipe will be about 95°F.

In reality, however, most parents only briefly warm up cold wipes with their own hands, if at all, before using them on their baby. Those who do own warmers tend only to use the warmed wipes in the room where the wipe warmer is kept. And we have yet to meet a parent who actually carries their wipe warmer with them when venturing out of the house. Realistically speaking, most babies are not afforded this luxury and get used to cool wipes right from the start.

 TEMPERATURE TRIVIA

While we're on the subject of temperatures and heated wipes, we thought we'd point out for the sake of comparison that a toasty hot tub is set at 104°F and indoor swimming pools are usually around 84°F. And lest we leave room for misinterpretation, let us emphasize that we are *not* suggesting you take your newborn in either but simply offering you a frame of reference.

Changing Diapers

Location, Location, Location

Wherever you choose to change your baby's diaper—whether it's on your brand new changing table or next to you on your bed—you'll want to prepare the area so that everything you need is accessible. At a minimum, this means a diaper and some wipes. While changing tables are clearly the norm when it comes to location, and some people, one of us included, even opt to have more than one around the house, you should be aware (if you aren't already) that they aren't inherently necessary. If you decide that you don't want your diaper changing to be limited geographically by where your changing table happens to be, then also consider keeping diapers accessible in convenient locations around the house (and in the car once you start to venture out). That way, you can limit how far you have to go to take care of business. Some people opt to use a simple diaper changing pad in lieu of the table, and the floor, bed, couch, or even the back seat of your car can easily serve the same purpose once you are comfortable with the routine. That said, some particularly messy episodes might require not only a new diaper, but also an extra pair of hands, a new outfit, and even a trip to the tub. On such occasions, you'll be much better off if you've chosen your "changing station" in close proximity to your supplies.

The Technique

Before starting to change your baby's diaper, keep in mind that some babies have a tendency to pee as soon as they are exposed to open air. By keeping them relatively covered as much as you can during the course of a diaper

change, you can help keep yourself, your changing surface, and your baby's clothes from getting unnecessarily wet.

If your baby is cooperative, which most babies are at least until they learn how to roll (somewhere around 4 months), you can first lift her legs with one hand and place a clean diaper under her bottom with the other. Make sure you have the picture side of the new diaper in front and the side with the tabs underneath. *Then* unfasten the old diaper and wipe your baby's bottom with the front (inner side) of it as you remove it. While you clearly don't have to wipe with the old diaper before taking it off, doing so can often remove a significant amount of poop before you reach for your first baby wipe. If the old diaper isn't overwhelmingly messy, leaving it folded over on itself but still under your baby's bottom can help prevent her still-dirty bottom from getting the new diaper soiled before you've had the chance to clean her up, and also serve to absorb any new pee that may present itself during the uncovered stage of the diaper change.

Next, wipe your baby's bottom and surrounding dirty areas with a baby wipe, moist tissue, or washcloth. Then remove the old diaper along with the wipes from underneath your baby and find a "safe" place to set them so that you don't end up with your baby's foot in poop, or find yourself with a new mess to clean up after accidentally knocking the diaper and its contents to the floor.

Securing the new diaper simply involves making sure that the front of the diaper is centered between the legs and pulled up to at least the

 A WORD ON THE PERILS OF LOOSE-FITTING DIAPERS

Many of you will know precisely what we are referring to when we suggest that you use caution not to let the back of the diaper sit too low or loose on your baby. This plumber-style method of diapering (no offense to plumbers intended) leaves way too much room for less than desirable contents to escape your baby's diaper. And even if you quickly become a master diaper changer with impeccable technique and flawless fit, beware of those well-meaning friends (and pediatricians) who are likely to pay less attention to the end result of their diaper-changing efforts than you do!

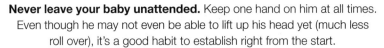

DIAPER CHANGING SAFETY CONSIDERATIONS

Never leave your baby unattended. Keep one hand on him at all times. Even though he may not even be able to lift up his head yet (much less roll over), it's a good habit to establish right from the start.

Avoid changing table falls by strapping your baby securely. If you use a changing table pad, make sure that it is secured to the table as well. These measures are not, however, substitutes for staying within arm's reach.

Talcum powder, when inhaled, can cause damage to a baby's lungs. If you choose to use baby powder, buy one that is talc-free. First carefully rub a little onto your hands and then apply it to your baby's bottom.

Keep plastic bags, safety pins, and any other potentially harmful tools of the trade out of your baby's reach.

same level in the back that it is in the front—usually around the level of the belly button. Check to see that the tabs are evenly secured in the front so that there aren't any gaps around the hips. Also, to help prevent leakage, make sure that the fringe around the legs isn't tucked into the diaper's elastic edges.

Disposable changing pads, available in most drugstores and sometimes referred to as bed liners, can be helpful in protecting your changing table, crib, bed, floor, or wherever else you may choose to set up shop. These are especially good when you're away from home because they can be used first as a changing pad and then to wrap the dirty diaper for a quick and easy disposal. If you're at home and don't mind a bit of extra laundry, a towel can easily serve the same purpose.

A Word on Boys

Baby boys are notorious for indiscriminately spraying their parents, grandparents, and pediatricians. By simply being aware of this inherent hazard, in addition to holding your hand, a diaper, or a tissue over your baby's penis as much as possible during a diaper change, you can limit the amount of time you leave yourself vulnerable. If you do find yourself caught in the line of fire, take comfort in knowing that it happens to the best of us. While it may not help you much, those of us in the medical profession who have been peed on more than once find it somewhat comforting to also remind ourselves that urine is, after all, a sterile bodily fluid. If you can get the diaper on without being doused but find yourself nevertheless with urine sneaking out of your baby boy's diapers, also try aiming his penis downward before covering it with the diaper.

A Word on Girls

Baby girls obviously have more "nooks and crannies" to deal with in their diaper areas, and as a basic principle, you shouldn't forget to look in them for hidden poop. That said, it is not necessary to wipe vigorously in an attempt to remove all of the normal white discharge that is commonly found between the folds of the labia. In fact, doing so can cause undue irritation.

For many of you, this will be stating the obvious, but in hopes of promoting good hygiene and potentially decreasing the likelihood of

 UDOS: UNIDENTIFIED DIAPER OBJECTS

Many parents are at a loss when they first find clear or yellowish beaded gel-like particles in their infant's diapers, but you can rest assured that there is usually a simple (and harmless) explanation. Sometimes the materials used to make the inside portion of the diaper have a tendency to form little gel-like beads when the diaper becomes over-soaked. Simply changing your baby's diaper more frequently can stop them from appearing.

Also common are small harmless crystals that are made in the kidney that tend to appear during periods of relative dehydration. For this reason they are occasionally discovered along with pee in the diapers of newborn boys and girls. They too can be clear solid or gel-like crystals, or leave an orange- or pink-tinged stain on the diaper.

And finally, it is not uncommon for newborn girls to have some pink or even bloody stains appear in their diapers during the first few days or weeks. The bleeding, which is caused by exposure to mom's hormones before birth, typically resolves on its own but can really throw new parents for a loop in the meantime.

If you have any concerns about unidentified objects or discolorations appearing in your baby's diaper, be sure to consult your baby's physician.

urinary tract infections, we also feel compelled to remind you that baby girls should be wiped from front to back to avoid spreading poop into the region around the opening where the pee comes out (called the urethra). Sure, the poop may already have made its way there without your help, but at least you won't be adding to the mess.

Disposing of Diapers

Several manufacturers are in the market of selling diaper disposal systems designed to cut down on the odor associated with dirty diapers. These systems generally use built-in deodorizers, plastic bags, and airtight containers to seal off the smell. While many parents swear by them and love to use them, the main complaints some parents have about these systems include inadequate elimination of odor once things start to get smellier and the added expense of buying replacement bags. They also tend to be less useful for parents who choose to change diapers in a variety of locations around the house instead of at the official changing station where the disposal system is typically kept.

It comes down to a matter of personal preference, how sensitive your nose is, and how often you take out the garbage whether a special odor-eliminating diaper disposal system is worth the extra money. Parents who conclude that mildly wet or soiled diapers don't actually smell too much may choose to use the disposal system to dispose of only the truly smelly diapers. Others find it just as easy if not easier to toss the smelly diapers into one of the zillions of extra plastic grocery bags (or newspaper bags or bread bags or…) we all seem to accumulate. Doing so helps minimize the smell of the diaper enough that it can be placed in a regular garbage can in your house or in a trash container outside. Once your baby starts having more solid and stinky poops—which tends to happen when solid foods are introduced, if not sooner—you'll find it very worthwhile to dump any solid poop into the toilet first.

The Medical Side

Diaper Rashes

Quite simply, anything that appears as an irritation or rash on the skin in the diaper area is a diaper rash. While there are several types and causes

IT'S A WRAP

If you haven't figured this one out yet, the simple technique of folding up a dirty diaper before disposing of it is actually quite useful. Simply take the old diaper and lay it flat with the inside facing up and the tabs out to the sides just as you would if you were spreading out a new diaper to put on your baby. Place any wipes you may have used into the center crotch area. Lift up the front portion of the diaper and roll it up like a sleeping bag. Once it is bundled up into a compact roll, take the side tabs and fold them over the rolled up part to keep it closed and its contents well contained. This technique not only saves space and decreases odor, but also limits your likelihood of spreading poop around.

of diaper rash, they fortunately don't seem to show up too often during the newborn period. That said, the 2 types you are most likely to become personally familiar with are caused by contact irritation and yeast. Contact with pee or poop can sometimes be enough to cause irritation of the skin. In other instances, a type of yeast known as *Candida albicans* is responsible for causing considerable redness and irritation. *Candida* is very commonly found in moist, warm areas, which helps explain why it primarily targets the diaper area—one of the most likely spots on a baby's body to be excessively moist. When *Candida* finds its way into the inside of an infant's mouth, it also can cause white plaque-like spots, a condition that is referred to as *thrush.* Changing your baby's diaper regularly (every couple of hours during the day) and allowing her skin to air-dry before putting on a new diaper can definitely decrease her likelihood of getting a yeast diaper rash.

Treating Diaper Rash

The treatment of diaper rashes depends on the underlying cause. If irritation is to blame, simply getting rid of or limiting your baby's contact with whatever is causing the irritation—whether it is a particular type of soap, detergent, or even just irritating poop—is often all that is necessary. Additionally, the use of zinc oxide creams, ointments, or petroleum jelly–type products that provide a protective barrier over the skin can help to limit the amount of contact and the severity of the resulting irritation. And lastly, mild over-the-counter anti-inflammatory steroid creams such as

AN OUNCE OF POWDER

Baby powder serves the basic purpose of reducing moisture and potential irritation in skin folds, and is often used not only in the diaper area but also under arms and in double (or triple) chin folds. While some parents commonly use baby powder, others (ourselves included) have never bothered. If you do choose to combat moist creases with baby powder, be sure to apply it carefully so that your baby doesn't end up lying in the middle of a powdery cloud. And even more importantly, buy talc-free baby powder (the most common alternative being a corn starch-based powder) because talcum powder can cause a chemical irritation and pneumonia in the lungs of babies who inhale it.

hydrocortisone can often help reduce redness and pain but parents should always be sure to discuss the use of this type of treatment with their doctor before using it. This is in part because of the possible harm that improper or prolonged use of steroids can cause to the skin, but also because of the potential for steroid creams to worsen a rash if it caused by yeast. Yeast infections require specially medicated antifungal creams—some of which are over- the- counter and others that can only be purchased with a prescription.

baby bath basics

While it is true that you are solely responsible for all of your newborn's nooks and crannies, you may be relieved to know that the task of bathing your baby does not necessarily need to be added to your daily routine just yet. The fact that you need to work around your newborn's drying-up umbilical cord stump actually gives you a bit of a "break-in" period—giving you a good reason to get used to sponge baths before trying your hand at more frequent and full-fledged baths. After all, it can be daunting and challenging to handle a slippery bundle of body parts that don't follow directions. As you get the hang of giving your baby a bath and no longer have to accommodate a crusty old umbilical cord, we hope you'll find that it becomes a less stressful and more enjoyable activity for everyone involved.

To Bathe or Not to Bathe

Contrary to popular belief, babies do not need to be bathed every day—especially as newborns. As we enter parenthood, we should all consider ourselves fortunate that we are given a few months in which to become comfortable with our baby-bathing duties before our children effectively figure out how to make themselves truly messy. It's really not until babies start crawling around in dirt, sandboxes, or even just on the kitchen floor (depending on how dirty yours is), and begin to explore baby foods—routinely ending up with more smeared on their faces than in their mouths—that they warrant frequent full-body washes. Until then, however, you have the practical option of focusing your attention on a relatively limited number of parts. Your primary area of focus predictably will be the diaper area—and, of course, the surrounding areas, the size of which will depend on whether your baby has taken to having blowouts (see "What Goes In

Must Come Out" on page 61). Other areas to pay particular attention to: around the mouth and anywhere there are skin folds. While some of you may be looking at your newborn and thinking to yourself that there are few, if any, skin folds to be found—rest assured that they will soon appear. The present-from-birth and all-too-often-neglected armpit and groin folds are likely to be joined in mere weeks by double chins and thigh folds. If you make a habit of regularly spot-checking these hot spots and cleaning them as needed using a wet washcloth, you really won't have to bathe your baby every single day. In fact, bathing a couple of times a week is often enough. With that as a lead in, it's high time we move on to the practical details involved in achieving cleanliness for all.

The Bathing Part

Tub Timing

When it comes to deciding when during the day is best to sit down (or kneel or bend over) and give your baby a bath, it is simply a matter of personal preference and convenience. From a practical viewpoint, we suggest you consider timing your baby's baths around your work schedules, your baby's sleep schedule, your own bathing schedule, or before or after feeding. If you opt for after, you may want to wait awhile to let the contents in your baby's belly settle a bit and allow any spitting up, peeing, or pooping to happen preferably beforehand. One time-tested tip we have to offer you is that babies really do respond well to routines, and while you don't need to cling to a set schedule at all costs—there's definitely nothing wrong with accommodating a trip out of the house or visiting guests—over time you and your newborn are likely to benefit from a comfortable routine. Our personal favorite, and one we highly recommend starting sooner rather than later: Offer breast or bottle first, follow this with a relaxing warm bath, and then take a few moments of cozy time curled up with a good book and your baby on your lap before bedtime (see "Books and Babies" on page 181).

Conditioning

This is not a reference to conditioning of your baby's hair (if, in fact, he has any, which we will address later), but rather conditioning newborns to water in general—the look, sound, and feel of water splashing around.

While there are certainly several bath-time safety measures we will address that you'll want to educate yourself about, you need not be timid about occasionally getting water in your baby's eyes or ears. Newborns are fully capable of blinking away splashed or even a bit of poured water. And to tell you the truth, few seem to actually mind it. That's why we have become convinced that there is such a thing as being too careful about splashing around newborns. From what we've seen, babies who grow up without ever being splashed with a few drops here and there, hearing the sound of the shower spraying, or getting a bit of water in their face every now and then are more likely to grow into toddlers who are afraid of water, put up a fight at bath time, and struggle through hair washing.

 WATER IN THE EARS

As far as ears are concerned, your baby's ear canals dead-end at the eardrum (as do your own). What this means for bathing purposes: Water is conveniently blocked from getting into the middle ear. It also means that having a little water in one's ear canals every now and then doesn't cause middle ear infections (otitis media) and may even help keep them clean of wax.

Stocking the Deck

If you buy into our philosophy of parenting preparedness, a good portion of the thought you put into bath time will be in the form of forethought. It's important to have anything and everything you think you'll need within arm's reach before getting down to business. Never leave your baby alone in the bath even for a minute to get supplies, answer the telephone or doorbell, or any other reason. Whether the "deck" is the edge of your bathtub or the counter next to the kitchen or bathroom sink, you'll want to come equipped with all of the bath-time supplies you're going to need before, during, and after. Some of the most useful supplies to have on hand include

- **Water.** Seem obvious? Of course you need water, but we suggest you make a habit of filling whatever tub you choose to use *before* putting your baby in it. In general, we've found that a water level in the tub of about 3 or 4 inches is easiest to work with—full enough to get the job done but not so full that you (or your baby) are going to make waves.

You may also find that limiting the amount of water you put in the tub will make your number one job of keeping your baby's head above water logistically easier.

- **Soap and shampoo.** Washing your baby with plain water is fine, so long as you remember to adequately rub and rinse problem areas (the notorious diaper zone and skin folds). Many parents, however, opt for a foamier form of cleaning, in which case there are plenty of baby soaps, body washes, and shampoos from which you can choose.

- **Washcloth (or two).** We have found many an adult is unaccustomed to using a washcloth in his or her daily self-hygiene regimen. This is the reason we thought we would state what may be obvious to others of you: Washcloths are quite useful for sponge baths and baths alike. We like to use them wet for cleaning and dry for wiping off.

- **Towel (or two).** It's pretty safe to say that no one likes to step out of a warm bath or shower into the cold air. Babies are no exception. In fact, they are often the most vocal about their dislikes, and you're likely to be met with considerably more enthusiasm if you plan for your newborn's quick escape from the tub to a warm, dry towel. Feel free to use the cute little hooded baby towels if you are so inclined, or simply opt for a regular bath towel. We should point out that for newborn babies, many parents find adult-sized towels more difficult to work with for wrapping purposes than the custom-sized baby towels—just too much towel to work with and considerably more towel than you actually need. Other than that, we suggest you go with your intuition and use towels that are soft, absorbent, and cozy. Remember that if you're going to be laying your baby on a towel during a sponge bath, you'll definitely want to have a second one designated for drying off.

- **Moisturizer.** Despite the fact that most newborns have dry, peeling skin, most of them, if not all, don't need moisturizers. In fact, some moisturizers are likely to cause rashes when applied to the sensitive skin of a newborn. That said, if it makes you feel better to apply a moisturizing cream, ointment, or lotion to your baby's skin, don't hesitate to discuss with your pediatrician which ones are best. In general, it's thought to be best to use moisturizers that are hypoallergenic. When it comes to effectiveness, sticky, oil-based moisturizers tend to get the job done better than those that are water-based (see also "The Drying Effect of Water" on page 140).

- **Diapering supplies.** Remember that it is a newborn's prerogative to poop wherever and whenever they feel like it, and you may well be met with a mess just before or after putting your baby in the tub. Coming to the tub prepared means coming with baby wipes, a clean diaper (or two in case of diapering mishaps), and any diapering supplies you typically use.
- **Change of clothes.** Your newborn is likely to appreciate any extra effort you make to get her out of her damp towel and into a clean diaper and warm, dry clothes because we have yet to find a newborn who likes to lie around naked, especially when wet.

Bathing Around the Cord

Having to avoid getting your baby's umbilical cord stump wet is going to be a short-lived nuisance, because dried-up cords typically fall off within the first 2 to 4 weeks. To the best of our knowledge, there's no serious medical reason why you need to keep your newborn's umbilical cord stump 100% dry at all costs—there's no direct connection to anywhere and nothing to panic over if you should accidentally get it wet. What we can tell you, however, is that cords usually need to dry up before they fall off, and wet cord stumps can be quite messy and gooey: in other words, an all-around general nuisance. With that in mind, most parents find it easiest to stick to sponge baths until the momentous day of cord detachment arrives.

 PRELUDE TO A BATH

If your newborn is still the proud owner of a pesky little umbilical cord stump, has a healing circumcision, or even just for those days when you don't quite have it left in you to fit a full bath into your routine, you'll find that sponge baths make for a great alternative. With your baby lying on a towel spread out on a flat surface or placed in a baby bathtub with or without a little bit of water at the bottom, simply take a warm, damp sponge or washcloth, add a little bath wash if you like, and then gently dab or wipe—targeting especially those areas in most need of cleaning. Rinse with a clean, wet sponge or washcloth; follow up with a dry towel or washcloth; and voila—squeaky clean.

The Technique

Whether you choose to bathe your baby in an infant tub, bathtub, shower, or sink, here are some practical principles common to all.

- **Full support.** Once you've gotten yourself and your baby situated and your supplies ready, you'll likely find it easiest to use your non-dominant arm and hand to support your baby's head and back as needed (eg, use your left hand for support if you're right-handed). By reaching behind/ under your baby and then holding on to his opposite arm throughout the bath, you will help to ensure that he will have your unwavering support, while you will still have your preferred/more functional hand free for cleaning. Using a plastic cup, washcloth, tub sprayer, or your free hand, you can then wet your baby's body from the head down with clean warm water.

- **Heads down.** When you work from the top down, it helps keep areas that were already rinsed clean from getting soapy again.
- **Focus on the face.** Wipe your baby's face with a clean, wet washcloth, using the corner of it to also clean the outer part of the ear and behind the ear.
- **Hair it is.** If your baby has any hair and you think it actually warrants washing, then add a small amount of all-purpose baby wash or shampoo to your palm or a washcloth and rub it into your baby's hair. When rinsing, simply tilt your baby's head back slightly to avoid getting soap or shampoo into his eyes or ears.
- **Lift and separate.** Remember to lift and separate as best you can any folds in your baby's neck, armpits, and groin.
- **Soap talk.** If you're going to use a mild soap or baby wash, put a small amount on the washcloth or your hand and gently rub it onto your baby's body from the neck down. For safety's sake, we highly recommend keeping your holding hand soap-free to prevent a slippery situation. If you get soap on your baby's hands, try to rinse them off fairly quickly before your baby decides he wants to rub his eyes or chew on his fingers.
- **Bend at the knees.** As you finish up, carefully hoist your baby out of the tub or basin without putting too much strain on your back. By bending at the knees and hips, or situating yourself comfortably on a stool or chair (or toilet, depending on the configuration of your bathroom), you can avoid unnecessary aches and pains.
- **No hands-free options.** For safety's sake, always keep at least one hand and both eyes on your baby (see "Undivided Attention" on page 142).

It's a Wrap

Especially if you are bathing your baby solo, you'll definitely want to have a towel set out within arm's reach before you start.

- **The lap wrap.** When you're ready to take your baby out of the tub, lay a towel vertically on your lap or other firm surface (a plastic baby bathtub works well, assuming you didn't use it for the actual bath). Simply grasp your baby under the arms and support her head carefully as you place her on her back just enough below the top of the towel that you can cover her head with it. Then flip the remaining (longer) part of the towel up over her body and gently pat her skin dry.

- **The upright wrap.** Try holding your baby's towel vertically against your chest with part of it hanging just over your shoulder. Pick up your baby carefully and hold her up against your chest. Wrap her by bringing the bottom of the towel up over her feet and legs. Once you get comfortable with the technique, you can hold your baby against your chest facing outward, bring the towel up under her chin, and then use the excess cloth draped over your shoulder as a bath hood. You may find this technique easier to master while sitting down, although standing is also OK if you're comfortable with it. Once you've done the quick wrap and dry, you can move your bundle to a more convenient location to safely finish diapering and dressing.

 THE DRYING EFFECT OF WATER

The fact that water itself can dry out the skin—yours and your baby's—may come as a surprise, but it's true. The drying effect takes place when wet skin is exposed to air and the moisture subsequently evaporates or is rubbed off. You can counteract this drying effect by simply bathing your infant less frequently, patting dry with a towel instead of providing a vigorous post-bath rub-down, and applying a moisturizer to skin while it is still damp—a technique which is thought to help lock moisture in the skin. However, many pediatricians will tell you not to bother with lotions, creams, or ointments for the first month or so. This is not only because newborn skin can be more sensitive, but because it is predictably dry and flaky, and almost invariably resolves on its own if you simply ignore it and let it run its course.

Have Tub Will Travel

Baby bathtubs are quite popular these days, and you will undoubtedly have plenty to choose from—from rigid, to inflatable, to collapsible and from sponge-like to those made of soft or hard plastic. While it is entirely possible to live without a baby bathtub, most parents find them quite practical, not to mention relatively inexpensive and multipurpose.

- They allow you to bathe your newborn on a counter, on the floor, in a sink, or in the bathtub (the tub-within-a-tub technique)—basically, wherever you are most comfortable.
- Many baby tubs are designed to "grow" with your baby—making use of newborn inserts that can be removed for extended use as your baby gets bigger.
- Even after your baby graduates from baths in the baby bathtub, it can still prove itself useful as a towel wrapping station or a safe place to set your wet or towel-wrapped baby after a bath. Some are even specifically designed to convert into other useful toddler "tools," such as a sturdy step stool.
- Once you become comfortable with the nuts and bolts of baby bathing, you may decide to take baths or showers with your baby—a somewhat risky business (see "Caution: Slippery When Wet" below) but cases in which baby bathtubs prove to be very logistically convenient, safe, and waterproof places to set babies before, during, and after.

Caution: Slippery When Wet

It is definitely not our nature to scare new parents. Instead, we want to introduce and reinforce a few simple but extremely important bath-time safety measures that will keep you and your baby from getting in over your heads. It probably goes without saying that the reason bathing an infant can sometimes seem like a daunting prospect is because there are some definite (albeit avoidable) risks involved. It's hard to miss the fact that babies are slippery when wet, much less ignore the occasional evening news story about an infant or child being unintentionally scalded or drowning unattended in mere inches of water. The good news is that most childhood injuries in general are preventable, and those related to bathing are no exception. In the committed spirit of tub safety, there are several hard-and-fast rules well worth committing to memory and putting into practice from day 1.

Hot Tubs

- **It's a matter of degree.** The ideal bath water temperature is thought to be somewhere between 95°F and 100°F, while water warmer than 105°F is considered to be too hot and cooler than 90°F too cold. In contrast, many water heaters are installed at 140°F to 150°F. *At 140°F, it only takes 3 seconds for a child to get a third-degree burn.* Before you christen your baby's tub, we suggest you pay a quick visit to your water heater and make sure that the upper temperature limit is set no higher than 120°F—a temperature at which you should be able to hold your hand under a running stream of hot water without getting burned. While most parents have heard this advice at least once, very few actually follow through. We suggest you make yourself one who does.
- **Fill 'er up first.** Run the bath water first. Turn off the water, and *then* put your baby in it. Having water flowing directly into the tub when your baby is already in it is an unnecessary risk because the temperature of running water can be inconsistent and hot water controls can be bumped.
- **Know what your baby's getting into.** Make it a habit to always test your baby's bath water on your own skin (preferably on a more sensitive area such as your wrist or elbow) *before* putting your baby in it. Testers and bathtub thermometers are also very easy to find and to use. Either way, you'll be sure to know exactly what you're both getting into.
- **Don't just go with the flow.** Anti-scald devices designed to stop (or slow) the flow of dangerously hot water are recommended as yet one more way to ensure you and your baby can keep your cool at tub time. We're told they are best found at plumbing or hardware stores.

Undivided Attention

Regardless of how much or how little water you have in your newborn's bathtub, you'll need to offer him at least one hand of support at all times and keep both eyes focused on the task at hand.

CHAPTER 13

clothing and accessories

The Big Picture

We all tend to have one thing in common as parents when it comes to baby clothes. Whether you're the type of parent who is looking forward to shopping for baby attire or you happen to have very little interest beyond having your baby's clothes fit properly and adequately serve their purpose, you will inevitably dole out a sizable amount of money on your child's wardrobe. For a glimpse of the big picture, consider that the average parent in the United States spends an estimated $10,000 to $15,000 to outfit his or her children—an amount that equals 6% to 8% of the total estimated cost of raising a child to the age of 17.

This chapter is especially meant for those of you who haven't had much, if any, experience outfitting and dressing infants prior to becoming a parent. Even if you have picked out baby apparel as gifts for other people's children before, let us just say that you're likely to find that you take a hugely different approach once you're faced with choosing (and paying for) your own infant's attire.

Learning the Layette of the Land

We wanted first to include a basic run-down of what's available in the world of baby wear and help you get a sense of what your baby might realistically need in the days and weeks ahead. The term layette itself comes from the French word for drawer or trunk and, technically speaking, it describes a baby's full clothing wardrobe, bedding, and accessories. Nowadays, the term is actually used much more loosely. You'll find that newborn sleeper gowns are sometimes called layette gowns, and many manufacturers market coordinated sets of baby clothing—often accompanied by matching accessories (such as hats, booties, and blankets)—as layettes. These conveniently coordinated set versions of a layette are especially useful as a quick gift. While there's no reason you can't buy some for your own baby if they catch your eye, be aware that you'll probably pay a premium for items you could most likely purchase individually for less.

With that in mind, here is a description of some of the more commonly found items in the baby clothing department, and our opinion on their usefulness.

 ONESIES DEFINED

As far as we know, credit for the term Onesies goes to Gerber, the baby product manufacturing company that first used it to describe their baby undershirts that snap at the crotch. Just as many other brand names—Kleenex, Xerox, and Coke to name a few—seem to have taken on lives of their own, Onesie is often used generically to describe all brands of snapping undershirts, and sometimes even entire 1-piece outfits (which we consider to be more accurately called rompers when worn as outdoor wear or sleepers when used for nightwear).

- **Undershirt Onesies.** These are handy in cooler weather as undershirts during the day and at night, and can also double as stand-alone outfits in warmer weather. Some look quite a bit like undershirts, while others are fancier and come in a variety of colors or complete with patterns and cutesy sayings emblazoned on the front (or rear). We suggest using the same rule of thumb as many adults do when buying themselves underwear: Buy enough to last you at least as long as it will take you to do laundry…and then buy a few extra for good measure.

- **Pajamas/sleepers.** While your baby is still young, you may find that you don't venture out of the house all that often. Even when you do, dressing your baby in sleepwear (as opposed to a fancy outfit) is not only convenient, but also socially acceptable. Most parents of newborns don't end up making much of a distinction between their babies' daytime and nighttime outfits. If you plan on using sleepers as your baby's primary clothing, then we again suggest you take into account leaky diapers, spitting up, and other common bodily function mishaps when calculating how many to buy.

- **Wearable blankets and baby gowns.** Wearable blankets typically zip up the middle or side, look like long- or short-sleeved or even sleeveless shirts at the top, and resemble sleeping bags at the bottom. Gowns are similar but often come in lighter weight material— sometimes with buttons instead of zippers up the front and often with an open elasticized bottom. Either type allows for use overtop a Onesie or other appropriate infant attire, and can prove particularly useful in the early weeks for easy access, and for keeping your baby well-covered in lieu of a baby blanket (see "Baby Bedding, Bumpers, and Blankets" on page 106).

- **Socks.** There's not a whole lot of enlightening information to share with you about baby socks that you don't already know from your own sock experiences, so we'll just point out a few quick considerations. When you do go shopping for baby socks, consider how many of your own socks you lose over the course of a few months. Then picture them smaller and with a much greater tendency to disappear or fall off tiny feet and you'll realize why we suggest buying quite a few. If you find that you like using them under (or even over) pajamas and footed outfits in addition to covering bare feet, then add a few more to your shopping list. You won't need to search for no-skid bottoms until your baby starts walking, but you will want to make sure you buy socks that are well elasticized to maximize the likelihood that they'll stay on.

AN OUTFIT A DAY...

...is rarely enough for most babies. If you buy baby clothes with the expectation that your newborn will only wear one a day, then we predict that you will be doing laundry very frequently. What with spit-up and leaky diapers alone, you may find yourself going through at least 2 (if not 3 or maybe 4) outfits on any given day.

Size Matters

After preemie and newborn sizes, just about all baby clothes come with relatively age-specific size labels starting with 0 to 3 months and continuing up in 3-month increments throughout the first year. This approach to sizing seems very straightforward—until you actually have a baby of your own and start putting the labels to the test. You'll quickly find that one manufacturer's idea of newborn doesn't always match another's, and that many newborns don't fit in newborn-sized clothing at all. Some may fit into size 0 to 3 months from day 1 and size 3 to 6 months within weeks of being born. While it's theoretically possible to take a baby into a fitting room and try clothes on to see if they fit, we find the thought of actually doing so quite comical and have yet to meet anyone who has ever done it! If you want to come away with a few practical pieces of sizing advice, rather than reserving a dressing room, we suggest you consider the following:

- If a label reads 3 to 6 months, an average-sized baby is more likely to fit in it around 3 months of age. We definitely don't recommend holding your breath for it to fit at 6 months.
- Look for tags that offer weight and height guidelines as well as age ranges, as they can give you a better sense of how the clothing will actually fit your baby.
- Remember that sizing varies by brand. Just as with adult clothing, some brands run big and others run small. Once you become familiar with one or several brands, you'll have an easier time gauging what size your baby needs relative to the specific brand.

SUPERSIZING

Right from the start, you'll discover that you're able to get longer wear out of your baby's clothes if you supersize them—or, in other words, buy big. Onesies are well suited for being worn big, especially if you use them as undershirts because there's no law that says they have to fit perfectly. Well-elasticized cuffs at the wrists and ankles of rompers, shirts, and leggings help keep sleeves and pant legs from hanging way over your baby's feet and/or hands, allowing him several inches' worth of room to grow (which translates into extra months' worth of wear). Just make sure they aren't uncomfortably tight or binding. Outfits or pants with attached footies can also be worn big if you simply put socks over the footies—a simple but ingenious way to keep your baby's feet snugly inside them.

Profiles in Color

Before buying a lot of clothes for your baby, we suggest you give some brief thought to whether you consider yourself color casual or a color conformist. If it's all the same to you, then you may as well limit the number of outfits you buy in baby blue and pastel pink in favor of more gender-neutral colors (pastel yellows and greens and primary colors)—especially if you don't know whether you're having a boy or a girl or see more children in your future and hope to use your baby clothes more than once. On the other hand, if gender-neutral clothing is unappealing to you and the mere thought of an onlooker mistakenly referring to your yellow-clad baby boy as a beautiful little girl horrifies you, then you may be better off opting for the more gender-definitive pinks or blues.

Principles of Practicality

Think back to your pre-parenting days and the last time (if ever) you purchased a cute little baby outfit. Did you opt for one with cute little ribbons? Splurge on matching dress shoes or the color-coordinated hair bow (which, on a side note, we have decided should more appropriately be called a head bow because most babies are significantly lacking in actual hair)? Well, many of these eye-catching features may be cute, but also tend to be impractical. We're not by any means saying that we haven't succumbed to temptation and bought adorable but inconvenient outfits for our own infants, or that there's no place for them in your baby's closet. It's just that as you find yourself faced with the reality of day-in and day-out dressing, not to mention coping with changing weather, frequent diaper changes, and even more frequent washings, you are also likely to find that practicality is a priority. In the spirit of practicality, here are several fundamental principles to consider.

Easy Access

It's exceedingly easy to disregard the access factor the first couple of times you set out to buy clothes for your baby, but the moment you're faced with dressing and undressing your baby several times a day—including as a result of the middle-of-the-night blowouts (you know, the occasional explosions that defy even the most absorbent and well-secured diapers)— you'll instantly gain a new appreciation for easy access.

- **One piece or two.** There are definitely benefits to both 1- and 2-piece outfits. In terms of easy-on, easy-off, many parents find that 2-piece outfits are more convenient. This is especially true for those late-night diaper changes that end up requiring a full wardrobe change. Once you've tried to remove a soiled 1-piece outfit over your baby's head without making more of a mess, you too may decide to go for 2 pieces instead of 1. A benefit of 1-piece outfits is the fact that they involve, by definition, fewer pieces to coordinate. One-piece outfits also generally keep babies more reliably covered. Bottom line on 1 versus 2: personal preference prevails.

- **Zippers, snaps, and Velcro.** These are generally easier to do than buttons—especially in the middle of the night or when you're on the go.

   ZIPPITY DOO OW!

If you think it hurts to zip your own skin, think about how you'll feel if you accidentally zip your baby's skin. We suggest getting into the simple but highly effective habit of lifting the fabric and zipper away from the skin and putting your finger under the zipper whenever you zip.

Newborn Dressing for the Beginner

If you haven't had any experience holding or otherwise handling babies before, it's quite understandable that figuring how to get arms and legs going in the right direction while properly supporting your newborn's head and getting everything snapped and secured may take some practice. We've come across enough new parents who are embarrassed to admit they aren't comfortable dressing their babies that we decided to include this step-by-step tutorial.

1. **Positioning.** Lay your baby down on her back, as if you're going to change her diaper.
2. **Head support.** Gently put one hand behind her head and neck for support.

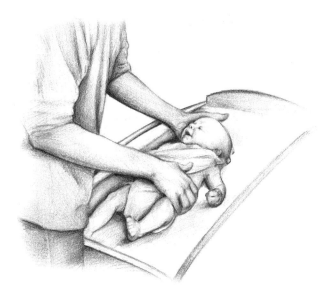

3. **Over the head.** With your other hand, put the neck opening over your baby's head and gently pull the clothing down over her head and your supporting arm. Then let her head rest on the changing area while you remove your arm from underneath.

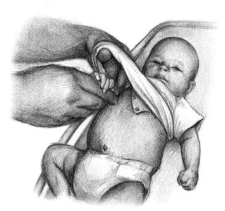

4. **Limbs.** One by one, guide each arm through the armholes. For sleepers and rompers with zippers or snaps down one leg, it is generally easiest to put the leg in the side without the zipper/snaps in first because it tends to be a tighter fit. Then put the other leg in.

5. **Securing.** Fasten any zippers, snaps, or buttons. If you've chosen an outfit with back snaps or buttons, consider picking your baby up against your chest or simply lay her on her belly to access them.

 ## REMOVING SOILED ONESIES WITHOUT ADDING INSULT TO INJURY

If you find yourself faced with a massive blowout—the kind where poop is up your baby's back and onto his clothes—we suggest you first place your baby on a towel, changing table, or disposable pad. Next, put a washcloth, wipe, or paper towel against the area of dirty skin and leave it there. Roll up the soiled piece of clothing so that the mess is well contained inside. Then carefully remove each of your baby's arms and lift the rolled-up outfit over your baby's head. For some outfits, you may actually find it easier to pull the clothes down over your baby's waist and legs instead of up and over. Once undressed and having done your best to minimize the mess, you can finish cleaning up and redressing your disrobed baby.

Comfort Is Key

It shouldn't come as a surprise to you that your newborn is just as likely as you are to appreciate wearing soft fabrics and well-designed clothes that don't scratch, poke, twist, or irritate. On the surface, decorative collars, frills, bows, and lace can definitely add to the appeal of an outfit, but cute isn't always what it's cut out to be. Be sure to consider whether added frills might get in the way or, worse yet, irritate your baby's skin. Additionally, the more ornate an outfit is, the more challenging it will probably be to clean.

Keeping Hands Covered

Newborn outfits often have fold-over sleeves that allow parents to keep their babies' hands covered during the period when infants have a disconcerting tendency to scratch themselves on the face with tiny yet rapidly growing fingernails (a problem we'll cover in more detail in "Nails, Nails Everywhere" on page 300). Their usefulness is generally limited, however, to the first couple of months at most. Once your baby begins to try using her hands and gains control of the flailing movements typical of her first few weeks, you'll definitely want to uncover her hands and let her explore.

Safety Considerations

You'll want to always take safety into account when choosing baby clothes. Fortunately, there aren't too many hazards lurking out there when it comes to baby clothing if you just put the necessary forethought into your purchases. An organization called the CPSC (Consumer Product Safety Commission) provides safety standards for clothing as well as other baby and consumer products, and routinely issues recalls to alert the public about potentially unsafe items. In addition to directing you to the CPSC Web site (www.cpsc.gov) for the purpose of identifying specific products as potentially unsafe, we've listed below some good general baby clothing safety considerations.

- **Safe at sleep.** Baby sleepwear should be flame-resistant and/or snug-fitting. That said, not all pajamas for babies come with a flame-resistant or flame-retardant finish. After determining that loose-fitting clothing could catch fire more easily, the CPSC required in 2000 that all tags and labels on children's sleepwear alert potential purchasers if they are not flame-resistant and therefore need to be snug-fitting. In other words, check the labels.
- **No strings attached.** Simply put, anything in which a baby could potentially become entangled is best left on the rack. While prevention measures have made it far less likely to find potentially dangerous outfits in the stores, items with strings or large, loose hoods should be carefully scrutinized before purchase. The CPSC recommends that no strings whatsoever be used in the neck or hood region and advises shortened drawstrings (measuring no more than 3 extra inches at either end) at the waist.
- **Loose object liability.** Get in the habit of evaluating baby clothes for small and potentially removable objects. The most obvious, of course, are buttons. It's amazing how many small 3-dimensional objects you can find attached to baby clothing in the name of fashion these days. If it isn't securely fastened, be sure to avoid or remove anything your child could choke on should it come loose.

Cleaning Baby Clothes

Washability is definitely something to consider. Be sure to look at the labels not only for size, flame-resistance, or snug-fitting information but also for washing instructions. Unless you relish the thought of hand-washing a lot of baby clothes and frequently replacing those that don't hold up well, we suggest you give some serious thought to the durability and washability of the baby clothes you buy—especially your baby's everyday outfits, Onesies, and sleepers.

- **Washing.** Because some newborns may have sensitive skin (and because you don't know who has handled the clothing and with what before it made its way into your possession), it's generally a good idea to wash all clothes prior to using them. An exception might be outerwear such as coats and jackets that don't have much contact with the skin (and tend not to wash and dry easily). As a helpful hint, consider putting small items such as socks in a mesh bag for washing and drying and remember to fasten any Velcro tabs (such as on bibs) before tossing them into the fray to avoid snagging other clothes.

- **Detergents.** It is a common recommendation that baby clothes should be washed separately, using special "baby" detergents that supposedly leave fewer residues and are therefore less likely to cause skin irritation. In reality, we've found that many if not most parents simply toss their baby's clothes in with the rest of the family's laundry without causing any problems. That said, it is worth paying attention to the fact that detergents in general don't strip away the flame-retardant properties of sleepwear, but soap flakes can. Given that information, you can choose your detergent as we do—buy one that smells good and gets the dirt out, and only feel compelled to invest in a milder "baby" detergent (or hypoallergenic/fragrance-free "adult" detergent) if your baby develops any signs of skin irritation.

- **Stain removal.** The best approach to managing stains made by breast milk, formula, spit-up, or poop is to try wiping or rinsing off the offending substance as best you can while it's still relatively fresh. We realize that this may be easier said than done—especially if you find yourself in the middle of a diaper change or feeding with a clothing stain that is settling itself in for the long haul—but if you can remove even some of it with a baby wipe or soak the clothes in some water and detergent, you'll be glad you did. We also suggest stocking your laundry room with a good stain remover and designating a place for soaking stained or soiled clothing.

As Good as New

Having told you it's a good idea to wash your baby's clothes before using them, let us point out one important caveat. Instead of washing them all well in advance (which many parents do before their babies are even born), we suggest you wash a couple and leave the tags on the rest until you are ready to use them. By getting into this habit, as well as keeping all your baby-clothing receipts in a convenient place, it will be easier for you to return those you end up not using. Believe us when we tell you that there's probably not a parent out there who hasn't bemoaned the number of outfits that have gone unworn in their baby's closet. Even if you're not able to return or exchange an outfit at the store where you bought it, unused clothing that have their tags still on retain a significantly higher value at resale or consignment shops, on eBay, when donating to charity, or—dare we say it (lest we be perceived as publicly admitting to it)—if you are tempted by the thought of re-gifting.

These Shoes Weren't Made for Walking

Because most babies don't walk before their first birthdays, you may be wondering why one might need shoes as an infant. The fact of the matter is that you really don't. Until your baby reaches the point where she's pulling up to a standing position (which probably seems impossible to imagine at this point but will happen before you know it), the only reasons we can come up with for needing shoes are to keep socks in place, help keep feet warm, or to look good in pictures if you or your family consider bare baby feet to be unacceptable in an otherwise "formal" portrait. If you do decide to buy shoes for your newborn, we suggest soft, roomy ones that are easy to put on and allow for plenty of wiggle room without falling off.

NEW MOMS DON'T WEAR SILK

OK, so maybe some do, but as for us, we sure stuck to plaid (flannel pajamas, that is); sweats; and other practical, comfortable, easily washed, no ironing or dry cleaning required clothes for several months after our babies were born. We have put together our own quick list of things to consider and watch for when laying out your own new-parent attire so that you too will be dressed for success.

Dress like your baby. Especially during this time when you're spending most of your waking (and non-waking) hours tending to your newborn, we highly recommend choosing soft, comfortable clothing over frills and fancy duds. As you make your selections, remember to keep an eye out for inopportunely placed zippers, buckles, snaps, or any other adult clothing accessories that could end up scratching, poking, or irritating your baby. And remember, unless you want to devote extra time, attention, and money to keeping your own clothes stain-free and clean, we strongly suggest adding "machine washable and dryable" to your own clothing checklist.

Easy access. This is especially applicable to you breastfeeding moms. Whether you opt for specially designed (and accordingly priced) breastfeeding attire or simply a loose-fitting shirt and an accommodating bra is up to you, but it's a safe bet you'll find yourself more at ease with your new role if you aren't at the same time wrestling with your wardrobe.

Comfort. We can't emphasize this enough: Make yourself comfortable. Now is not the time to worry about snapping up pants and zipping up jeans if drawstrings or elastic waistbands feel better.

Personal style. Bottom line advice: Don't expend any more time and effort on pulling your outfits together than you need to make yourself feel good. Some of us feel just fine about how we're handling new parenthood even as we lounge around for the first few weeks in ponytails, sweats, and T-shirts. Others, we have found, find themselves feeling further removed from the life they used to lead and more like they aren't rising to the challenge of new parenthood unless they get up and make themselves outwardly presentable. Either way, whatever works for you, wear it!

CHAPTER 14

taking care of yourself

Have you ever noticed that flight attendants routinely recommend that adults traveling with small children take a moment to strap on their own oxygen masks first before tending to their child(ren) when faced with a loss of cabin pressure? Well, not unlike this standard announcement, we make a point of telling all new parents we encounter (which now includes you) that you shouldn't expect to do a perfectly wonderful job of tending to someone else's needs (namely, your newborn) if you completely neglect your own. We're not suggesting regular days at the spa and weekly pedicures here (although we think one of the all-time best presents to receive as a new mother is a gift certificate for a relaxing massage). No, we're talking the basics—as in hygiene, food, and sleep. While we're well aware of the fact that many of the take-home messages we've included in this chapter have been said before (including several suggested elsewhere within this very book), we think they're worth drawing your attention to as much more than side comments or afterthoughts in the grand scheme of new-born parenting.

Tending to Your Own Activities of Daily Living

Try to allot time for your own activities of daily living, not the least of which include such seemingly simple tasks as brushing your teeth, bathing or showering, and getting dressed in the morning. Those of you who have yet to have your babies may be laughing at this advice and wondering "how hard could the completion of such basic tasks possibly be?" We are quite confident in telling you that we are not the only ones who found ourselves routinely going on upwards of 36 hours with bad breath, wearing the same clothes, and in need of much more than a quick deodorant application. Unless you sincerely don't mind sitting around in pajamas all day with fuzzy teeth, attending to your own basic hygiene each day, getting a bit of fresh air, and offering yourself a change of scenery or a little extra time to do some grooming every now and then in lieu of housekeeping or doing dishes, for example, often works wonders in helping new parents feel accomplished and in control.

Supplying Yourself With the Strength to Carry On

It's unreasonable for you to expect yourself to keep up with the pace of new parenthood without providing yourself with adequate nourishment, regardless of whether you're asking your body to nourish your newborn as a breastfeeding mom. Anything you can do in the early weeks (if not months) to make mealtime easier and less effort-intensive, the better. If you don't exactly have anyone volunteering to do all your grocery shopping, prepare you gourmet meals, and bring you breakfast in bed, we highly recommend considering the following time- (and sanity-) savers:

- **Hydrate.** Remembering to actually sit down and drink can be a bit of a new-mom challenge. We recommend building this necessary habit into your daily routine by simply grabbing a bottle of water or drinking a glass of whatever healthy fluid you choose each time you sit down to feed your baby. Now we're not saying that you can't indulge in your caffeinated and/or alcoholic drink of choice every now and then, but when it comes to keeping well hydrated (especially as a breastfeeding mom), you'll be better served by keeping a good stock of water, milk, and 100% juices close at hand.

- **Splurge.** Whether splurging means buying more prepared foods (fresh or frozen) or indulging in take-out (better yet, home-delivered) meals, it's entirely possible to do so without overindulging in a lot of fried fast foods. You most likely will pay a bit more, but you may also find it seems like a small price to pay for the convenience of getting the tasks of food shopping and preparation off your plate.

- **Stock up.** Accept and even suggest the gift of freeze-and-heat casseroles or other premade meals from friends and well-wishers. If no one is offering and you have not yet had your baby, then now is the ideal time for you to prepare a few (dozen) of your own. It's also useful to keep plenty of relatively healthy "adult" snacks around the house, as well as having them available to take with you if and when you find yourself on the go (see "Thinking Outside of the House" on page 193).

- **Streamline.** Consider using disposable (or very easy to clean) plates and utensils for awhile if keeping up with doing dishes is not your strong suit. Try to enlist the help of others to take over any preparation and cleanup involved, regardless of how much or little there is to do to get meals on and off the table.

In Search of Sleep

Getting rest is a great way to help your outlook on life, not to mention your physical condition and general sense of well-being. It is therefore an unfortunate and sometimes even painful fact of new parenthood that getting an 8-hour stretch of sleep quickly becomes a distant memory and your nights will undoubtedly be interrupted for the next few months. Nevertheless, we want to reassure you that it is possible to compensate, at least to a certain extent.

- **Get your priorities straight.** Start by making sleep a priority— ranking well above entertaining and doing dishes or housework—on your to-do list.
- **Partners in sleep.** Make every attempt to follow the age-old adage to sleep when your baby sleeps. Granted it's not going to be 8 hours at a time, but then again, beggars shouldn't be choosers. Besides, it's amazing how good it can feel to get an extra hour or two of sleep when you're functioning under conditions of relative sleep deprivation.
- **Set the mood.** If you're the type of person who can sleep anytime, anywhere if you're tired enough, then you can skip this tip. For the rest of us who need peace and quiet to fall (and stay) asleep, do whatever you can to create a sleep-conducive setting for yourself, whether it's simply finding a quiet room with a door you can shut while someone else takes over baby duty for a while or investing in light-blocking shades.

Find New Friends

In no way are we saying that you need to forsake the friends you've already got for new ones now that you are (or are about to become) a parent. It's just that we find new parents aren't always aware of just how big and broad the "parenting world" is. The support you stand to find if you simply look around in your own neighborhood, community, or even on your computer can work wonders for giving you an almost-instant and understanding support group. These are people who, like you, are quite likely to benefit from sharing the joys, as well as the occasional rude awakenings, of parenthood. Whether you find your support on a mom blog or from the parents next door, the bottom line is that having friends who can really relate is an invaluable part of parenthood.

PART IV

activities of daily learning

INTRODUCTION

We now know that the early learning experiences you offer your new-born can literally connect neurons, influence brain structure, and ultimately have a lifelong impact on your baby's potential. Sound like a big responsibility? Well, it is. But before you scramble to find the latest greatest baby video or put the classical music CD on continuous play, we hope you'll read the following few chapters in order to gain a better understanding of which learning experiences really make the most difference. While we address some of the "formal" learning activities parents often ask about—including books for babies, classical music, sign language, baby videos, and more—we are true believers in the notion that just about every seemingly routine interaction you share with your newborn over the next several weeks and months will qualify as an activity of daily learning for your baby. By sharing what we know about how babies think, learn, and communicate, we hope you'll learn something new and valuable as well.

CHAPTER 15

baby brain basics

We are parenting realists, and as such, we are well aware of the day-to-day realities of new parenthood. But just as we plan on reminding you to take time to preserve some of the guaranteed-to-be-priceless memories of the next few months (see "Thanks for the Memories" on page 333), we also want to make sure you take a moment or two to look past the piles of diapers, Onesies, and wipes and marvel at the potential of your newborn's brain power.

Making the Connections

What modern-day neuroscience now reveals about the way the baby brain works and develops is truly remarkable. By the time you find yourself heading home with your newborn most, if not all, of his brain cells (*neurons)* will have already been formed. Yet his brain will still be the most immature organ in his body and weigh only 25% of what it will by the time he reaches adulthood. As your baby grows and develops, the cells in his brain will be busily making lots and lots of new connections (called *synapses)*. So many, in fact, that by 8 months it is estimated he will be the proud (and now babbling) owner of hundreds of *trillions* of synapses—a number that's hard to even comprehend. Infancy isn't just about building connections, however. The baby brain also becomes more efficient over time by strengthening connections that are used frequently while "weeding out" others that aren't. What do all these neurons and synapses mean to you in what we realize may be a very sleep-deprived state? Let us summarize the extensive literature as best and concisely as we can by simply saying that you will play a very influential role in your baby's brain development. How newborns develop—right down to their trillions of neurons and synapses—is believed to be significantly shaped by all of their day-to-day activities, experiences, and interactions.

 THE BABY BRAIN BEFORE BIRTH

The first brain cells, or neurons, are thought to develop very early in pregnancy, forming at the mind-boggling rate of 250,000 per minute as early as the fourth week of gestation. While a baby's basic senses begin to develop early in the last trimester (which accounts for the ability to respond to a clap, tap, sound, or friendly nudge from the outside), it isn't until right before birth that babies are thought to begin feeling, thinking, and remembering. When it comes to influencing your unborn baby's brain development, the most important takeaway message is that nutrition, certain infections, drugs, alcohol, and stress during pregnancy all can have a significant effect.

The Secret to a Smarter Baby

As parents, we all want happy, healthy babies. Not only that, we want them to be smart. For anyone entering parenthood today, this desire seems to translate into a trip to the toy store and a significant blow to the baby budget. The difference between what we're now going to share with you, however, and all of the claims you're guaranteed to find on every make-your-baby-brilliant product lining today's store shelves is that we aren't selling anything (other than this book, which you've presumably already bought), and you don't need to spend a penny to accomplish the noble goal of making your baby smarter. That's right, despite the hype and marketing, for the most part we're not buying it. There just isn't convincing scientific evidence out there that all of these expertly marketed, highly sophisticated forms of baby brain stimulation, with all of their bells, whistles, and on/off switches, lead to any more advanced brain development. As you approach your own baby's activities of daily learning, we suggest you start by remembering that the real baby Mozart never had CDs, DVDs, *or* iPod playlists! What, then, is the secret to a smarter baby? We're happy to report that the answer is, above all else, the loving interactions that you (and your baby's other caregivers) will share with your baby over the upcoming days, weeks, and months.

The Best Learning Activities for Babies

Perhaps the most important message we hope to get across is that you don't need to put undue pressure on yourself when considering what to do with your baby. The types of activities we're talking about are simple, but to help make sure we're all on the same page, we've put together a quick list to get you started.

- **Time for a talk.** Sound simple? That's because it is. While some new parents feel a bit funny about talking to babies who can't talk back, this isn't the same as talking to yourself. Whenever you take the time to talk to your baby while changing his diaper, tell him about your plans for the day or just comment on whatever it is that comes to mind. The nuances may be lost on him for a while, but he'll definitely be listening and learning.

- **Take a walk.** Not only does taking a walk get you both some fresh air and you some exercise, but it gives you plenty more interesting things to talk about and describe to your baby. We're both fans of front-pouch carriers or slings, as they offer you the close contact that is even more conducive for carrying on a conversation. (For more on taking your first trip out of the house, see page 193.)

- **Sing, sing a song.** One of the classic Sesame Street songs says it perfectly: Don't worry if you're not good enough for anyone else to hear, just sing, sing a song! Your newborn will not only cut you some slack if you happen to sing off key, but will instantly become your biggest fan.

- **Imitate.** Start by sticking your tongue out and you may be surprised to find that your newborn copies you. Move on to making some exaggerated facial expressions and repeating sounds your baby makes, and before long you'll find that she'll imitate you as well!

- **Stay in touch.** Massage is a great way to stay in touch with your baby. Anyone who has ever had one will agree that it is relaxing. But beyond just relaxation, touch is a particularly important part of how young babies experience the world, and massage can be a true bonding experience—whether you make it up as you go along or buy a book on the art of baby massage.

- **Read a book.** The entire reading-with-your-baby experience is custom-designed to foster both fun and learning, from the close contact of being held, to hearing the sound of your voice, to watching the pictures and pages go by. In your baby's first months, however, don't worry too much about pictures, because it's the time you share and the sound of your voice that your baby will care about most. In fact, we suggest you take this opportunity to read aloud whatever *you* find to be the most interesting, since it will only be a matter of months before your baby will expect to have a say in which book(s) you read! As enthusiastic supporters of books for babies, we've also included an additional chapter on the subject for your reading pleasure (see page 181).

 OVEREXPOSED

In your quest to be the best parent you can be, it's important to remember that you don't need to (ie, shouldn't) set up a jam-packed schedule of constant singing, reading, walking, and talking. The fact of the matter is that the simple activities of daily living—right down to the diapering, feeding, bathing, and changing of clothes—expose babies to lots of exciting and "educational" sights, sounds, and smells. All this new and interesting stimulation can really add up, so remember to give yourself, and your baby, a break. You both will need time each day to relax!

do you understand me now?

Forgive us for stating the obvious, but one of the most noticeable characteristics of all newborns is the simple fact that they just don't talk— a lack of words that can easily leave them misunderstood and you scratching your head asking them "What, exactly, do you want?!" As the proud but potentially perplexed parent of a newborn, it's safe to say that you'll need to adopt a somewhat different approach to communicating with your newborn. Sure, you'll still be able to use *your* words from day 1, but establishing a mutual understanding is going to take some time and some new parental powers of observation. We hope the following section will help you understand what your baby is trying to tell you, and help you appreciate each coo and babble that gets you one endearing step closer to an ongoing conversation.

Look Who's Talking!

"Mama" and "dada"—2 words that are guaranteed to sound like music to your ears. After all, they represent not only one of the most memorable steps babies make toward talking, but a 2-syllable recognition of all your devoted love and attention. While it will be many months before your baby will be able to master this milestone, it certainly won't be your baby's first when it comes to language development. Below are some of the significant stepping stones that will lead up to the day when your child will actually be able to talk (and talk back!) to you.

- **Newborn:** Crying is really going to be your newborn's primary form of vocalization. While crying is admittedly less than perfect in conveying what babies want or need, it's definitely a start.

- **8 weeks:** Cooing and babbling begins. These crowd-pleasing skills will symbolize your baby's first more formal attempts to vocalize, soon to be followed by actual consonants and vowels.
- **6 to 8 months:** Your baby will happily use his voice for making sounds and even some more elaborate streams of babble, but no words yet. The much-anticipated "mama" and "dada" are sure to surface—albeit arbitrarily mixed in with other sounds and, we should note, with "dada" typically being uttered first if only because it's easier for babies to say (ie, with no implications of parental preference!).
- **1 year:** By a year, be prepared to celebrate not only your baby's first birthday, but also the long-awaited "mama" and "dada," now being used intentionally to refer to you! You can also anticipate hearing some simple exclamations like "uh-oh," as well as a few single words. And while there's sure to be plenty of animated babbling and attempts to imitate words, don't expect your baby's self-expression to string together into full sentences just yet.
- **18 months:** Your ears will likely be graced with the sounds of at least several stand-alone words. Your toddler may even be able to put 2 words together—such as "all done"—in order to more meaningfully convey his wishes. Rest assured, however, that your toddler understands far more words than he can speak.
- **2 years:** Now we're talking…as in 2- to 4-word sentences and the start of real conversation (along with a whole lot of repetition). Before long, you'll have a hard time remembering the sounds of your newborn's silence!

To sum it up: While it may take well into toddlerhood before your baby is able to put her thoughts, feelings, and demands into words you can understand, she'll be communicating with you long before then.

CAN YOU HEAR ME NOW?

It's very important to note that hearing plays a critical role in language development and learning. As a parent, you can look for simple but meaningful signs that your baby is hearing OK as you talk, laugh, and play together—including noticing that your baby startles to loud noises and starts turning her head toward the sound of your voice. That said, be aware that in addition to your observations, universal newborn hearing screening is recommended for all infants. For more on this important subject, see "Sound Advice for All Newborns" on page 283.

these hands were made for talking

While you may not have come across it just yet, baby sign language seems to have become a mainstay of mainstream parenting these days, at least among a significant handful of proactive parents and child care providers. As a trend that has been picking up momentum over the past 20 years, signing with babies is based on the simple observation that children can be taught to use their hands to "talk" long before their mouths can catch up. Sure, you've got a ways to go (ie, 8 or 9 months) before your newborn's dexterity will let her fingers do the talking, but that doesn't mean you can't start learning some basic baby signs in the meantime. Here are a few reasons why we approve.

- **Breaking the language barrier.** From what we've seen in our own children and others (including in Laura's educational child care center), infant sign language really does deliver on its promise of improved communication. This is a particularly appealing promise for new parents, given that there's a well-recognized gap between what babies and toddlers *want* to say and what they are capable of saying. It only makes sense that young children who lack the verbal skills necessary to say what they want, feel, or need experience frustration—especially in the period between 8 or 9 months (when babies start to really know what it is they want) and 18 to 24 months (when they typically start to speak their mind). In other words, if basic sign language can help babies use their hands to better express themselves at as early as 8 or 9 months, it can mean the bridging of this otherwise months-long communication gap.

- **Fun for all.** Signing with babies can also offer an opportunity for plenty of positive interaction, and anything that increases parent-baby bonding is a good thing in our book. One creative idea we love: Start learning and adding signs to your musical repertoire of popular baby songs such as Twinkle Twinkle and Old MacDonald. Long story short, if you approach signing with your baby as an interactive and rewarding activity, then it's guaranteed to be all for fun and fun for all. In fact, if it's not fun, then you shouldn't be doing it.

Signs of the Times

There's nothing wrong with teaching young children to "recite" the ABCs of sign language, but the most useful signs—especially for infants and toddlers—are going to be those that convey more than just the letters of the alphabet. Signs you'll want to start with are those that are the most meaningful or serve to describe the things your baby most often sees, does, or wants. The following is a list of favorites we've put together in order to give you a better feel for some common signs of the early childhood times. Start by learning these and you're sure to get the conversation started: airplane, baby, ball, bird, blanket, book, cat, cup, cold, daddy, diaper, dog, done, drink, eat, go, good night, happy, help, hot, hurt, I love you, milk, mommy, more, nap, no, outside, please, sit, sleep, star, thank you, up, water.

Tips for Getting Started

While signing isn't exactly a must for new parents, it isn't exactly difficult to learn, either. Books and videos on baby signing abound, and it's easy to see why so many parents swear by it, why child care centers include it in their infant and toddler classrooms, and why it has become so commonplace as an activity of daily learning. Here are some big-picture tips to get you started.

- **Be patient.** The baby-signing trend is based on the observation that babies taught simple signs at 6 or 7 months of age could begin using them to communicate at as early as 8 or 9 months. While there's no reason you have to wait until your baby turns 6 months to get started, we encourage you to be realistic in your expectations for any true signs of success.

- **Speak up.** Be sure you don't cut back on the amount of time you spend talking with your baby. As long as signing does not take the place of speaking, it won't get in the way of your baby's learning to talk with her words as well as her hands.
- **Make it a habit.** As with much of the learning your baby will be doing, repetition is key. For a better shot at success, make signing a daily habit, not a one-time lesson.
- **Sign it like you see it.** Use signs to describe routine activities and common objects that make up your baby's world.
- **Don't be heavy handed.** Don't worry if your baby doesn't get the signs quite right or doesn't pick them up right away. Remember the goal here is to have fun communicating and *lessen* frustration, not add to it!
- **Share your signs.** Be sure you share your signs with your baby's other caregivers so that everyone can join in on (and understand) the conversation once your baby begins to sign. And if your baby's child care provider is going to be the one teaching your baby sign language, be sure to ask for a quick tutorial so you will understand what your baby wants when she starts signing to you!

 THE ABCS OF AMERICAN SIGN LANGUAGE

While the popularity of signing with babies who don't have any hearing problems seems to be relatively new and trendy, the use of sign language itself is not. American Sign Language (ASL) has been developed and used predominantly in the deaf community for hundreds of years. In fact, it is now considered to be not only one of the most complete sign systems in the world, but the fourth most used language in the United States.

CHAPTER 18

fun and games

Parents often ask us questions regarding what toys are best for their babies—Can my newborn even see them yet? (The quick answer is yes, but for the more detailed answer, see "The Eyes Have It" on page 279.) Do they have to be red, white, and black? Should they play music and flash lots of colorful lights? We believe that the best way to answer questions about baby toys is to help you first understand play itself. After all, play is often said to be the "work" of children, which by definition makes their toys the fundamental tools of their trade. That said, playing for babies is really the same thing as learning, and we've already given you our two cents on what the best learning activities are for babies. With that in mind, what makes a toy truly educational is not how much it costs or its color coordination, but its ability to entertain and encourage your baby to explore, engage, and interact. It's a principle that's well worth taking to heart now (not to mention remembering over the next several years when you are faced with countless toy temptations).

Safety First

According to the Consumer Product Safety Commission (CPSC), bigger is better when it comes to safety and baby toys. While bigger toys are just as enjoyable, they don't present the choking hazard that small toys or toy parts pose to babies and children all the way up to age 3. There are specific products, or "testers," on the market that can help you determine which toys and other little objects that may be strewn around your house stand to be choking hazards. For a free and convenient gauge, you can also grab a toilet paper roll. Anything small enough to fit through one of these testers or a toilet paper roll is simply too small for your baby to play with because it could all too easily make its way into her mouth and potentially cause choking or block the airway.

 ## BLACK AND WHITE AND RED ALL OVER

Young babies are known to see bright colors and high contrasts best. We imagine that's why manufacturers of baby toys often include lots of black and white (for contrast), mixed with a splash or two of bright red color in many of their "educational" toys for babies. While this makes good sense, and we've seen everything from mobiles, balls, and toys to bed sets and floor mats in this cute and popular baby motif, in reality you really don't need to limit your baby's color palette for the purposes of meaningful play.

What to Look for in a Toy

Babies rely primarily on their 5 senses (seeing, smelling, hearing, touching, and—yes—tasting) to play and explore. If you keep this concept in mind, it will serve you well when selecting the best toys for your baby.

- **Eye catching.** Babies typically prefer objects with bright colors, high contrast, simple designs, and clear lines.
- **Shakes, rattles, and rolls.** Your baby's exploratory efforts will be rewarded with both sounds and movement.
- **Touchy feely.** Remember to let your baby explore various textures. Think soft, smooth, fluffy, and fuzzy.
- **Holds its own.** Look for toys that will be easy to hold so your baby can get a good grasp.
- **Drool resistant.** As soon as they're able, babies use their mouths to explore their world. Fortunately, there are plenty of baby toys today designed with this in mind.
- **Stands up under pressure…**not to mention all of the pushing, pulling, dropping, and smushing that baby toys are inevitably subjected to.

BOOKS AS TOYS

Whoever invented board books was, in our opinion, brilliant. By making books durable, colorful, *and* designed to stand up under the scrutiny of inquiring mouths, board books clearly fit the bill as ideal baby toys that are both readily available and relatively inexpensive. For more about books for babies, see page 181.

Be Pro-Active

When it comes to toys (and, ultimately, learning), active play always wins out over passive entertainment such as watching a TV. Although your newborn certainly won't be getting a full-fledged workout just yet, she'll be moving more in a matter of mere months. As she does, offer her toys that she can reach for and hold, look at, listen to, wave, shake, chew on, make noise with, and more. An activity mat that you put on the floor can make an excellent fitness center for your new baby as she learns about the textures and sounds of different objects as well as works on her depth perception skills by trying to grab such items as hanging rings and plastic mirrors.

The Perfect Fit

Finally, be sure to offer toys to your baby that are at an appropriate level for her development. While you may love the idea of building Legos together, she won't yet have the required dexterity (or self-control to avoid eating the pieces) to make them a good fit. If a toy is too advanced (or too simplistic) for a child, they will quickly lose interest or get frustrated.

 DON'T JUST THINK INSIDE THE BOX

There's a poignant truth to the observation that children are often more entertained by something as simple as a box than the expensive, sophisticated, well-researched toy or game that came inside of it. That's because a box can offer open-ended opportunities for creative play. We certainly don't recommend giving your baby a box to play with just yet (wait a couple of years for that), but it will serve you well throughout parenthood if you simply remember that a toy can really be anything that safely engages and entertains your child. Sometimes the best toys in life really are for free!

CHAPTER 19

books and babies

No good parenting book—even one written expressly for the parents of newborns—should be without its very own section addressing the subject of books for babies. Maybe you're already acquainted with the kinds of baby books we're referring to: the classic *Goodnight Moon*, *Mama Do You Love Me?*, *The Very Hungry Caterpillar*, and *Goodnight Gorilla*. If not, we're here to tell you that you're in for a good time. That's not to say you have to sit down and start reading to your baby the first night you get home from the hospital, nor do you have to choose certain books just because they are board-book bestsellers, considered classics, or because they happen to be our personal favorites. Rather, we want to encourage you to start sharing the joy of reading books with your baby as soon as you start to settle into your new parenthood routine. Ultimately we hope you will come away with a deep appreciation for the fact that when loving parents share books with their babies, babies develop an early and positive attachment to books (as well as to their parents) that can last a lifetime.

Reasons to Read

It is often said that children spend the first several years of their life learning to read, and the rest of their lives reading to learn. We wholeheartedly agree with this statement, but find that it is likely to be lost on new parents who have yet to even crack open *Brown Bear, Brown Bear*, much less plot out their children's future course to academic success. That said, we do want to make sure that you know just how much more to reading there is than what you may recall from your grammar school days, when reading was wedged in with 'riting and 'rithmetic. Especially when it comes to reading books with babies and young children, there are some pretty inspiring reasons to read aloud, all of which we hope will help you realize that it's not just about the book.

Instilling a healthy habit. Just about every parent we know wants their children to be able to read well and, more importantly, grow up with a love of reading. We are also big believers in the notion that healthy habits are more easily introduced sooner rather than later. Put the two together and you'll discover that introducing books to your baby early and often will help ensure that books become both an integral and enjoyable part of her daily life.

Bonding through books. Reading with your baby offers you both the perfect bonding experience. The process of reading aloud is an important part of early learning and literacy by exposing babies to new words, pictures, and even the taste and feel of the board books they'll soon grow to know and love. Add yourself to the experience, however, and what you'll end up with is something much bigger than the sum of the parts. That's because your warmth, voice, and undivided attention are exactly what your baby needs to grow up feeling safe and secure. The time you spend each day setting everything else aside and cradling your baby in your arms to read a good book or two (or three) will be invaluable.

Making memories. Reading books with your baby inevitably involves plenty of the silly sounds, exaggerated voices, and funny faces you are likely to make to enhance your storytelling adventures, all of which will add up to some very memorable moments. Sure, those moments from your baby's first months will undoubtedly be recalled in much greater detail by you than your baby, but over time the stories you share as well as the time spent reading them are sure to hold a place of prominence in both of your memories.

Books at bedtime. Whether a child is 4 months, 4 years, or a full 14, we routinely prescribe books at bedtime. That's because we've often discussed with parents the fact that short of drugging children (which, for the record, we don't condone!), you can't force a toddler—or teenager, for that matter—to fall asleep any more than you can convince a newborn to sleep through the night (see "Sleeping Like a Baby" on page 89). We are convinced, however, that one of the best things you can do is establish a predictable bedtime routine that includes books, as it will serve you and your baby well for years (if not decades) to come.

Showered by Books

If you ask us, there's no better way to decorate a nursery than lining your baby's bookshelf with a new collection of favorite children's books. Reach out to friends, family, and anyone else you can think of (ie, anyone who has ever had or cared for a young child) and ask them to share the name(s) of their favorite children's book. Start collecting a few just for fun in anticipation, and remember to put them on your baby registry. If you're fortunate enough to have someone offer, you can even suggest a book-themed baby shower.

The Developmental Milestones of Early Literacy

Some parents choose to read to their newborns even before they can hold their heads up or focus their eyes on the pages. We occasionally hear of those who start even sooner—reading to their unborn children through uterine walls. Our take on this head start? Although babies are thought to be able to hear well before they are born (see "Sound Advice for All Newborns" on page 283), we wouldn't count on it making your baby significantly smarter or more well read. If you enjoy it, though, then by all means read away in anticipation of the day when your baby will be able to join in the fun more actively. The good news is that you won't have to wait too long. Just as there are well-defined and eagerly anticipated "motor milestones" that include rolling (4–6 months), sitting (7–9 months), and walking (anywhere from 9–15 months), there are equally well-defined and important milestones of early literacy. For the sake of making this short and sweet, we have decided to list just some of the many book-related behaviors of early childhood, many of which have been developed by Reach Out and Read (see page 184), so you can be sure to celebrate them in the months to come.

3 months: *Let the games begin.* Your baby will begin to babble and imitate sounds, as well as smile at the sound of your voice. With his head held higher than in months past, he should now be developing a better grasp not only of what you're reading to him (or at least the expressions on your face), but also at the books themselves as he learns to swipe at objects and attempt to bring them to his mouth.

6 to 12 months: *Taking an active interest.* Between the ages of 6 and 12 months, your baby will develop many new skills, including the ability to sit up tall with his head steady and grab at pages. Don't be surprised if books all end up in your baby's mouth, as this is not only to be expected, but a good sign that he is interested in books and wants to explore them further. This is the time to invest in some board and bath books, if you haven't already, as they stand up the best to new teeth and baby drool, and also contain plenty of color, simple objects, and the photographs of faces that babies prefer.

12 to 18 months: *A hands-on experience.* Not only will your baby be able to sit without support, allowing him both hands free for holding books and turning board pages (albeit several at a time), but he's likely to demonstrate his already well-developed love of reading by carrying his books around, eagerly handing them to you to read, and answering your questions of "where is the…?" by pointing to pictures with one finger. At this age, toddlers also learn to recognize when a book is upside down (which, if you've never thought about it before, is actually a fundamentally important step toward reading!).

18 to 24 months: *Taking charge.* By now your baby will not only have turned into a toddler, but also a true book connoisseur adept at turning his own board pages (although paper pages may still take a while to master). Ask "what's that?" and your toddler is sure to respond with the names of

---

 REACHING OUT TO READ

As one of the country's leading nonprofit early literacy organizations, Reach Out and Read (ROR) is committed to reaching families with children between the ages of 6 months and 5 years, especially those living in poverty. ROR promotes early literacy and school readiness by distributing books to children at each well visit in more than 4,500 hospitals and health centers across the country. After 20 years and with more than 50,000 trained pediatric health care providers, this program now effectively serves nearly 4 million children who as a result are more likely to be read to and enter kindergarten with larger vocabularies, stronger language skills, and hopefully a love of reading that will last a lifetime. You can find out more information about the organization, early literacy, the importance of reading aloud, and a list of doctor-recommended books for babies at www.reachoutandread.org.

familiar pictures. Pause before completing the sentence in a favorite book and your toddler will finish it for you. Listen in and you'll even hear him taking over your role as storyteller as he starts to recite the stories he knows best to his own loyal listeners (ie, dolls or stuffed animals).

The Best Books for Babies

You may be expecting us to share with you our own favorite baby books, but we decided it would be far more useful to tell you that the best books for babies are quite simply those that you and your baby enjoy most. Early on it won't really matter what you read. That's right—feel free to read aloud the Sunday paper, the latest issue of your favorite magazine, or a book club selection you will otherwise never find the time to finish. Your baby is sure to enjoy the sound of your voice and share in your enthusiastic narration. As your baby starts to develop some interests of her own, make sure you stock up on plenty of durable books designed to hold their own in the face of plenty of touching, tasting, teething, and drooling. You'll find plenty to choose from in the board-book section, but also look for cloth books and waterproof bath books that also fit the bill. As for what's inside, young babies seem to be particularly partial to photographs of faces. As your child's repertoire grows, add books with colorful pictures of recognizable objects and animals, as well as books with fanciful rhythm and rhyme to your baby's growing collection.

CHAPTER 20

the sounds of music

In recent years, everyone from hopeful parents to well-meaning politicians seem to have jumped on the classical music bandwagon—embracing the notion that something as easy as listening to classical music can make babies smarter—an intriguing concept that almost certainly contributes to the fact that everything from mobiles, crib toys, and music boxes to teddy bears play favorites from classical composers such as Mozart, Bach, and Beethoven. While the relationship between these musical maestros and your baby's brain may not be exactly what it was billed to be when the Mozart Effect was first "discovered," music (classical music included) can and should be an enjoyable part of your baby's early experiences.

 A CLOSER LOOK AT THE MOZART EFFECT

Much of the parenting lore about classical music's ability to build a better baby brain—most commonly referred to as the Mozart Effect—seems to stem from a single study published in *Nature* in the early 1990s. Based on the results of this study, which found that college students who listened to Mozart scored better on an intelligence test than those who didn't, the popularity of classical composers seemed to skyrocket in the popular press and the parenting world. Within years, scores of classical CDs had found themselves a permanent home in nurseries and on baby registries all over the United States. In 1998 the governor of Georgia even started distributing them to every newborn in his state. Was classical music the secret to success for making babies smarter? Not exactly. A closer look at the original study reveals that the so-called Mozart Effect only showed a very short-lived (on the order of 10–15 minutes) improvement of a very specific type of intelligence (spatial reasoning) in a very few college students. Furthermore, the improvements weren't reproducible (in humans or in monkeys, for that matter!), and were never tested in babies.

The Case for Classical Music

Just because the Mozart Effect may not be what it was originally thought to be, that's not to say you need to shut off the CD player and have your baby listen to the sounds of silence. What does seem to be the case for classical music is that

- It has a more complex musical structure than most contemporary pop, rock, or country music.
- Its increased complexity is believed to stimulate areas of the brain responsible for spatial reasoning.

Given what we know about how repeated exposure can lead to new and more well-developed connections in babies' brains, it seems there are still plenty of reasons to believe that music makes a difference.

Music for Your Baby's Ears

When picking music for your baby, don't choose classical (or any other musical selections, for that matter) simply because of its anticipated ability to boost your baby's intelligence, but rather for enjoyment. The reality is that you can play just about any type of music for your baby, as long as she seems to enjoy it and you keep the following simple tips in mind:

- **Turn down the volume.** Babies' ears are sensitive to sound and loud music can cause damage.
- **Sing along.** Even if your pitch is off and you can't remember all the words, the presumably enjoyable interaction you will share with your baby each and every time you sing with her is sure to overcome any lack of musical talent.
- **Set the tone.** Music can set the stage for routine daily activities. Put on some upbeat music and your baby will soon learn that it's play and "dance" time. Many parents also find that consistently playing certain soothing tunes at bedtime can go a long way toward calming babies down and getting them in the mood to fall asleep.

CHAPTER 21

Media Matters

In this day and age of high-tech, multimedia everything, we feel obliged to at least briefly direct your attention toward a few media matters of particular parenting importance. While you may not need to teach yourself how to use your television set's parental controls just yet, controlling how much time your baby spends in front of a screen is a responsibility you should assume right from the start. TV, DVDs, computer games, and electronic toys have made their way into early childhood in a big (and potentially concerning) way. The "educational" DVD and video market alone is a multibillion dollar industry, and an estimated two-thirds of infants and toddlers spend an average of 2 hours a day in front of a screen. In fact, it is estimated that children today spend more time watching television than doing any other activity besides sleeping.

Getting Poor Reception

While the jury is still out when it comes to whether television (or DVDs or computer games) for children are fundamentally "good" or "bad" (or somewhere in between) when it comes to their activities of daily learning, there are many valid reasons why TV-watching babies and toddlers are causing considerable concern—not the least being the sheer numbers we're talking about. It has been estimated that 75% of toddlers and preschoolers watch television every day. At the same time, research suggests that for children under 2, none of it is actually beneficial to learning and, in fact, may be potentially harmful. As researchers, pediatricians, and parents alike tune in to these numbers, questions are being raised about the negative impact of television on everything from play and behavior to IQ and language skills. To be fair, we should point out that the news about television isn't all bad. In fact, high-quality educational programs (along the lines of

Sesame Street, Blue's Clues, or *Dora the Explorer*) for children *over the age of 2* have shown some benefit—especially in fostering improved language skills. As the parent of a newborn, we imagine this may seem like a topic of less immediate importance to you than, say, watching your baby's umbilical cord in anticipation of it falling off, but we can assure you that watching (and limiting) your baby's exposure to screen time is a topic well worth tuning in to sooner rather than later.

No TV for the Under Two Set

The fact that so many babies and toddlers are watching television is somewhat surprising, given that the American Academy of Pediatrics (AAP) has long and decisively discouraged *any* media use or screen time for children under the age of 2. This includes television, computers, and all of the numerous DVDS and videos marketed as educational for babies and toddlers. Although this recommendation has been met with understandable resistance in the parenting world (along the lines of asking devoted football fans to forego watching the televised Super Bowl), it is important to note that it is based on some very real concerns. Most importantly, we know that what infants and young children really need most are positive interactions *with real, live human beings.* Unfortunately, there's very little way to look past the fact that TV-watching under the age of 2 is a 2-dimensional and, for the most part, passive pastime.

   THE BABY EINSTEIN CONTROVERSY

If you haven't come across any of Disney's Baby Einstein products yet, chances are good you will, as they include a group of exceedingly popular videos that cater to very young viewers—playing classical music (*Baby Mozart*), making reference to world literature (*Baby Shakespeare*), and alluding to acclaimed art (*Baby Van Gogh*)—all to a reported tune of hundreds of millions of dollars in annual sales. Babies seem to love them, and parents often swear by them. What's the problem? Quite simply: Their potentially misleading claims of educational benefits, not to mention that their target audience most definitely includes children under 2. In 2009, presumably in response to considerable pressure, the company actually offered a full refund to anyone who purchased the videos under the false assumption that they were guaranteed to make their baby smarter.

TV Guide for Kids

In order to help you figure out your own strategy for how the likes of Dora, Blue, and Big Bird will most appropriately fit into your baby's future schedule, we wanted to leave you with the following TV and screen-time guidelines from the AAP:

- Avoid television altogether until your child reaches the age of 2.
- Once your child reaches the age of 2, limit TV and other screen time to 1 to 2 hours per day of *quality programming*. That means age-appropriate, informational, educational, and nonviolent— *not CSI* or even the evening news!
- Turn off the TV during meals.
- Monitor what your child watches and discuss the content with her.
- Keep your child's room television-free.
- Make sure you ask about (and limit) your child's exposure to television in child care, as well as at home.

It All Ads Up

On a final note, remember that when your child does start to watch some television, it's not just the show's content you'll need to keep an eye on. With ads taking up nearly a third of an entire program's time, it is estimated that the average American child views 40,000 television commercials each year, with 80% of those being for fast food, candy, cereal, and toys. Being able to skip this sort of unwanted marketing to children is one particularly compelling reason why parents opt for only allowing their children to watch prerecorded shows, where you can simply skip over the commercials, and/or DVDs, where there aren't any.

PART V

thinking outside of the house

Looking for a Way Out

Having a new baby around the house tends to make even the most routine of pre-parenthood tasks require a bit more forethought. Many of you will find yourselves perfectly content to head home and remain there until you feel you've mastered the primary new-parent challenges of feeding (yourself and your newborn), sleeping, diapering, clothing, and maintaining a healthy state of household hygiene, to name but a few. Don't be surprised if "homeward bound" starts to feel just that—a bit binding. Looking at the same 4 walls has a way of making some new parents start to get a little stir crazy, leaving them longing to get out of the house—somewhere, anywhere, just out. Whether you decide to venture out of the comfort zone of your own home early on or weeks down the road, of your own free will or out of necessity, and with or without your newborn in tow, we wanted to put together a set of basic considerations to help you feel properly prepared.

Dressing for the Occasion

Yes, your baby's relatively large head is a surefire source for heat loss. No, you shouldn't take your baby out of the house without bundling him appropriately. And no, you won't want to venture out and expose your newborn to direct sunlight. Before you spend any time trying to memorize the endless "don'ts" involved in stepping out, we suggest you focus on a few general wardrobe issues and pieces of advice. By becoming familiar with and then applying them, you will significantly reduce the number of "don'ts" you need to commit to memory before safely and comfortably exposing your newborn to the outside world.

- **At a loss.** Whether you're headed outdoors or in, your newborn is going to benefit from a covered head for several weeks to come. That's because relative to the rest of their bodies, newborns have impressively large heads—a characteristic that not only makes them completely dependent on parental head support, but also leaves them prone to significant loss of body heat from their uncovered heads.

- **Anticipation.** It's next to impossible to go anywhere and be able to rely on predictable climate control. Regardless of how much faith you have in weather forecasting or the person in charge of the thermostat, your best bet will be to come prepared with several layers of easy-on, easy-off clothing.
- **Overshadowing.** Ideally, you'll want to keep your newborn out of direct sunlight to prevent sunburn. Additionally, we suggest you provide some guaranteed shade by dressing your baby in a thin layer of clothing and a wide-brimmed hat even in warm weather. If you cannot avoid the sun, be sure to apply sunscreen (at least 15 SPF) to any small areas of exposed skin, such as your baby's face and the backs of her hands.

All Dressed Up but Now Where to Go?

You're certain to find a lot of advice regarding taking your newborn out of the house with you. In reality, there are really only a few basic principles in action here, with the rest tending to be a matter of opinion as opposed to expertise.

- **Less is more.** You are going to be better off if you choose to go to places with fewer people around. Close contact with a lot of people tends to be one of the most predictable hazards when it comes to the spread of germs. Enough said, at least until you reach the "Fever: Trial by Fire" chapter (page 303).
- **An easy out.** Our advice to you—consider starting small when you first leave home. A walk around the block is a great example of a doable first choice (weather and neighborhood permitting). Not only does it tend to be a relaxing way to get back on your feet gradually, but babies often like the soothing motion, you're less likely to find yourself in close quarters fending off unwanted well-wishers, and it leaves you an easy out should you need to abort the mission and retreat back home for any reason— diaper blowout; fatigue (your own); or a hungry, crying, or otherwise unappreciative baby.
- **Overwhelming success.** Heading out of the house can be quite an adventure for a newborn. And depending on your newborn's tempera- ment and tolerance of stimulation in general, you may find yourself with a crankier-than-usual baby at the end of the day. For some new-

borns, even a quick trip to the grocery store can feel like a day spent at the amusement park. Any routine you may be working toward stands a chance of being thrown off kilter a bit by such stimulation. We by no means want to imply that heading out of the house is the wrong thing to do. Instead, we want you to set your expectations appropriately, test the waters, and plan your approach accordingly. It is entirely possible to end up with an overwhelmed baby but still feel the outing has been a success.

- **Timing your travels.** This is a subject we address specifically as it relates to airplane travel in "Flying the Family-Friendly Skies" on page 227, but it really is a concept you'll want to apply whenever you choose to leave the house—with or without your newborn. Have faith that what now seems like orchestrating a grand production will soon become a routine you fall into.

 IT'S ABOUT TIME

You may increase your odds of being met with success when you head out by taking into account a few time-tested recommendations.

Just after a feeding. Given that we've spent many pages addressing how unpredictably and frequently newborns tend to eat, let us just say that planning your day around your newborn's anticipated feeding schedule may not always go as planned. Nevertheless it's worth a shot.

Off-hours. Go where the crowds aren't, or at least to places at times when it's not as crowded.

When you're well rested. You're probably now thinking this means we recommend no outings in the foreseeable future. To clarify, we don't mean well rested in the pre-parenthood sense of the phrase, but rather in a relative sense. You're bound to have good days/nights and bad ones. We simply suggest giving yourself time to catch up if you've just finished a bad one.

You've got coverage. Venture out when someone can cover for you at home or go along with you and lend a hand with logistics.

Don't Leave Home Without Them

Despite the catchy heading, technically speaking there aren't many items that we consider a must-have before taking your baby out of the house, especially if you're not planning on strolling far from home. There are, however, definitely some useful items we've found best to have on hand, and others that we feel have earned their characterization as modern-day conveniences. Here are a few thoughts and suggestions for when you're ready to get on the go again.

- **Diapering supplies.** It's Murphy's Law of Newborns that if you don't have a diaper within arm's reach at all times, babies are all but guaranteed to poop the first chance they get.
- **Accommodating change (of clothing).** Expect to need at least one complete change of clothing—definitely for your newborn, but quite possibly for yourself as well. Blowouts, leaks, and spills are far less stressful if you've planned ahead.
- **Food for thought.** Newborns don't care how recently they've been fed before setting out on an adventure. The minute you and your newborn step out the door, any semblance of a feeding schedule you may have achieved within the confines of your home has the distinct possibility of flying right out the window. In short, you'll never regret being prepared to feed your baby on the go. With that in mind, we suggest you flip to our "Into the Mouths of Babes" section (page 1) for a more in-depth look at what supplies you might want or need for either feeding option—be it breast or bottle.
- **Baby carriers.** Right off the bat let us tell you that we love baby carriers. They offer new parents a comfy, cozy, baby-friendly, hands-free option. While there are many, many options readily available (including carriers that go in front of you, backpacks that go behind you, and slings that drape across you), we are going to narrow our discussion a bit to issues that apply specifically to newborns.
  — *Weight limits.* Some baby carriers aren't designed for use by small infants. If you plan on using one early on, double-check the lower weight limit first.
  — *Support.* As we've mentioned elsewhere in this book, babies are born with poor head control and neck support. Be sure to choose an appropriate carrier for your baby's development and motor abilities.

— *Comfort level.* Not all baby carriers are created equal when it comes to comfort. You'll want to consider ease of use—how comfortable you are strapping it on and putting your baby in it—as well as how comfortable you find the carrier to be. Remember to factor in how much you plan on using the carrier, because some are perfectly comfortable at first but quickly become less so when put to the test by heavyweights.

— *Price points.* Factor in cost to determine if you're getting what you pay for. This really is a personal preference. Some parents consider the more expensive, Cadillac-equivalent baby carriers to be well worth the price they must pay for them—especially if they are easier to use and as a result, end up being put to more use. Others find that the more economical models serve their purposes just as well.

- **Strollers.** From the basic umbrella stroller to a top-of-the-line double jogging stroller, parents these days have nearly unlimited options to meet their needs—whether it's transporting your baby through a shopping center, going on a daily jog, or strolling a colicky baby down the hallways of your own home (a "remedy" that, in some parents' minds, even justifies the purchase of an extra stroller specifically for use indoors!). You may ultimately find that having a few different strollers is worthwhile—a lightweight umbrella stroller for quick trips or to use when traveling, a sturdier stroller for outdoor errands, and a jog stroller if you're the athletic type (or want to look or feel the part)—but for the time being, you'll want to narrow your scope a bit and look for strollers that are appropriate for newborns.

  — *Rate of recline.* In general, newborns need strollers that offer a fair degree of recline because their development does not yet allow them to sit upright and hold their heads high. Some stroller seat backs even recline completely to aid with napping—a feature whose usefulness extends well beyond the first few weeks and months. Most jogging strollers, on the other hand, aren't recommended for use during the first 5 or 6 months because they aren't designed to recline (although some have secure enough harnesses and positioning for younger babies).

— *Canopies and covers.* Whether it's windy, rainy, or sunny out, some type of stroller canopy is guaranteed to prove useful in protecting your baby from the elements. Some cover more than others, so consider the weather variations in your area. These may also help your baby sleep while in the stroller, and keep well-intentioned but nevertheless germ-covered hands from reaching in and touching your baby.

— *Travel systems.* A car seat and stroller may come as a matching set, or a special attachment can allow car seats of various makes to hook on securely to a stroller. Each of these options allows for easy transfer of your baby from car to stroller and back without requiring you to remove her from her seat. If you don't plan on keeping your baby in her car seat while strolling, this option is unnecessary. If you do plan on taking advantage of the convenience of (potentially) uninterrupted slumber in the car seat, just be aware that there is growing concern among experts that allowing infants to spend extended amounts of time in their car seats (and seats in general) may not be good for infants for a variety of reasons. What counts as "extended amounts of time"? Unfortunately, we don't have an answer for you (because there isn't one yet), but we suggest that in addition to never leaving your infant unattended in a child safety seat, you don't get into the habit of relying on it as a prolonged sleep site.

 SIT BACK AND STAY A WHILE

You may find it interesting to know that traditional Chinese and Indian cultures actually dictate that new moms not leave the house for about a month after childbirth. This gives mothers time to slow down and recuperate from childbirth—something that can be healthy for mom and baby (but in our opinion, would lead us to develop a serious case of cabin fever).

Taking Your Own Sweet Time

Now that you've read about the preparation that can help with venturing outside the home, you may actually decide that you're not quite ready to do so. That's OK too. In fact, there may be days where you don't even feel like showering or changing out of sweats or pajamas. If you have the luxury of being able to hang out at home (and perhaps let others come to you), enjoy it while you and your baby can.

Leaving Home Alone

Want to know where I (Laura) went the first time I left home without my newborn when she was only about a week old? Target. Want to know what I needed to get there? Nothing. I, like many new parents, just started to feel a gradually increasing need to get out of the house and get some time to myself—if only for a brief while. Whether you're more likely to be enticed by the thought of a walk in the park than a visit to a nearby retail establishment, we strongly recommend seeing what you can do to make it happen if and when the urge strikes you. Start by finding and enlisting trusted help to take over baby duty and give you a chance to do whatever it is (within reason, of course) that you think will help make you feel like you're not trapped or missing out. You may well find that getting some occasional alone time out of the house is invaluable in refreshing your perspective and outlook on your new life.

CHAPTER 22

car safety

Buckling Up So You Can Enjoy the Ride

Buying an infant car seat has become an integral part of the official entry into parenthood—ranking right up there with getting a prenatal ultrasound and picking out nursery furniture. Knowledge about how to keep our children safe in cars has improved dramatically since our own parents were faced with the same task. After all, we've come a long way from the days when new babies were brought home inadequately secured in nothing more than a parent's loving arms. Only a generation ago, parents had to be convinced to even buy a car seat, much less use one. Today, none of us would dare leave home without one. As you join the ranks of proud parents, you will inevitably become well acquainted with car seats. Not only are they guaranteed to be part of your everyday parenting routine for many years—long after teething, colic, strollers, and diapers have all come and gone—but making sure your child is always secured properly in a car seat constitutes one of the most important measures you can take to help ensure your child's safety. You may notice that we have temporarily put aside our joking tone a bit in this section on car seats—something we did intentionally for the sake of offering you a serious, useful, and hands-on look at how to get it right.

HOW TIMES HAVE CHANGED

A quick historical look at the evolution of automobile safety may help you understand why there is a generation of grandparents (and even parents) out there who still need to be convinced to buckle up!

1965: Lap belts first required in passenger vehicles

1971: First federal standards for child restraints (car seats)

1973: Lap/shoulder belts required in front seats

1989: Lap/shoulder belts required in both outer positions of the back seat

1996: Phase-in of air bags and requirement that all seat belts come with a locking mechanism

2002: Nearly all new vehicles and child seats equipped with universal tethers and anchors—a system referred to as LATCH
(more on LATCH at the end of the chapter)

Before Leaving the Hospital

Buying a car seat for your baby will certainly be one of the most important purchases you'll make, and one that you will need to make before your big day arrives—or at least before you leave the hospital. All 50 states now have laws requiring the use of infant safety seats in the car, and it has become standard hospital policy that parents must always have one in their possession before taking their new babies home. Showing up with an infant seat, however, is not the same as knowing how to use and install it correctly. We strongly recommend that you plan ahead, take time to educate yourself, practice installing the seat in your car(s) and, if possible, schedule a time before your due date or as soon as you can after your baby is born to have the seat checked by a certified child passenger safety technician (more on this at the end of the chapter).

Selecting the Perfect Seat

Although you may be hoping that this is the part of the chapter where we tell you exactly which make and model of car seat to buy, we're actually going to tell you a bit about what your options are and then give you the information you need to make the choice best suited to your needs.

THE "CAR SEAT CHALLENGE"

The American Academy of Pediatrics recommends that all infants born more than 3 weeks prematurely be monitored in a car seat—preferably their own—for at least 1½ to 2 hours before leaving the hospital. Taking this simple precaution helps determine whether the required semi-reclined position of the car seat puts the baby at risk for breathing problems or slowing of the heartbeat. If this car seat challenge test does result in any such concerning problems, doctors will likely recommend a temporary alternative such as an infant car bed, as described on page 209.

Your take-home message in a 4-criteria nutshell: *The seat you should buy is the one that (1) meets all federal standards, (2) is the right size for your child, (3) you can securely install in your vehicle, and (4) you will use every time your baby rides in the car.*

While manufacturers work very hard to appeal to parents' sense of convenience and style, safety should still be your number one priority when choosing a car seat. All child safety seats made and sold in the United States must meet certain federal safety standards (Federal Motor Vehicle Safety Standard 213)—a fact that must be referenced on each car seat label. If only ensuring your baby's safety were as easy as reading the label, but there's clearly more to it than that. Your next step will be to determine if the seat you select is the right one for your baby, and if it can be installed properly in your particular car. It would be nice if all car seats fit well in all vehicles, but incompatibility is unfortunately not uncommon. And while some stores gladly accept returns or allow exchanges, others may not be so accommodating. That means you'll want to carefully explore your options before purchasing.

An Overview of Your Rear-Facing Options

Infant-Only Seats

This type of seat is designed for use *only* in the rear-facing position and may be used only until your baby reaches the seat's upper height and weight limits. These typically range from 22 to 32 pounds depending on the seat (but with new seats soon to allow rear-facing use to as high as 40 to 45 pounds), or until the top of his head is within 1 inch from the top of the seat.

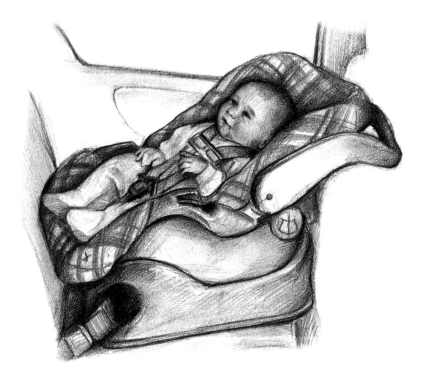

Advantages
- Carrying handles allow you to carry your baby around in the seat conveniently.
- Once installed, the detachable base remains in the car so that you don't have to reinstall the seat each time you take it out—simply click it back onto its base. Many seat manufacturers offer the option of purchasing additional bases if you want one in other cars.
- In most cases, the infant seat can be installed and used without a base. While the seat is not always as easy to install correctly when used alone, some actually fit better in the vehicle seat without the base. Having this option can be quite useful when traveling so you don't have to lug the base around, but be sure to follow the installation instructions carefully.

- Many come with stroller travel systems, where the car seat fits interchangeably with the base and with a stroller (which can also be used alone). While this allows for the much less disruptive transfer of a sleeping baby from stroller to car and into the house (see "Travel Systems" on page 200), be aware that you should not make a habit of leaving your newborn strapped in his car seat for extended periods of time when not riding in the car, since leaving babies in a semi-reclined position for long durations is not recommended.

Practical Considerations

- Be sure to also consider the lower weight limit for any infant seat you're considering. Many standard infant seats are only rated for use for babies above 5 pounds, which isn't low enough for some low birth weight or premature babies.
- Most babies reach the upper weight or height limits before their first birthdays and must be moved to another type of seat that has higher rear-facing capabilities (see "Convertible Seats" below) to allow infants to remain rear-facing as long as possible.
- As your child gets heavier, carrying her around in an infant car seat is likely to become less of a convenience and more of a physical challenge.

 CARRYING HANDLES

One of the most common mistakes parents with infant-only seats make is not putting the carrying handle in the correct position when the seat is being used in the car. While some manufacturers require that the carrying handles on their infant-only seats be put down behind the baby's head, others allow (or even require) their handles to remain up while in use in the car. As is true for everything to do with car seat installation and use, this variability reinforces the need for you to actually read your seat's instruction manual.

Convertible Seats

Convertible seats are so called because they can be used not only as rear-facing infant seats, but then "converted" to forward-facing toddler seats later on. Perhaps one of the most important things to consider when purchasing a convertible seat (in addition to what it offers in safety and compatibility) is its rear-facing upper weight limit. Most now offer the advantage of significantly higher rear-facing limits than some of the infant-only seats.

Advantages

- Higher rear-facing weight (as high as 40 pounds) and height limits allow for longer use rear-facing.
- They have greater potential longevity because they can later be used forward-facing (up to 60 pounds or more for some seats) after the child outgrows the rear-facing height or weight limits.

Practical Considerations

- Parents sometimes find that their newborns or small infants don't fit quite as well, presumably because they are designed to accommodate a wider range of sizes.
- They lack a carrying handle, detachable base, or stroller attachment.
- They are generally bigger, bulkier, and often more expensive than the infant-only seats. Seats are not only bigger, but also tend to be taller, making it even more important to check that they actually fit when installed rear-facing in the back of smaller cars.

THE AAP WEIGHS IN

The American Academy of Pediatrics currently recommends that infants remain rear-facing *as long as possible* within the limits of the seat. These upper limits will be determined either by the upper weight limit of the seat, or when the top of a child's head comes within an inch of the top of the seat (or to the level listed by the manufacturer). Fortunately, the important manufacturer-determined height and weight limits can be found on labels located on the side of car seats. For those of you familiar with the recommendation to keep your infant rear-facing until at least 1 year AND 20 pounds, be aware that this age and weight limit represents the bare minimum, and we have yet to find a parent who wants to settle for bare minimums when it comes to their child's safety. The longer your child can stay rear-facing, the better.

One Seat Fits All: Birth to 80 pounds

This type of seat can be used from birth (rear-facing with the built-in harness, usually 5 to 35 pounds) through toddlerhood (front-facing with the built-in harness from 20 or 22 up to 40, 50, or even 65 pounds), and all the way through booster seat age (used with the vehicle's lap/shoulder belt from 40 to 80 or 100 pounds). Forward-facing only combination toddler/booster seats (2 seats in 1) are also available but cannot be used in the first year or below 20 pounds.

Advantages

- Longevity—One seat fits all.

Practical Considerations

- Longevity—Some parents see little to no benefit in being stuck with the same seat for more than a year or two—especially those of us who have witnessed the wear and tear that milk, spit-up, and worse can cause to a car seat over the years. Additionally, as improvements are made in children's car seat safety and engineering, you may find yourself wanting the latest state-of-the-art seat long before your child outgrows this one.
- Even more so than with convertible seats, many parents and safety advocates have reservations about using all-purpose seats for newborns and small infants because, they argue, these large seats do not fit as well as infant-only seats.

Car Beds

We've chosen to mention this particular type of child safety restraint because some of you may come across one on the shelves of your local car seat retailer. Fortunately, far fewer of you will actually find yourself needing one. It's worth pointing out that car safety seats—"regular" infant car seats—are recognized to provide excellent protection for infants positioned rear-facing and are the preferred method of transportation. Car beds *are not recommended for general use.* Rather, they are only meant to be used when recommended by a health care provider for those infants who cannot breathe well in the more upright position of a regular infant car seat and must therefore be transported lying down. Most commonly, this applies to very small and/or premature infants. Car beds should never be bought secondhand or reused unless you are advised to by a child passenger safety professional. Unlike car seats, most car beds are designed for one-baby use—even if only used for a few days or weeks.

Used Car Seats—Considerations and Common Pitfalls

We'll admit it, buying a car seat secondhand seems at first glance like a very good way to get a great deal at a fraction of the cost. Before you decide to use one, though, we want to offer you some compelling reasons why we (and our child passenger safety colleagues) strongly discourage it. Unless you get a used car seat from someone you know and trust, you will have no way of determining whether it has been involved in a crash. Fact is, not all seats show outward signs of damage from a crash, but any seat that has been involved in a significant crash is considered to be unsafe for use. And if you don't send in the original registration card or later call or write with your contact information, the manufacturer of the seat will have no way of notifying you if there is (or has been) a recall. Additionally, used seats are often expired, are missing parts, or are without their instruction manuals. The take-home message when it comes to used seats? We strongly recommend out with the old, in with the new. The money saved by buying used may not be worth the potential price you'll pay.

The Key to Keeping Safe

The key to keeping your baby safe in the car lies not just in buying an appropriate car seat, but also in using it properly. Properly installed infant car seats have been shown to dramatically reduce the number of deaths in children younger than 1 year—by some estimates more than 70%. Yet some studies suggest that as many as *9 out of 10* car seats are not installed correctly. If you've already tried your hand at the task of installing one, you may have discovered that mastering this necessary task of modern-day parenthood is not exactly easy.

4 Rs of Installation

Just as with the 3 Rs of reading, 'riting, and 'rithmetic, the 4 Rs of maximizing your infant's safety in the car are not all there is for you to know—as is obvious by the rest of the information we've included in this chapter. That said, reading, rear-facing, recline, and recalls are definitely as good a place as any to start.

REPLACING CAR SEATS AFTER A CRASH

No one ever plans to get in a crash, it just happens! That's why your baby needs to be in a correctly installed car seat each and every time you set out on the road. We've found, however, that many parents are unaware of the fact that car seats involved in a crash may need to be replaced regardless of whether a child is in the seat at the time of the crash, or that their insurance is likely to cover the expense of replacing any car seat(s) deemed unsafe for use!

So which seats are considered unsafe for use? This is not a question you can or should answer alone. The National Highway Traffic Safety Administration (NHTSA) guidelines suggest that seats involved in minor crashes may be safe for use based on the following criteria:

1. No visible evidence of damage to the car seat when carefully inspected. This includes uninstalling the seat and taking the padding off to look for any cracks or otherwise hidden damage.

2. The vehicle is in good enough condition to be driven away from the scene of the crash.

3. The vehicle door nearest to where the child safety seat was installed at the time of the crash is undamaged.

4. None of the vehicle's occupants were injured.

5. No air bags deployed in the vehicle containing the child safety seat.

That said, it is very important to note that not all experts agree with these criteria. The bottom line: Car seat manufacturers should always be given the final say. In the event that you ever find yourself in a crash, call the manufacturer. Be sure to have any involved car seats in front of you when you call so you can provide the make, model number, and date of manufacture (all found on the car seat label), along with information about the crash. The manufacturer may decide to exchange the seat for you directly, or can provide you a written statement saying that replacement is deemed necessary for you to submit to your insurance company.

Reading

Unlike babies, federal guidelines require that all car seats come with an owner's manual. Yes, we realize that actually sitting down and reading an instruction manual is not exactly human nature (we plead guilty as well), but becoming a parent inevitably involves many changes, so just consider this one of them! There are so many car seats and so many different cars these days that it is virtually impossible to give you all of the information you need to install your own seat properly. While we intend to help you become well informed on basic safety principles, it is still essential that you take the time to read through your car seat instruction manual and your vehicle manual for the exact details that apply to you. If you happen to lose it, call the manufacturer's 800 number (required to be on every child restraint) or go to their Web site to download a new one.

Rear-Facing for the Long Haul

One of the most misunderstood concepts relating to car seats is the recommendation that all infants must be kept rear-facing until they reach at least 1 year of age AND 20 pounds. Parents and physicians alike have misinterpreted this advice, not waiting for both requirements to be met, and missing the emphasis on the words "at least." The fact is that if we could all ride around rear-facing in the middle of the back seat in a 5-point harness, we'd be a lot safer—as in 500% safer, according to a recent study of children under the age of 2! While this is obviously not realistic for adults, the American Academy of Pediatrics and NHTSA now recommend that children remain rear-facing as long as possible within the height and weight limits of their child safety seats. Fortunately, car seat manufacturers are rising to the occasion, and most convertible seats now on the market have rear-facing size limits of at least 30 to 35 pounds and as high as 36 inches or more, allowing infants the opportunity to safely remain rear-facing well past their first birthdays.

The reason for the rear-facing position is as follows. We know that most crashes involve frontal collisions. During a frontal collision, the crash forces are spread over a rear-facing infant's entire body as she is pressed into the back of her car seat. This is in contrast to the forward-facing child whose head and body are thrust forward with the full force of the crash. As we noted before, infants have very large heads in proportion to the rest of their bodies. They lack the neck strength and the reflexes that allow older children and adults to resist whiplash-type forces, so the rear-facing position is crucial in preventing brain and spinal cord injuries. Bottom line: Instead of asking "when can I turn my baby face-forward?" the question all parents of rear-facing infants should be asking is, "When do I *have* to?"!

 BUT HER FEET TOUCH THE SEAT

It may seem a long way off right now, but one of the most common concerns that parents seem to have about keeping their infants rear-facing is that their legs eventually grow long enough that their feet press up against the back seat. While we'll hand it to you that this may seem somewhat uncomfortable, in our estimation, and in keeping with the opinions of our child passenger safety–trained colleagues, it is a concern that should not take precedence over your goal of protecting your baby's brain and spinal cord—a goal that is best achieved rear-facing. Luckily, we find that babies and toddlers also happen to be much more accustomed to and comfortable keeping their legs bent than adults tend to be!

Recline

All rear-facing car seats need to be installed in a reclined position in order to keep babies safe. Just how far back, however, will depend on what your car seat manufacturer specifically recommends. Getting the seat installed at exactly the right angle (which ranges from 30 to 45 degrees) can pose a bit of an installation challenge, if for no other reason than the fact that many vehicle seats aren't level themselves. Fortunately, all rear-facing seats now come with a built-in mechanism (in such forms as a dial, ball, fluid level, or even just a horizontal line on the side of the seat) that can help guide your efforts. Many (but not all) infant-only seat bases also come with an adjustable reclining platform that can make securing the seat at the appropriate angle much easier. As a quick shopping tip, this is a feature we suggest you look for when deciding which seat to buy. If your baby's head still seems to flop forward or you can't get the angle quite right despite your very best efforts, be sure to contact a trained child passenger safety technician for additional assistance. And remember—more of a good thing is not always better: Too much recline, as well as too little, puts babies at serious risk.

BUT I CAN'T SEE HER FACE

Even though it is clearly safest to keep your baby rear-facing as long as you can, we empathize with parents who find it difficult to comply. Nevertheless, we want to stress that there really aren't many, if any, activities related to tending to your child that you can safely undertake while driving. Many safety advocates even discourage the use of back seat mirrors that allow parents to see their baby's face while driving because they inherently require drivers to take their eyes and attention off of the road. Our best recommendation: If you are so inclined, sit in the back seat next to your infant while someone else drives. Otherwise, take comfort in knowing that your baby's car seat is properly installed, focus your attention on what lies ahead, and commit to pulling over to a safe spot if and when you feel that your baby's demands truly warrant an immediate response.

Recalls

If you are like most of the population, you rarely (if ever) fill out manufacturers' product registration cards. Once you buy a car seat, however, it is very important that you do so because supplying the manufacturer with your seat's make and model number, along with your contact information, allows them to notify you in the event of a recall. And despite manufacturers' best efforts, recalls do occur. If you've already misplaced your registration card, be aware that there are other reliable ways to find out about recalls as long as you remember to look. You can refer to Web sites for NHTSA (www.nhtsa.gov, 888/DASH-2-DOT) and the Consumer Product Safety Commission (CPSC, www.cpsc.gov). You can also call in your car seat details and contact information to the manufacturer or submit them online.

Making Your Efforts Last

We want to emphasize that an important determining factor in keeping your baby safe is not just how secure you are able to make your car seat at installation, but rather how secure the seat is *at the time of a crash.* All too often, well-installed seats are able to work themselves loose because they are not properly locked into place. To avoid this, take a look in your own car and ask yourself how you're going to get the seat belt to secure the car seat. The following advice is meant to help you figure out the answer to this question.

And You Thought You Knew Seat Belts

Buckling your own seat belt is a task that we hope you do without much thought and one that requires little effort or understanding. When installing a car seat, however, a little more thought is generally required—hence our primer on vehicle seat belts.

Lap/Shoulder Belts

If you're using a lap/shoulder belt, you'll notice that it can be easily pulled out and then spooled back in again on what is called a retractor. When lap/shoulder belts were first introduced, they could be pulled out; however, once slack was allowed to spool in, the retractor automatically locked the lap/shoulder belts in so that they could not be pulled back out again. Consumers did not like the inconvenience of these automatically locking retractors, and as a result we now have lap/shoulder belts that only lock up when a sudden force is put on the seat belt. While most adults enjoy the comfort, there's a potential problem with installing car seats using seat belts that have only emergency locking retractors: They allow car seats to move just as freely as they do adults until the event of a crash.

Fortunately, 2 locking mechanisms have since emerged to address this problem. The first is a *switchable retractor*—one that affords an adult the comfort of a free-sliding seat belt, but that can easily be switched into the automatic locking mode by simply pulling the seat belt all the way out to the end. Once this seat belt is fully tightened and set to lock, it can't be pulled back out until the seat belt is first allowed to spool in completely.

The second mechanism is a locking latch plate (the metal and plastic part of the seat belt where the lap belt threads through and becomes the shoulder belt), which has the ability to lock the seat belt in place. If you have a relatively new car, it should come with either a switchable retractor or some type of locking latch plate. In the event that your car does not have either feature or you are simply unable to get them to work properly, only then will you need to figure out how to use a locking clip.

LOCKING CLIPS EXPLAINED

Locking clips are small, metal, H-shaped accessories that come with all infant car seats. However, in this day and age, a locking clip is rarely needed to ensure that car seats are held securely by vehicle seat belts. That's because unlike in decades past, today's seat belts generally have their own built-in locking mechanisms that can do the job. That said, many car seats these days have locking clips (also called lock-offs) conveniently built right onto the sides of the seat—an added feature that also helps ensure that they can be properly secured by just about any type of seat belt without the need for an additional metal locking clip.

Lap Belts

Lap-only belts are generally found in the middle of the back seat, as well as in additional seating positions of older cars. While they offer older children and adults no upper-body protection, they can safely be used to install infant car seats, which all come with internal harness straps. Some newer models of cars have lap belts that ratchet in and out on automatically locking retractors, whereas others function like airplane seat belts—with a locking latch plate that allows the length of the seat belt to be manually adjusted and then locked in place. Thread your lap belt through the guide slots provided on the car seat and secure it into the vehicle as tightly as possible.

Getting It Right Means Getting It Tight

Once installed, you should not be able to move your baby's car seat more than an inch from side to side (at the path of the seat belt) or away from the back of the vehicle seat. The trick to getting seat belts appropriately tight is to put your weight on the car seat base (if you're using one for an infant-only seat) or the car seat itself (while your baby is not in it, of course) and then give the already buckled seat belt an extra pull to remove slack. As you take your body weight off of the seat, it should be sufficiently secure.

LATCH

All new child safety seats and vehicles manufactured after September 1, 2002, must be LATCH-compatible. What does this mean? Well, LATCH

SEAT BELT TIGHTENERS

These devices, marketed as the easy solution to the challenges of securing car seats with seat belts, are unnecessary and have been noted on occasion to damage the seat belt (tearing or fraying the nylon webbing). In general, safety experts consider them to be potentially dangerous and, at best, unnecessary. Any claims about being "manufactured to the highest standards" you happen to see on the packaging of these products are misleading at best, since no federal standards exist for these nonregulated devices!

stands for <u>L</u>ower <u>A</u>nchors and <u>T</u>ethers for <u>Ch</u>ildren, and the driving force behind its creation was a desire to standardize the installation of all child safety seats to make it simpler and quicker and leave less room for error. LATCH involves the use of a top tether for forward-facing seats for older children and 2 lower attachments that can be used to secure rear- or forward-facing car seats to universal anchor points located in the car. While it was initially believed that LATCH would ultimately make the use of seat belts to install car seats (and most of the preceding information in this chapter, for that matter) unnecessary, this hasn't exactly been the case. In some instances, LATCH makes installation easier, but in others, correctly using the vehicle's seat belt works just as well (or sometimes even better). Either method is fine, as long as you choose just one (since more is definitely not better in this case), and the end result is a well-secured seat.

Top tether

Lower anchors

Securing Your Infant

After you have put time and effort into installing your infant's car seat, it is equally important to make sure that you know how to secure your infant in it. All infant car seats come with harness straps. There are small variations between brands, but the basic principles are the same. While harness straps should be threaded through the lowest level of harness slots for all newborns, you'll notice that most infant car seats have more than one pair of these slit-like openings. Because the harness straps must be at or below your baby's shoulders when in a rear-facing car seat, you'll want to remember to move the straps when her shoulders are at the level of the next opening. Some seats allow for easier adjustment of harness straps using an adjuster (usually a dial) that eliminates the need for harness re-threading.

Getting to the Points

All infant car seats now come with 5-point harnesses. This simply means that the straps used to secure your child safely in the seat attach to the seat over both shoulders, both hips, and one between the legs.

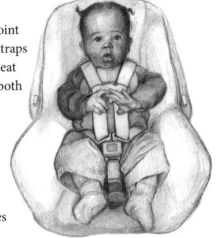

5-point harness

Once your baby is placed in the car seat and buckled in, the harness straps should not be twisted and should be snug enough that you can't pinch any slack in the straps at the level of your baby's collarbone. Any extra slack leaves your infant more room in which to move and, therefore, more susceptible to injury in the event of a crash. The fastener that holds the 2 harness straps together is called a harness clip and should rest across your baby's chest at armpit level.

A Word on Accessorizing

If you look in any baby store, you'll find an impressive array of products with which to "adorn" your infant's car seat. Before you find yourself lured into buying any, there are a few safety considerations to keep mind. Whether you've got your eye on a cute little car toy or a suction cup mirror, any items that are hard, rigid, and can't be secured well are best left on the shelf of the store or reserved for use outside of the car. The reason is simple—the potential for objects to become dangerous projectiles in the event of a crash far outweighs their possible usefulness or entertainment value.

 UFOS: UNRESTRAINED FLYING OBJECTS

At the risk of causing a flashback to high school physics, it is worth refreshing your memory about Newton's First Law of Motion. Quite simply, it states that things in motion stay in motion until acted on by an opposing force. Applying this concept to the context of car safety means that any and all loose objects in your car can easily become projectiles. It's well worth glancing around at what you have lying around, and then ask yourself what it would feel like to be hit with any of them at 60, 40, or even 20 miles per hour. You're likely to find that even the tissue box on your back dash looks a little more threatening in this context, and be convinced that it is well worth your time and effort to either restrain them or tuck them safely in your trunk.

Padding the Seats

Specially designed and readily available baby headrest cushions help prevent young babies' heads from flopping around in their seats, and are therefore especially popular among parents of newborns. That said, you shouldn't place any additional padding (including blankets and winter clothing) between your baby and the back of the seat or his harness straps unless it came with the car seat, lest it interfere with the seat's ability to protect your baby. Cushions and padding sold separately to fit around (but not under) the sides of your baby's head are acceptable, but if you would rather spare yourself yet one more purchase, then just roll up 2 towels and place them along either side of your baby's head instead (see picture on page 219). As your baby grows, remember that when any of these items become a nuisance or unnecessary, simply stop using them. If you feel your baby needs another layer of warmth and that your choice of clothing seems insufficient, you can secure him in his car seat first, then tuck a blanket or coat over him.

Location, Location, Location

Infants and Front Seat Air Bags

You're probably familiar with the golden rule that *infant car seats should never be placed in front of front seat air bags.* As a point of future reference, neither should young children. That's because air bags deploy at such great force that they can cause great harm, if not death, to infants whose car seats are placed in front of them. Granted, there are a few exceptions—such as trucks with air bag turn-off switches—but we want you to think long and hard and enlist the expertise of someone trained in child passenger safety before deciding that you qualify as an exception to this life-saving rule.

The Back Seat

It is recommended that all children under the age of 13 years sit in the back seat. The reason is quite simple—because it is almost always safer than the front. While the middle of the back seat is generally felt to be the safest and most protected location in the car, not all infant seats can or should be installed there. If the center back seat does not work, the next question many concerned parents ask is which side of the back seat is considered safer—the driver's or the passenger's? While there isn't thought to be a difference in relative safety, the passenger side often ends up being the side of choice for reasons of convenience. It's not uncommon for a rear-facing infant seat to get in the way of the vehicle seat in front of it, and most parents would rather have the inconvenience of having to scoot the front passenger seat farther forward than the driver's. When parallel parked, it also tends to be easier (and safer) to remove a baby from the car if she's on the same side as the curb.

The Impact of Side-Impact Crash Protection

While most crashes occur at the front of the car, it's well worth noting that close to 1 in 4 crashes are side-impact crashes. What makes side-impact crashes worthy of more attention, however, is their increased risk of serious or even fatal injuries. While there are not yet uniform, mandatory standards in place for car safety seat manufacturers to meet when it comes to testing how well their seats protect children in side-impact crashes, manufacturers and the National Highway Safety Administration are actively working to come up with them. Many manufacturers, aware of the added risks associated with side-impact crashes, are already testing their seats using their own (albeit varying) side-impact crash test protocols and making seats with added side-impact crash protection features readily available. In addition to keeping an eye out for new safety features and requirements, it's as important as ever that you remember to check your vehicle owner's manual and car safety seat manual to determine if the middle of the back seat is suitable for installing your baby's car safety seat, as this position is the furthest away from any potential point of side impact.

 GOING PRO

As you near the end of this chapter, we hope that you feel a bit more knowledgeable and confident in your abilities to keep your child safe in the car; but don't feel like you are now on your own. There are now tens of thousands of certified technicians across the country trained in child passenger safety. You can locate one in your area by simply contacting your state's department of transportation, local fire or emergency personnel, or a nearby children's hospital, or by looking for listings by ZIP code on the NHTSA Web site (www.nhtsa.gov), SeatCheck.org, or the National Safe Kids Coalition's Web site (www.safekids.org). Toll-free numbers such as the NHTSA Vehicle Safety Hotline (888/327-4236) and 866/SEATCHECK (866/732-8243) are also useful sources of information. You can also watch for local car seat checkup events advertised in your community. These services are usually offered at no cost, and just about all parents who take the time to have the techniques we've discussed presented in a hands-on setting find the experience to be invaluable.

A Little About Lots

As a parent, what you consider to be the most convenient spot in the parking lot may not just be determined purely by the distance from car door to store door, but also what lies between. Unless you are one of the lucky few who consider valet parking or a chauffeur as viable options, here are some thoughts to ponder when parking as a parent.

- **Curbside check-in.** Whenever possible, park along the curb so that you won't have to cross a busy parking lot and you'll be able to load and unload without another car pulling up beside you.
- **Last in line.** For those of you who have never considered the option before, parking at the end of the row and away from the crowds can offer you more space for unloading and loading babies, bags, and strollers. However, be aware that others may follow suit or cut across the parking lot from any direction while you attempt to manage your goods.
- **New parent parking.** Take advantage of "new parent parking" if any of your local area merchants have been so kind as to designate special parking spaces for new parents along with their disabled and "stork" (expectant mother) parking.
- **Out of harm's way.** If you can find a spot between 2 parked cars that has more than squeezing room on either side, you'll be better able to keep yourself, your bags and, most importantly, your baby tucked relatively safely out of the way of traffic.
- **Corralled.** Parking next to the cart corral not only allows for quick transfer of baby and goods from car to cart and back, but also lets you return your cart without leaving your infant unattended or in harm's way. However, we feel obliged to add that our husbands do not like this choice of parking spots—if only because it puts the cars at risk of being bumped, dented, or otherwise damaged by stray and misplaced carts.

 JUST SAY YES!

In some parts of the country, "Do you want help out with that?" is a commonly asked question in grocery stores these days—second only to "paper or plastic?" Before you selflessly decline the offer, take into account that an extra pair of hands to unload groceries will allow you to focus on securing your child in the car, and you'll undoubtedly be offered the luxury of having someone else put your shopping cart away free of charge.

Mr Carr's Words of Wisdom

Believe it or not, I (Laura) had a driver's ed teacher whose real name was Mr Carr. Of all his "take home and remember until parenthood" messages, one stood out above the rest—and that was to always, without exception, walk all the way around your car before getting in and driving off. Even before children are able to crawl or walk themselves into precarious positions, the potential tragedy of an infant left in a car seat on top of or behind a car is unfortunately not hypothetical. As a rule to live by, never set your baby in front of, on top of, or behind your car. Also look into some of the now-available vehicle safety features, including rearview cameras and sensors that help alert you to potential danger. And if you have to set aside the car seat or stroller momentarily while loading or unloading, consider opening a door and placing it in a spot on the side of the car where the open door will shield your baby from and deter oncoming cars.

Keeping Your Wits and Keys About You

Having experienced it firsthand, believe us when we tell you that getting locked out of your car with a hungry, crying infant can be a very traumatic experience—one that's even more traumatic if the baby is inside the car along with the keys! Acknowledging that parenthood often makes it harder to keep one's wits about them, much less stick to a routine, we strongly suggest that you make it a habit always to check for your keys before shutting the car door rather than randomly tossing them in a purse, in a diaper bag, or onto the seat of the car.

Maintaining a Perfect Attendance Record

As parents, we've gained a new appreciation of drive-thrus. Sure, they were convenient before we had children, but we never fully appreciated them until we were faced with all of the loading and unloading involved in even the most simple—and what used to be quick—errands. It's no wonder that parents are tempted to quickly run into a store, bank, or gas station without taking their infants along with them. Before you do, stop and ask yourself if you'd consider leaving a million dollars in the back seat of your car in plain view, even if the windows were cracked for air.

IN THE HEAT OF A FEW MOMENTS

The inside of a closed car on a 75°F day can reach temperatures well above 100°F in less than half an hour. In direct sunlight on a day when the temperature is in the mid 80s, it takes less than 5 minutes. Combined with the fact that a baby's body temperature increases 3 to 5 times as fast as an adult's, the heat of a few moments shut inside a car can lead to serious if not lethal consequences.

While we don't need to tell you (although we've found all parents like to hear it) that your child is priceless, we do feel obliged to reinforce for you the fact that carjacking-turned-kidnappings, heat stroke, and even worse calamities do happen in cars where children are left unattended. It is for these reasons that we urge you never to get in the habit of leaving your baby alone in the car, however briefly. It is as much a part of keeping your child safe as having a properly installed car seat!

BACK SEAT REMINDERS

As much as every parent would like to think it could never happen to them, we've all heard of infants being forgotten and left behind strapped in their car seats in the back of the car—sometimes with devastating consequences. More often than not, this nightmare scenario involves a change in routine, sleep-deprivation, stress, or any of a host of other factors all too common to new parenthood. Given that it's all too easy to imagine how this out-of-sight, out-of-mind situation could occur, we suggest making use of any of the tried-and-true ways that parents remind themselves whenever they have precious back-seat passengers in tow. Examples of such reminders from KidsAndCars.org, the advocacy group dedicated to keeping children safe in and around cars, include

- Keep a large teddy bear in your child's car seat and move it to the front passenger seat whenever your baby is in the back seat as a (big) visual reminder.
- Put something you'll need for work, such as your purse, your cell phone, or an employee badge, for example, on the floor of the back seat whenever you strap your baby in the back so that you won't ever leave the car with one but not the other.
- Make sure to coordinate with your child's caregiver(s) and let them know if your child won't be coming on any given day so that they know to call you if your child is ever unexpectedly late or absent.

CHAPTER 23

flying the family-friendly skies

In this age of upward mobility, a large number of new and expectant parents find themselves faced with what we consider to be an altogether new form of travel: airplane travel with a baby. As with just about every other aspect of parenting, this undertaking will inevitably involve a lot more advanced planning than the trips you used to take alone. In this section, we've included insights that apply specifically to flying with your baby—a topic we've found to be especially useful during the early weeks of parenthood when you're laden down with diapers, strollers, and car seats and still settling into sleep and feeding routines.

Timing Your Ticketed Travels

Most parents who find themselves planning airplane travel with their newborns wonder about the age at which it's safe and easiest (relatively speaking) to fly with a baby, not to mention which time of day generally works the best with a newborn's "schedule." First let us say that planning flight times around a young infant's sleeping and eating schedule is a noble idea and one worth pursuing, but one that does not always proceed according to plan—even for those babies who settle into predictable routines conveniently early in life. This is definitely where the phrase "even the best laid plans…" comes to mind. While we have found from personal and professional experience that there isn't one right answer to the question of when it's safest and easiest to travel, the fact of the matter is that newborns and young babies generally adapt pretty well to changes in sleep and eating schedules, including those necessitated by travel.

First in Flight

We have found no wiser advice than to take it easy on yourself after having a baby and devote your time and energy to establishing a comfortable routine. In this regard, airplane travel is not exactly conducive to rest and recuperation. Yet it is surprisingly common how often new parents end up faced with taking their newborns or young infants on an airplane. Whether you find yourself traveling by choice or because of a hard-to-cancel and far-away obligation, it should be reassuring to know that healthy term babies generally do just fine flying anytime after the first week or two. Parents, on the other hand, don't always fare so well. We recommend you think through your travel plans carefully before embarking on yet another journey, because setting out on your journey through parenthood is likely to require a great deal of planning and adjustment in and of itself. Especially during the time when your baby is younger than about 4 months, it's worth stopping and asking yourself whether the trip you are contemplating is optional. If not, then jump right ahead to the rest of the chapter for practical advice on how to go about flying the family-friendly skies successfully. If you're unsure, then it is up to you to decide how fatigued you are from your recent and ongoing induction into parenthood, how much you like (or dislike) to travel, what seasonal germs you stand a good chance of running into along the way, and whether your baby is likely to be accommodating. For young infants, how accommodating they are will be dependent on whether they have become relatively skilled at eating and sleeping in unfamiliar surroundings and whether they are very sensitive to stimulation.

 FLYING PREMATURELY

While commercial airliners are pressurized and the oxygen level in the cabin is carefully controlled during flight, premature babies whose lungs are not fully developed may be more sensitive to the effects of high-altitude travel. We haven't found a definitive answer as to when it is OK to travel with a premature infant, and therefore recommend you double-check with your baby's doctor before flying (or going to the mountains, for that matter), where the altitude's effect on oxygen concentration may be a factor.

Unwanted Parting Gifts

Even if you're ready to take on the challenges of air travel, consider the fact that airplanes are notorious for their close quarters—a factor that makes the spread of germs all the more likely. Even a good many adults find themselves with the lovely parting gift of fresh colds soon after flying. As discussed in the chapter we devoted to the subject, fever in newborns is more than just an inconvenience and needs to be taken seriously—requiring not only the involvement of health professionals but also the possibility of tests and treatment. In general, avoiding closed-in spaces—especially those filled with people who have the sniffles—is definitely in your baby's (and your) best interest. If you do fly with your baby, remember that taking extra precautionary measures such as stepping up your hand-washing or hand sanitizing, and shielding your baby from any direct contact with coughing or otherwise obviously ill travelers can help minimize your baby's (and your own) chances of catching whatever seasonal viruses happen to be out and about.

Sleeping en Route

Over the years, we've been asked or told about many home remedies rumored to be effective in getting babies to sleep on planes. As nice as it would be to have a calm, quiet, and sleeping baby throughout an entire flight, we simply haven't found any ingestible remedy that we can bring ourselves to recommend. Common sense, never mind our medical training, tells us that giving babies even a tiny spoonful of an alcoholic beverage or a sampling of a sedative—while often referenced in parenting humor—is a very bad idea in real life, however tempting it may seem under duress. The use of sedating over-the-counter children's medications (most notably antihistamines used to treat allergies and itchiness) in hopes of inducing sleep is also not recommended for young infants. For those of you who are still tempted, let us also forewarn you that some children actually have the opposite response and become hyperactive and irritable instead. If you are determined to use something to get your child to sleep on the plane—during infancy or in the years to come—then be very sure to talk to your baby's doctor about it first so you know it's safe and you have the correct dose. Then do a trial run at home so you can determine ahead of time how your child will respond.

Late-Night Flights

Once babies master the overall concept of sleeping in the first few months, we have found that they tend to sleep more reliably at nighttime than they do during naptime travel. That said, before you book a cross-country red-eye, give it your best guess as to whether your baby actually will sleep through the night if he's on a plane instead of in a crib, not to mention whether you'll be able to sleep as well. If you determine that both you and your baby are up for it, a late-night flight may be the way to go. Just remember to factor in some extra time for getting yourself *and* your baby settled in safe and sound once you arrive at your destination, because the additional parenting tasks—not the least of which include installing a car seat and setting up a crib—can add a fair bit to your overall travel time. If nothing else, having a baby along all but ensures that you won't have time to sleep in after a late night or early morning arrival, especially if your baby is well rested and raring to go.

Booking Your Flights

To Buy or Not to Buy

Yes, it's true…the Federal Aviation Administration (FAA) does not require the purchase of an airline ticket for any child younger than 2 years, and we openly acknowledge that from a budgetary standpoint, the option of traveling with a lap child (as the airline industry calls unticketed infants and toddlers) can be financially appealing. You should know, however, that safety experts across the country unanimously agree that forgoing the purchase of a seat for your baby is not an ideal way to save money, and the FAA strongly urges parents to secure all children in an appropriate restraint—a recommendation that inherently requires they have a seat of their own on the plane. Even if it remains optional for parents to purchase infants their own seats on airplanes, we want to strongly encourage you to save up and pay for the extra seat anyway if at all possible. Believe us when we say that we wish there were a good alternative, but knowing what we do about safety and airplane travel, we can't come up with one. Instead, we suggest you look around and take advantage of discounted seats that airlines sometimes offer for infants. We also recommend getting in the habit (if you aren't already) of signing yourself *and* your baby up for the airlines' frequent flier mileage programs. Even though it may take a while to get to the level of a free ticket, your baby's accumulated miles (as well as your own) can ultimately help soften the blow to your budget.

DISCOUNTS FOR THE UNDER TWO JET SET

Before purchasing your tickets, be sure to check with the specific airlines you intend to fly to see if they offer any discounted fares for children younger than 2 years. You may be pleasantly surprised with purchase prices of up to 50% less than the published adult fare. International flights may offer even larger discounts for "underage" fliers. In fact, these fares are not always limited to children younger than 2 years; some are even offered for children up to the age of 12 years.

Safety First

Securing your infant in a seat of her own in an FAA-approved car seat is an important step in committing yourself from day 1 to the idea that your baby's safety comes first. We're not saying that you can't unbuckle to change a diaper or take care of other baby business while in flight, but be aware that turbulence poses the greatest safety risk to passengers of all ages, and is unpredictable. Before you set out, you'll also want to keep in mind that not all car seats are FAA approved for use in aircraft, and those that are may still not fit in the airplane seat if they are wider than about 16 inches. Check for a label on your car seat that says it is FAA approved, and check with your airline if you're concerned about whether the seat will fit. You can also go to the FAA Web site (www.faa.gov/passengers/fly_children) for more details.

Sitting in the Lap of Luxury

Even if you love to hold and cuddle with your baby when you're at home, you may find that doing it for an entire airplane flight is somewhat uncomfortable. Also, many babies who would otherwise be content to sit in their car seats and entertain themselves or sleep tend to have much greater expectations when they are held.

AN OVERVIEW OF SEAT ASSIGNMENTS

For any infant or child who is going to travel in a child restraint seat on an airplane, the following seat assignments should be considered a must:

- All car seats must be secured in a window seat.
- The exit row is not an option for anyone who has a baby as a travel companion.
- Only use an FAA-approved car seat as evidenced by a label on the seat that verifies that it is, in fact, FAA approved.
- Be aware that the FAA recommends all infants weighing less than 20 pounds be restrained in a rear-facing car seat during airplane travel.
- For future reference, children from 20 to 40 pounds should still be restrained in a forward-facing seat, and not be switched to using just the airplane's lap belt until they reach 40 pounds.
- While there are alternative harness systems approved by the FAA for use by toddlers on airplanes, booster seats are not approved for use and should be checked or stored overhead.

If You Don't Opt for the Extra Seat

There are definitely those out there who would matter-of-factly tell you that if you can't afford to pay for an extra seat for your infant, you shouldn't be traveling. We too feel strongly about keeping children safe, but we also intend to live up to our claim that this is a book about the realities of parenting—and we know full well that not all of you are going to buy your babies airline tickets. While doing so is the only way to guarantee that your baby will be safely secured during a flight, we wanted to provide some tips about traveling with an infant if you haven't purchased a seat.

- **Playing the odds.** Even if you haven't purchased your infant a seat, it is possible on occasion to get one. Some regularly scheduled flight times are notoriously less popular than others. If you will be traveling with a lap child, consider booking yourself in a window seat on one of these typically less than full flights (such as overnight red-eyes) and take your chances that there will be open seats left. When you check in at the gate, simply ask the ticketing agent if there are any empty seats still available. If there are, chances are good that they will be middle seats, and you may be allowed to secure your infant's car seat in the window seat you had reserved for yourself and then sit in the adjacent middle seat without paying extra. If your flight does end up being full, however, you'll be asked to check your baby's car seat and proceed with your original plan.

- **Picking a seat on a full flight.** If finding an open seat is out of the question, then you'll want to decide which you think is going to be the lesser of 2 evils—a window seat that is out of the way but with less easy access to the aisle, or an aisle seat where you'll need to pay attention to a second set of body parts (your baby's, that is) to make sure that head, feet, and limbs don't get bumped by service carts or passers-by. In the aisle seat, you may also have to accommodate your middle- and window-seat neighbors' need to access the aisle. When traveling with your baby and another ticket-purchasing person, we suggest you book the aisle and window seats. Chances are better that the middle seat between will remain unoccupied, potentially allowing you to claim it for yourself and then secure your infant's car seat in the window seat as described above. If someone else does get assigned to the middle seat, you can virtually guarantee that person won't mind switching from the middle to an aisle or window seat, allowing you and your travel companion to sit next to each other with your baby on your lap.
- **Baby carriers.** Baby carriers (including slings) are very popular among flying parents, but they by no means offer the same degree of protection as placing your baby in a secured car seat during the flight, and the FAA does not approve them for use during take off or landing.

Other Seating Rules, Regulations, and Recommendations

Before your days of flying with your baby, your seat preference was probably based on proximity to the front of the plane, a desire for extra leg room, or an interest in seeing the sights out the window. Not so anymore. If nothing else, you will now be required to install your infant's car seat in a window seat so as not to block passengers from exiting the row, and opting for the exit row is no longer a possibility, because families traveling with small children aren't exactly the ideal people to perform the necessary exit-row duties in the event of an emergency.

As for the choices you do have when it comes to seat assignments, many parents vie for the opportunity to sit in the bulkhead rows located at the front of each section of the aircraft. These seats typically offer more space than is allotted between the rest of the rows and ensure that rear-facing infant car seats won't be in a position to interfere with the ability of the passenger in front of your baby to recline his seat. As an added benefit, you also don't have to go far to reach them. Now that we've extolled the virtues of bulkhead seating, let us point out that the odds of getting assigned to bulkhead seats are not that great, and you will likely have to sacrifice the convenience of stowing your diaper bag under the seat in front of you (because there is usually no allotted space) and store it in the less-accessible overhead compartment instead. If you find yourself in the likely position of considering your second choice in seat selection, you may find that there are benefits to the front and the back. Sitting toward the front of the plane is particularly useful if you're loaded down, whereas the back of the plane will get you tucked out of everyone's way once you make it back there, and is often just loud enough (from the sound of the engines) either to soothe your baby with background noise or to drown out any crying for all but those sitting closest to you.

Navigating the Airport

Arrivals

As the rules of 21st century air travel changed and airport security heightened, so did the challenges of navigating the airport with an infant. There was a day when we would have recommended that you simply pull up to curbside check-in before parking, leave one person stationed at the car with the baby, and have the other stand in line to check in. For obvious reasons, those days are long gone. Figuring out how to get everyone and everything checked in and to the gate on time takes a little more forethought these days. We've found that the easiest solution to this problem is to avoid the prospect of parking altogether and get dropped off whenever possible.

Divide and Conquer

If you do end up driving yourselves to the airport, you might want to consider the divide and conquer approach (assuming that you are not traveling solo). Drop off one adult with photo ID and ticket in hand at curbside check-in with all of the bags, including the carry-on(s). This leaves the parking parent less encumbered and more easily able to park the car expeditiously and hurry back with the baby to check in. If your parking pros-

STATISTICALLY SPEAKING

We advise you to buckle up your baby on the way to the airport as well as on the plane! The chance of injury from an automobile crash is much higher than that from airplane crashes or in-flight turbulence, yet in some states, babies are not required to be secured in car seats when riding in the back of taxis, limos, or shuttle buses. It makes us cringe when we hear about parents who tuck the car seat into the trunk of the taxi with the luggage, thinking, "It's just a short ride to the airport."

pects look particularly grim, you may want to consider dropping off your baby as well—especially if you don't have a stroller or baby carrier. That way, if you find yourself heading to the remote corners of the economy lot, you'll avoid the frustrating dilemma of how to secure your baby safely on the shuttle, because quite often you just plain can't. The final key to success with the divide and conquer approach is to be sure to set a clearly defined meeting place before parting ways.

Security Checkpoints

Many airlines now require that even infants without a paid ticket receive a boarding pass. This helps with their inventory of passengers and weight estimates of each airplane load. Be sure to let the airline agent know, at the time of booking and when checking in, that your infant is traveling with you. The security personnel will check that each passenger has a boarding pass and photo ID if applicable.

 LET SLEEPING BABIES LIE

As inconvenient as it may seem, safety regulations may require that you lift your baby out of her car seat when going through security so that the seat and your baby can be properly inspected—even if your baby is sleeping contentedly. When walking through the metal detector, you may even be asked to carry your baby at arm's length in front of you to prove you are not concealing any objects (other than your nursing pads) between your bodies.

Leave the Pointy Parenting Objects Behind

Most adults have become quite accustomed to leaving potentially dangerous objects (tools, weapons, flammables, and even butter knives) at home as but one of the post-September 11th security changes—but don't forget that this "absolutely no sharp objects on board the airplane" principle may apply to your baby's nail scissors and other grooming supplies as well. By substituting a cardboard emery board for a pair of sharp-pointed metal nail scissors, for example, you'll avoid having them confiscated. Fortunately, most baby supplies are not considered to be security risks. Just be aware that all carry-on baggage, including diaper bags, strollers, car seats, and any other baby items, must go through the x-ray machine and/or be inspected by a security officer. Check the Transportation Security Agency's Web site at www.tsa.gov/travelers/airtravel/children for full details.

Ease on Down the Terminal

When making the seemingly endless trek through airport terminals with an infant in tow, it's best to make the most of modern-day conveniences such as rolling luggage, Smarte Cartes, and your baby stroller or baby carrier. Smarte Cartes typically run $2 to $4 and in most airports can be rented using cash or a credit card. Unfortunately, in some airports, Smarte Cartes are only allowed up to the security checkpoints, at which point parents are left to their own devices to find ways to get their belongings gracefully to the gate. In a bind, we've been allowed to use a spare wheelchair to hold carry-on bags and free our hands to hold our babies, tickets, and ID—just make sure to ask permission first and leave the wheelchair at an acceptable location. If you have a long way to go to reach the gate, are really heavily loaded, or especially if you have a lightning layover, by all means request to be picked up by one of the airport's indoor electric carts.

Gate Checking Baby Gear

Gate checking is an option well worth knowing about as a parent. If nothing else, it allows you to use your stroller to make your way through the entire parking lot and airport, right up until the time you're about to set foot on the plane. Just be prepared to collapse or fold it up (after making sure nothing will fall out of its pockets, trays, or baskets) when you reach the security checkpoint. At the gate you will be given a claim ticket for your

GETTING THINGS ROLLING

Rolling backpacks make for a perfect example of a relatively simple but well thought out design that we can only assume was invented by a parent. Even if it wasn't, we recommend that you consider investing in one for use during travel. Many are big enough to hold the same amount of stuff as a rolling carry-on suitcase, but the added hands-free feature of the shoulder straps can be invaluable—especially if you're going it alone.

tagged stroller and then asked to leave it at the end of the Jetway as you board. If everything works the way it is supposed to—which it usually but not always does—your stroller should be waiting for you immediately outside the plane as you get off or shortly thereafter. We've found gate checking to be so convenient that we made a habit of checking even the small umbrella strollers that can fit in the overhead compartments for the simple reason that doing so gave us one less item (or three) to lug on board. As for the "deluxe" strollers that allow the infant car seat to attach, we found them invaluable.

All Aboard

Walking up to the gate with a baby and all of your travel accessories should be enough to cause everyone but those we consider to be truly cold-hearted to offer sympathetic glances, in some cases assistance, and—in what has become less common but no less appreciated—the option to pre-board. The privilege of getting on first used to be a luxury that was granted to anyone and everyone traveling with children. It seems, however, that not all airlines believe in pre-boarding anymore and when they do, it can feel a lot more like a 2-second head start than a luxury. The good news is that you do have some options.

- **Boarding last.** Your first option is to pass on pre-boarding and instead wait until last to get on the plane. This works especially well for parents who aren't going to require a lot of overhead space, find it stressful to be solely responsible for blocking 100 other passengers from their seats, or who simply don't relish the idea of entertaining their infants in a confined seat on the plane for any longer than necessary.

- **Send ahead or go your separate ways.** This is what we like to think of as the (relatively) hands-free option. Whether you are traveling with another adult or need to seek the assistance of an airline employee working at the gate, consider sending someone ahead with your car seat, carry-on suitcase, stroller, and/or any other bulky items without which you can manage until closer to flight time. The 30 extra minutes or so that this is likely to afford you and your baby in the gate area instead of being stuck in your seat(s) can make quite a difference—especially for an awake and demanding baby.
- **Stand up for pre-boarding.** If you definitely want to get on the plane and get settled in, then don't be shy about broaching the subject of pre-boarding even if it seems to have been "overlooked" by the gate attendants. While a few airlines seem to have lost a little bit of their family-friendly charm, it is still challenging to find a ticket agent who is comfortable turning away a loaded-down parent and infant at the front of the line just because their row number has yet to have been called.

Please Remain Seated

You already know our strong bias toward having a purchased seat for your baby. If you have followed through and chosen to buy one or just lucked out and taken over an unused seat, then by all means make sure to use it during as much of the flight as possible. Quite often, babies decide to voice their disapproval of having to sit in a car seat loudly enough that their parents feel obliged to remove them to stop the crying. Before you give in too easily, try to treat flying in an airplane as you would a trip in the car. Just as (we hope) you wouldn't dream of setting out for a drive without first securing your infant safely in his seat in the car, use the same approach on the airplane. Your baby will be safer and you'll increase the likelihood that, as he gets older, it won't occur to him to complain about being restrained on the plane.

Dressing for Success, Not a Flight of Fancy

Those of you who are frequent air travelers are undoubtedly well acquainted with the concept of dressing for the occasion. For one, there's the unpredictability of cabin temperature. We highly recommend dressing yourself and your child in easy-on, easy-off layers so that you are prepared

TURBULENCE

According to the Federal Aviation Administration, turbulence is the most common cause of non-fatal injury in passengers and flight attendants—about 60 people per year are injured by turbulence while not wearing their seat belts. While it is more likely to occur when the aircraft is above 30,000 feet and tends to be worse in the winter than in the summer, turbulence can occur out of the blue, at any altitude and in any season—even in clear blue skies.

for whatever in-flight conditions you may find. In making your selections, remember that easy access and comfort are key—even for you, but definitely for your baby. If you consider this an opportunity to show your baby off in a frilly new dress or a fancy new outfit for this venture out into the real world, it will quickly become apparent that function was meant to overrule fashion when it comes to infant airplane attire (and, we would argue, the rest of childhood). Simply put, elastic-waist pants, zip-up outfits, or easy-snap crotches are far easier than tights and lace or button-up-the-back Onesies when it comes to diaper changing—especially when faced with doing it in cramped quarters.

Carry-on Contents

Believe us when we say it's well worth it to pack with your baby in mind. One of the major differences in traveling with kids is that you inevitably lose claim to a significant amount of space in your carry-on suitcase—at least until several years down the road. The basic goals underlying your suitcase-stuffing efforts should be that when you're done, you will be well prepared but at the same time weighted down by as few carry-on bags as possible. If everything you choose to bring along as carry-on items fits easily in your bag(s), it will significantly decrease the likelihood that you will leave a trail of belongings in your wake. That said, there are quite a few supplies that you won't want to board without—several of which we have listed for you on the following page.

- **Diapering supplies.** When it comes to changing diapers on airplanes, expect the worst and don't assume the airline will have the supplies you need. If your baby usually poops twice a day, expect the pleasure of 3 or 4. And if they're usually semi-formed, expect liquidy leaky ones—just because good old Murphy (and his "it's bound to happen" laws) said so. We highly recommend giving priority in your carry-on or diaper bag to plenty of extra diapers, a hefty supply of wipes, and some small plastic garbage bags (grocery store plastic bags work quite well). If you don't end up needing them, that's great, but carrying them along with you is a small price to pay for not being caught empty handed. Remember that flight attendants should not be expected to touch or discard diapers for sanitary reasons since they are the ones handling everyone's food. You can either dispose of the diapers—sealed in a plastic bag to minimize the odor—in the lavatory or pack them in your diaper bag to toss when you land. If you run out of plastic bags, the airsick bags work well as backup. Also consider packing a travel-size antibacterial hand sanitizer in case you are unable to get to the sink.
- **Change of clothing.** Think about how many outfits your baby typically goes through in a day, double it, and make room for them in your carry-on. And then consider doing the same for yourself, because you aren't likely to enjoy sitting in clothes that bear the fresh stains of parenthood any more than your baby would. Also remember to leave space in your carry-on for any extra layers you and your baby may shed during the trip.
- **Additional supplies.** You will undoubtedly know your baby well enough to know whether leaving home without a pacifier is going to spell disaster. Making room for a favorite blanket, stuffed animal, or other attachment object is also a good idea if your infant is old enough to care about them. Be sure to tuck in an adequate supply of tissues and paper towels, and then proceed to pack anything you might actually want for yourself in whatever space you have left.

IN-FLIGHT CHANGING CHALLENGE

While the availability of pull-down changing tables in airplane lavatories are logistically invaluable for in-flight diaper changing, they unfortunately are far from universal.

Yet diapers will inevitably need to be changed, and the ability to change your baby's diaper on your lap will therefore be a handy skill to master in anticipation of any airplane flight. The underlying principles are essentially the same as those described in the diapering chapter (page 117), but there are a few extra considerations that will make in-flight diapering go more smoothly. First and foremost, for the sake of your fellow travelers, we strongly suggest that you make every effort to limit your lap changes to significantly wet diapers and save the smelly ones for the lavatory. That being clearly stated from the outset, practice laying your baby on your lap with her head resting near your knees and her bottom toward your stomach. It is a particularly good idea to use the method of slipping a new diaper under your baby's bottom before taking the old diaper off when your lap is serving as the changing table. Now more than ever, you'll also want to keep "things" covered as much of the time as possible to avoid being caught in any crossfire. Have wipes and a bag readily available for quick cleanup and sanitary disposal. As a side note, solo lap changing is entirely possible, but an extra pair of hands sure is nice for expediting the process and reducing the likelihood of a mess. Based on the rules of airplane etiquette, however, we suggest you refrain from seeking assistance from any of your in-flight neighbors unless, of course, they happen to be traveling with you.

In-Flight Feeding

As hard as it already is to eat a meal comfortably on a tiny tray table if and when you're offered one, traveling with your baby will likely add to the mealtime challenge. The first challenge is managing to eat your own meal; the second is feeding your infant in cramped quarters with the likelihood of onlookers 6 inches away. You may find that this is all the more reason to get your baby his own seat, freeing up space for your own meal and having a place to either secure or hold him while he's eating. Be aware that tray tables rarely, if ever, can be put all the way down flat in front of a rear- and sometimes even a forward-facing car seat.

Breastfeeding in 6 Inches of Personal Space

Breastfeeding on airplanes presents its own unique set of obstacles. If your baby's car seat is in the window seat, you are in the middle seat, and a complete stranger is on the aisle encroaching on your shared armrest (which, as you know, is not just hypothetical), nursing comfortably may seem like an oxymoron. Here are a few suggestions that can help.

- **One-sided.** If the flight is short, nursing on just one side while saving the other for later when you get off the plane may be an acceptable option.
- **At an angle.** The close quarters greatly limit a breastfeeding mother's chance of privacy. Simply angling your body so that you're facing the window before trying to breastfeed can help minimize the degree of exposure.
- **Covering up.** For the sake of modesty or convenience, it is well worth your while to wear easy-access clothing such as a breastfeeding shirt or a loose-fitting top layer over a button-down or untucked shirt.
- **Layering.** Use your outer layer, a blanket, a magazine, or even the back part of your baby carrier as a practical way of obstructing the view.
- **Stalling.** Nursing in the lavatory may seem like a reasonable last resort, but suffice it to say that it generally poses a huge inconvenience for fellow passengers and isn't exactly hygienic. In other words, we don't really recommend it.

In-Flight Formula Preparation

Short of taking along the more expensive but ready-to-feed formula, the best way to have plenty of easily prepared formula on hand is to put premeasured amounts of dry powdered formula into several of your baby's bottles and seal them with nipples and lids. As an important forethought, be sure your bottles are completely dry before putting the formula in them, because a few drops of water left inside a bottle can make the powder stick to the sides in a manner reminiscent of cement. Needless to say, this can make future bottle cleaning a much more challenging proposition. Once the premeasured powder is sealed in dry bottles, tuck the bottles into your carry-on bag (or purse or diaper bag). Whenever it's time to feed your baby, simply add the appropriate amount of room-temperature water to each bottle.

And even though airlines still reliably offer beverage service on just about all flights, you can't count on the timing. That's not to say that most flight attendants aren't quite accommodating, but there are inevitably going to be times (during take-off and landing, for example) when they are going to be unable to respond to your baby's urgent insistence. Instead, play it safe and bring along at least one extra bottle of water of your own. That way you won't have to worry about refrigeration, heating, or the timing of beverage service to be able to appease your suddenly starving child.

 ## GOING WITH THE IN-FLIGHT FLOW

For anyone who has traveled by air in the many years since September 11th, you're probably all too familiar with the requirement that all fluids packed as carry-on must be in 3-ounce or smaller containers, all of which must collectively fit in a single quart-sized plastic bag. The good news for traveling parents is that the Transportation Safety Administration now allows for baby-related exceptions. What does this mean? It means that medications, baby formula and food, breast milk, and even juice are allowed in reasonable quantities exceeding the usual 3-ounce limit, and they do not need to fit in the zip-top plastic bag. While we can't tell you just how much is considered "reasonable," we can tell you to expect that these items will be inspected and possibly even tested (but not tasted) as you go through security.

In-Flight Troubleshooting

As frequent fliers, we often received wary looks from fellow passengers as we boarded planes with a baby (or two or three) and took our seats. We're not sure which is more stressful: being the passenger who first realizes he will be seated next to someone else's crying baby, or being that baby's parent. Fortunately for all involved, however, many young babies actually do travel well in flight; quite often it tends to be the crawlers and toddlers who get antsy and upset when confined, but that's a different book altogether.

High-Altitude Crying

Babies of all ages do cry for various reasons, so in the space constraints of aircraft, try to be resourceful when trying to calm your crying child. As you do, take comfort in knowing that the drone of the engines usually limits how far a crying baby can be heard. Keeping your own cool can go a long way when you're trying to soothe your baby and have to remain seated. Check the usual suspects and respond accordingly: Is your baby hungry, wet or dirty, cold or warm, bored? If it's bright outside, try closing the window shade; if your baby wants a view, show her the one outside the window or in the pages of the airline's magazine. If all else fails, try not to let a few dirty looks bother you and be assured that most people sympathize with the parents of a crying infant. After all, everyone was a baby once, many have had to try to quiet one in a public place at some time in their past, you're unlikely to have to face any of these people ever again and, lastly, they'll get over it.

The Ears Have It

Before we discuss ear pain on airplanes, let us first offer you the reassurance that a great many babies never show the slightest signs of discomfort. Until you know that your own child (and you) will be spared, the thought of a baby screaming because of ear pain is easily and understandably one of the most dreaded aspects of air travel. And from firsthand experience, we can tell you it tends to be all the more disconcerting when that baby happens to be your own. Any of you who have flown before know that ears can be quite sensitive to changes in pressure. Switching to pediatrician mode for a moment, this is because the outer ear is separated from the middle ear by a thin membrane called the tympanic membrane, or ear drum. Experiencing a difference in pressure across this membrane causes a sensation that as many as 1 in 3 passengers (children more so than adults) experience as temporary muffled hearing, discomfort, or even pain. Unfortunately, having a stuffy nose or a head cold can increase a child's chances of ear problems. For an adult, chewing gum or yawning is often all that is needed for the middle-ear pressure to return to normal and make plugged-up ears "pop." Perhaps part of the reason that babies tend to be more vocal than adults about the changing pressure in their ears is because chewing gum is simply not an option and we have yet to meet an infant who can yawn on command. If your baby has a cold or ear infection, discuss with your pediatrician whether you should give him an infant pain reliever. Unfortunately, decongestants have not been proven to help, and in fact are not recommended for use in infants. For children with significant ear discomfort associated with a cold and/or ear infection, it may simply be best, if possible, to postpone flying. If your travel plans are not flexible enough to cancel because of a cold, just be aware of your increased odds of dealing with ear pain when you do hop aboard.

Sucking Away One's Sorrows

Once on board, it's useful to know that there is a practical and realistic alternative to the traditional gum-chewing approach (which, for obvious reasons, is absolutely contraindicated at this age regardless of your level of desperation) that works very well for babies when it comes to relieving ear pressure. That alternative is sucking. Pediatricians, flight attendants, and seasoned parents alike commonly suggest offering a bottle, breast, or pacifier during the times when the pressure changes in the cabin are likely to be greatest—during takeoff and initial descent. You'll notice we said *initial* descent, not landing. That's because the pressure change is typically most noticeable as much as a half hour or more before landing, depending on a flight's cruising altitude. The higher up you are, the earlier in the flight the descent usually starts. If you generally don't tend to notice your own ears popping and the captain doesn't announce plans for the initial descent, you can always ask a flight attendant to let you know when it would be a good idea to try to get the sucking started. If sucking doesn't cut it and your baby seems to be bothered, stay calm and try rubbing his ears and singing a soothing song. Even if you find that nothing short of reaching solid ground (and normal air pressure) works to calm him down, remind yourself that you've done everything you can, and that most babies who have difficulty with ear pain on airplanes tend to outgrow it.

 OUT OF EARSHOT

Airplane cabin noise levels can range anywhere from 60 to as high as 100 decibels, and tend to be louder during takeoff. Using cotton balls or small earplugs may help to decrease the decibel level your baby is exposed to, and as a result make it easier for her to sleep or relax.

These Shoes Were Made for Wearing

As you make your way through airports and on and off airplanes, one thing's for sure—you'll be very grateful for comfortable shoes. And for those of you who were recently pregnant—just when you thought you'd seen the last of swollen feet, think again. Sitting for hours on a plane is a well-known cause of sluggish blood flow and swollen feet. Also misleadingly referred to as economy class syndrome, poor circulation and blood clots (called deep venous thrombosis, or DVT) resulting from air travel can affect people sitting anywhere in the airplane, not just in the coach cabin. As you focus your attention on changing, feeding, soothing, and entertaining your baby, conventional wisdom suggests you keep your shoes on (lest you're unable to get them back on) and be sure to stretch your feet and legs frequently throughout the flight.

CHAPTER 24

choosing child care—
insider tips for all those who care

As you sit down and enjoy the anticipation of bringing your newborn home, the last thing that may come to mind is the thought of turning around and putting your baby's care into someone else's hands. Yet the fact of the matter is that many of us are faced with doing just that, whether our maternity leaves end at 6 weeks, 6 months, or even 6 years. That's why we've added this chapter on choosing child care. In addition to both of us being pediatricians who have helped parents including ourselves navigate the world of child care, I (Laura) also happen to have some additional and relatively unique insights to share as the owner of a 200-student educational child care center that provides care for children starting as young as 6 weeks.

Finding Child Care That's Right For You

The search for quality child care is hugely important—not only for reasons of health and safety, but also because whoever cares for your baby ultimately stands to play such a key role in your baby's activities of daily learning (see page 161). In this chapter, we'll help you better understand the various types of child care, know what to look out for and, ultimately, how to recognize high-quality care when you see it. Of course, the challenge doesn't stop there, because finding good child care isn't the same thing as being able to get your baby into it!

The Early Bird Gets the Crib

If you haven't already begun your search for child care, it's safe to say that now's the time. One of the most compelling reasons to focus your attention on your future child care needs now—regardless of what stage of pregnancy or parenthood you're in—is simply that finding the right child care can take time, and space may well be limited. Let's face it—finding an infant spot in a high-quality child care setting or finding the ideal nanny can be downright competitive. In some places around the country, babies' names are put on waitlists months before their anticipated arrival—sometimes before parents have agreed on a name (or, in some instances, even conceived!). Regardless of whether your child care plans involve employing the watchful eyes of friends or family, day care in someone's home, or a child care center, we highly recommend starting your search and making preparations as far in advance as possible. While you may find this chapter seems to focus more on center-based care, a majority of the principles and standards of health and safety that we want to share with you can (and should) be applied to all child care providers.

 HOW MUCH WE REALLY CARE

The answer to just how many children in the United States today are in child care is simple: lots. To elaborate, an estimated 60% to 70% of children under the age of 6 are in some form of child care, and by the time they reach 6 years, 84% of all kids have been enrolled in some form of care—a percentage that adds up to approximately 12 million children at any given time.

Who Cares?

There are several child care options from which you can choose. The following is a basic overview of each of the general types, along with some useful information about how each is structured, staffed, and regulated.

Child care centers. Child care centers provide care for groups of children. They are typically defined as large or small based on their maximum capacity. With only a few exceptions, child care centers regardless of size are required to be licensed by the state in which they're located. The minimum health, safety, and training requirements that must be met varies by state. While licensure alone doesn't guarantee quality, it can play an important role. Parents often turn to center-based care because there are multiple caregivers (which improves both safety and reliability); regular inspections; and it affords additional space, equipment, and organized activities. Also of note, research has shown that children attending child care centers experience fewer injuries than those cared for at home. Prices for center-based care can vary significantly by center, location, and age of child (to give but a few examples). Of note, church and temple day care centers and preschools may or may not be exempt from your state's licensing regulations, so be sure to carefully evaluate them as you would any other child care setting before enrolling.

Family child care. In general, family child care providers offer child care services in their homes. Like child care centers, all states set minimum health and safety standards for family child care providers as well. Parents who opt for family child care are often those who find the home-like environment appealing, and tend to favor the typically smaller numbers of children and single (or relatively few) caregivers characteristic of family child care. Additionally, this type of care may prove to be a bit more flexible and less expensive than center-based care. Of note, children in this setting have been shown to have a higher incidence of injuries than either in centers or in their own homes. While you may be tempted to choose one based on word-of-mouth recommendations from friends or colleagues, be aware that not all states require family child care providers to get criminal background checks or have ongoing training, so make sure you do your own checking.

In-home caregivers. In general, this category of caregivers refers to nannies, au pairs, and/or housekeepers who provide care in the child's own home. This type of child care isn't as well regulated and only requires minimal health and safety training. While it may seem quite pricey to enlist the services of an agency, nanny placement agencies (both local and online) typically provide extensive and very valuable services including thorough background checks, reference checks, interviews, etc. Parents may find in-home care a more convenient arrangement than having to drop off their child elsewhere, and are often willing to pay more for the convenience. However, the same issues of reliability and dependence on a single caregiver that arise with family-based care apply to in-home care as well. The fewer the number of caregivers, the more you'll want to have a good backup care plan in place. Also keep in mind that in the government's eyes, hiring a caregiver means that you have become a household employer, with all of the many insurance, legal, tax, and payroll implications that come with it.

 ## ACCOUNTING FOR IN-HOME CARE

Hiring an in-home caregiver has some significant financial implications that are often overlooked by new, unexpecting parents. Not only do you need to take into account what sort of vacation pay or insurance coverage you're going to offer (and pay for), but you'll need to factor in the government's expectations of you as well. That's because according to the IRS, when you hire a household employee, there are a lot of required things you must do, including (but not limited to)

- Find out if the person can legally work in the United States.
- Determine if you need to pay state taxes.
- Withhold social security, Medicare, and federal income taxes.
- Get an employer identification number (EIN).
- File and submit very specific tax forms.

To find out exactly what is involved in the process and to make sure you get it right, we strongly suggest you get informed guidance from a well-respected placement agency and/or obtain a current copy of the IRS' *Household Employer's Tax Guide.* You won't want to leave your baby at home (in someone else's care) without it!

Care by relatives, friends, or neighbors. This type of care is fairly self-explanatory and is not characterized by any given location, but rather by who is providing the care. What may come as a surprise is that some states actually require friends and family members who are going to serve as providers to undergo a screening criminal history check, and several require minimal health and training safety similar to other forms of child care. Schedules, budgets, transportation, and a greater trust of friends and/or family members can all factor into deciding on this type of child care. While trust and familiarity can be a huge bonus with this type of care, be sure you still make it a point to sit down and discuss important aspects of your child's care to make sure you're all in agreement. While you'll certainly want to acknowledge what a great job your child's grandparents (presumably) did raising you or your spouse, for example, you'll want to also discuss how several important things have changed since then—not the least of which include such important safety practices as back sleeping (see page 90) and using car seats (see page 203).

> **A LICENSE TO CARE**
>
> Of the roughly 12 million children in child care, about 3 million are cared for in unlicensed and therefore unregulated settings. Be sure to check that the provider you choose for your child has a current license to provide child care services in your state.

Trust More Than Your Gut

Your gut instincts should definitely play a role in your search for someone you trust to be nurturing and to provide your child with the best care whenever you aren't around. Word of mouth can also provide invaluable insights. But don't stop there. Unless you take your child to a place where you are sure that all of the background sleuthing has been done for you (such as in licensed child care centers), always put in the extra time and effort necessary to ensure that your gut feeling rests firmly on additional and reassuring facts. In our book, these efforts should always include

- **Interview.** Meeting potential providers face to face is invaluable. You get to ask your questions and gauge how comfortable you are, not only with the provider's answers but with the provider herself.
- **Check references.** You may feel like you're just going through the motions, but you'd be amazed to hear what many a parent (or employer) has heard when they've called on references. Sometimes it's just the glowing feedback you'd expect. Sometimes you'll get an unexpected and eye-opening earful. Either way, at least 2 reference checks are a must. If you're considering a child care center, remember to ask other parents and staff about their experiences.
- **Go online.** For good or for bad, in this day and age we all have a digital footprint. When it comes to finding a trustworthy provider for your child, you'll want to make sure that she hasn't taken any concerning steps in the wrong direction. It takes almost no time at all to Google

someone or search out their Facebook page. We recommend you do so to see if there's any information the prospective provider forgot to share with you.

- **Back it up with a background check.** A nationwide background check doesn't come for free, but can be invaluable. By working with a government or private agency, you can find out if a prospective caregiver is listed in the child abuse/neglect or sex offender registries or if she has any record of federal or state offenses.

Qualifications and Considerations

Given all we now know about the importance of early brain development, early childhood education, and learning, we firmly believe that dedicated child care providers deserve to be treated (not to mention compensated) as professionals and that they should be well trained. The fact of the matter is that child care providers today are playing a hugely important role in shaping our children's first and very important experiences. The more education and training child care providers have, the more children have been shown to benefit.

A matter of degrees. Ask if caregivers have a degree in early childhood or a related field, if they have done any sort of special training, and/or if they routinely attend workshops or educational conferences. All of these forms of professional development increase the likelihood that your child will be well cared for.

 CDAS DEFINED

Some child care providers attain what is commonly referred to as a CDA (Child Development Associate). This is a national credential that requires the completion of 120 hours of child care training in 8 content areas that span everything from planning a safe and healthy learning environment and establishing productive relationships with families to emphasizing principles of early childhood learning, behavior, and development.

Attention to turnover. One of the biggest challenges in child care is retaining high-quality providers and reducing turnover—a noble and valuable goal based on the fact that we know young children thrive best when they can develop strong and lasting bonds with their caregivers. That's why every "choosing a child care" checklist you're likely to come across includes inquiring about how long caregivers have been at a given center or providing care in their homes. The longer the better, but bear in mind that low turnover of qualified caregivers comes with a cost. For child care centers, we recommend you ask what benefits, such as paid time off, vacation pay, insurance, and savings plans staff are offered and then be willing to factor these staff-retaining factors into what you're willing to pay.

Accreditation. Child care accreditation generally indicates a greater commitment to health, safety, and providing high-quality care, as the voluntary standards required for accreditation typically exceed those required for licensure. The 2 largest organizations that provide child care accreditation are the National Association for the Education of Young Children (NAEYC) and The National Association for Family Child Care (NAFCC).

Child Care by Numbers

There are several important numbers you'll want to take into account in your quest for quality care.

- **Ratios.** If this is your first introduction to this all-important concept, "ratios" in child care simply refers to how many children any particular caregiver is responsible for. For example, one baby, one caregiver would give you the appealing ratio of 1:1. In general, the fewer children per adult the better, because young children thrive on lots of attention and require a lot of care. That said, unless you go the route of a personal in-home nanny or caregiver, your baby will likely be sharing his caregiver's attention with at least 2 or 3 other infants. While a 1:3 ratio (one adult, 3 babies) is considered ideal, 1:4 is a much more likely scenario, even in high-end centers. As you set out on your search, be sure to ask (and observe) how many babies are watched by a single adult.

- **Group size.** In the case of group size, bigger isn't better. Even if the overall ratio of adults to children is appropriate, younger children do better in smaller groups. In other words, an infant room that limits the group size to 8 babies (with 2 caregivers) is likely to be calmer and safer—and therefore considered better—than one that has 12 infants and 3 teachers.

- **Cost.** No discussion of child care numbers is complete without a discussion of the cost of child care. While this is a very broad subject that is impacted by a whole host of other factors (including geography, type of care, etc), in the context of ratios and group sizes, the reality is that fewer children and more dedicated staff members come at an expense. As you consider your options, it will be important to keep in mind that all of the numbers in the child care equation have to add up: If you want lower ratios, you'll undoubtedly pay more for them.

 RECOGNIZING QUALITY WHEN YOU SEE IT

While a lot has been speculated, said, and written about how parents should go about determining which child care is best, research offers us a closer look at which characteristics, when put to the test, actually serve as the most reliable indicators of quality. Quite simply, if a child care provider or center consistently meets the well-defined guidelines listed below, children in their care are more likely to be a safe and healthy.

- Appropriate supervision at all times and positive, consistent discipline
- Nurturing care
- Low staff-to-child ratio and group size
- Frequent hand washing and safe, hygienic diaper changing techniques
- Qualified director and teachers who understand the needs of children and participate in ongoing staff training
- Well-established policies regarding safe storage and administration of medications as well as immunization requirements
- Emergency plans that include regular fire drills and a reliable method of contacting parents in the event of an emergency
- Safety as a clear priority, as evidenced by such features as safe storage of any toxic substances and a safe outdoor playground

If you are interested in more detailed information, you can go to the National Association of Child Care Resource & Referral Agency's (NACCRRA) Web site at www.naccrra.org and find their downloadable booklet for parents entitled *Is This the Right Place for My Child?: 38 Research-Based Indicators of High-Quality Care.*

Health and Safety Considerations

Just about everything we've included in this book regarding your newborn's health and safety applies not only to you, but to anyone who will provide care for your baby. While the principles are generally the same, there are some health and safety topics specific to child care that we want you to be familiar with ahead of time.

In Sickness and in Health?

One of the concerns (fears) we hear most often about child care is about germs and what recurrent illnesses can do to send child care–dependent parents into despair. That's why we want to give you a healthy perspective on this topic. First, let us say that what you've heard is probably true: Children who attend child care often do get exposed to more germs and as a result, get sick more often—somewhere on the order of 7 to 10 times a year with more occurring during germ-sharing (cold and flu) season. But it's worth noting that this isn't just a result of child care, but of being around lots of other young children. Let's face it, young children (and even some adults) just can't be relied on to keep their germs to themselves. That said, there are definitely things that can be done to limit the spread of germs in child care, not the least of which is frequent hand washing (especially after wiping noses, playing outside, and trips to the bathroom or diaper changing table), routine cleaning of toys, and well-defined exclusion criteria for when children (and providers) are too sick to attend. Be sure these types of measures are in place and enforced. Also take some comfort in knowing that children who've attended child care have also been shown to get sick less frequently when they get to elementary school!

Safe Sleep in Child Care

Safe sleep is something you'll definitely want to discuss before entrusting anyone to put your baby down to sleep. That's because while all of the infant safe sleep and sudden infant death syndrome (SIDS) prevention recommendations prevail (see page 91) as much in the setting of child care, if not more so, only half of states have any sort of requirement that babies be put to sleep on their backs. We feel obliged to emphasize this point because research suggests that infants in child care are disproportionately at risk for SIDS. Before you panic, rest assured that this is not an inherent risk of child care itself. Our sound sleep advice: Be certain that any and all of your child's caregivers are trained on and follow the exact same back sleeping and safe sleep recommendations (see page 91) that you do! This really matters, because if babies have parents who diligently put them to sleep exclusively on their backs but then have a caregiver put them to sleep on their tummies for the first time, they have been found to be at 18 times greater risk for SIDS.

Food for Future Thought

Having dedicated our time to writing an entire book called *Food Fights: Winning the Nutritional Challenges of Parenthood Armed With Insight, Humor, and a Bottle of Ketchup,* we are clearly committed to focusing your attention on the expansive subject of childhood nutrition. For the time being, let us just say that in child care, what's on the menu matters. Even though solid foods may seem a long way off, just remember that it will be as important for your baby's other caregivers to pay careful attention to how much, how often, and what your child eats as it is for you. Nutritious meals and planned menus, along with attentive caregivers who routinely hold babies to feed them and staff members who sit to eat family style meals with older children, all add up to a healthier environment for your child.

Playing It Safe Outdoors

While the thought of your baby running, jumping, and sliding may admittedly seem a long, long way off, playground safety should nevertheless be on your radar screen as you set out to select a safe child care center. While playgrounds are vitally important in offering plenty of opportunity for physical activity and outdoor play, they are also one of the highest risk areas for injuries. For now, we'll simply say that sturdy playground structures, safe surfacing, good supervision, clean age-divided play areas surrounded by fences, and developmentally appropriate equipment are all worthwhile considerations.

TRUE LIFESAVERS: CPR AND FIRST AID

Consider CPR and first aid training to be an absolute must for anyone who cares for infants and children—yourself included. While almost all states require child care providers to have CPR certification and first aid training, be aware that in some states, only one trained caregiver is required to be present at any given time. We recommend you ask not only how many caregivers have completed CPR and first aid training, but check that all certifications are current. Also inquire about what sort of backup plan is in place if the certified caregiver(s) is going to be absent.

PART VI

just for the health of it

No newborn parenting book worth its weight in diapers would be complete without an explanation of the most common medical aspects of newborn care, including a basic overview of the working parts, important signs of illness, and things you can do to keep your baby healthy. The fact that we are both parents and pediatricians puts us in the relatively unique position of understanding what you are likely to want to know about ensuring the health and well-being of your precious new baby.

For most new parents, this begins with the simple yet sometimes bewildering task of anticipating what you'll need and appropriately stocking your medicine cabinet with the necessary tools of the newborn parenting trade.

 WHAT'S IN YOUR CABINET?

Stocking your medicine cabinet in anticipation of your baby's arrival will give you some extra peace of mind that you are well prepared to tend to whatever you may be faced with—from tiny toenails to first fevers and stuffy noses. While there are no hard and fast rules about what constitutes a well-stocked medicine cabinet, here's our streamlined list of suggested staples (with more detailed descriptions of their appropriate use included later in this section).

- **Baby nail clippers.** Adult-sized clippers are not advised.
- **Cotton balls and/or swabs.** We can think of numerous uses.
- **Thermometer.** And yes, we mean the rectal kind.
- **Fever reducers.** Not to be given lightly, but definitely good to be prepared with acetaminophen (eg, Tylenol) on hand for first fevers.
- **Medicine syringe.** Useful but not mandatory, since infant medications come with measuring devices.
- **Bulb suction and saline drops.** It's best to avoid overuse, but when used appropriately, stuffy noses don't need to leave you feeling helpless.
- **Diaper cream.** Can wait, but certainly convenient to have on hand and likely to get used.
- **Petroleum jelly.** Multipurpose, safe, and bound to be used on various occasions.

We also aim to offer you the most pertinent medical information pediatricians want all newborns' parents to be familiar with before they head home—most notably fever and jaundice. Having already included the obligatory disclaimer that we cannot and should not take the place of your own pediatrician, and having read far too many superficial checklists and questionnaires in parenting magazines on how to find your baby the "perfect" doctor, we decided to start out our "Just for the Health of It" section by offering you some practical (and more in-depth) "insider" advice. This includes how best to approach the task of picking out a health care provider you will be happy to call your very own and work in partnership with for at least the next 18 years!

CHAPTER 25

finding the right baby doctor— a view from the inside out

As pediatricians and parents, we wholeheartedly agree with the current trend in which parents "interview" pediatricians to find the one that best suits them. After all, you can expect to pay a visit to your chosen health care provider at least 6 times during your baby's first year—and that's only taking into account the standard number of well-baby visits. It's worth starting out on your "mission" to find just the right one by keeping in mind that pediatrics, just like parenting, isn't always an exact science. When it comes to the art of pediatrics and parenting, you will undoubtedly come across a wide range of styles and opinions on what's best—whether you're discussing the use of antibiotics, feeding, approaches to colic, or how to handle sleep problems. Beyond finding someone who is well trained in the science of pediatrics, it will clearly be to your advantage to make sure that the person (or group of providers) you choose shares your own personal parenting philosophy and style.

Your Quest for the Best

We have every intention of including the specifics of what you can and should look for in your search for the "perfect physician." Before we do, we thought we'd toss in a little reality check: There's no such thing. That's because physicians are people too, and to date we have yet to meet a person—ourselves included—without quirks and flaws (real and perceived). Just like everyone else, doctors have good days and bad. Some are superb communicators and others are men and women of few words.

Some have families and children, some don't. Some have breastfed while others don't have breasts (which, for clarification, is not a commentary on breast size but on the difference between the presence or absence of a Y chromosome). Some work part-time while others put in unbelievably long hours and take call 24/7. Yet none of these traits alone guarantees you that you've found a model of perfection. Instead, we recommend that you take all of them into account and then factor in personality so that you end up finding someone you can really relate to. Remember—the doctor that seems perfect in the eyes of other parents may not be at all right for you. On a personal note, one of the hardest parts about beginning in private practice after finishing our pediatric training (aside from being bombarded with questions to which we were never taught the answers and trying to stick to some semblance of a schedule) was coming to grips with the fact that not everyone who came to see us was going to like us or our parenting philosophies. Over time we came to realize that it's just plain unnatural to see eye to eye with everyone—whether you're a parent or a pediatrician! The key is finding a good fit for everyone involved.

Let the Search Begin

The second or third trimester is an ideal time for you to start considering whom you want to serve as your baby's health care provider. Ask around to find out who in your area is well liked, well trained, and conveniently located. You'll find that in addition to friends, neighbors, and family members, obstetricians are often a great source for recommendations. So are the nurses in labor and delivery and the newborn nurseries—most of whom interact with area pediatricians on a regular basis and know which ones are the most skilled and which have the best bedside manner.

Choosing Among Health Care Providers

You will find that we tend to refer to babies' health care providers as pediatricians in this chapter (and throughout the book) as a matter of convenience. It's important to note, however, that there are several types of health professionals who are qualified to care for babies and children.

- **MD and DO.** If doctors have an MD after their names, it simply tells you that they attended a "traditional" medical school. Others have the initials DO after their names—a designation that tells you they are

BACKGROUND CHECK: THE AAP

Now is as good a time as any to familiarize yourself with the AAP because you're bound to come across these 3 letters at just about every turn in your search for reliable information and all-around parenting enlightenment. AAP stands for the American Academy of Pediatrics—a professional organization of about 60,000 pediatricians, pediatric medical subspecialists, and pediatric surgical specialists throughout the United States, Canada, and Latin America. If you happen to spot the letters FAAP after a doctor's name, it tells you that he or she is a Fellow of the American Academy of Pediatrics—a title bestowed on just over half of the AAP members in recognition of passing the pediatric board exam (which we can tell you from personal experience is no cake walk). As the authoritative source on health issues for children, the mission of the AAP is to attain optimal physical, mental, and social health and well-being for all infants, children, adolescents, and young adults.

graduates of osteopathic medical schools. MD and DO medical schools train physicians, and both types of doctors can go on to do pediatric residency training specializing in the care of children. While there are some differences between these 2 types of physicians, both are educated about normal human health and disease conditions.

- **Board-certified pediatrician.** Board-certified pediatricians are physicians who have graduated college, completed 4 years of medical school, and have at least 3 years of "on-the-job" training (residency) in pediatrics. To become board certified, pediatricians must also pass a rigorous examination given by the American Board of Pediatrics (ABP). To remain board certified, pediatricians have to maintain ongoing education in pediatrics, demonstrate quality patient care, and hold a valid medical license. These certification requirements help ensure that certified pediatricians (including specialists) have sufficient knowledge and skills to provide quality care for children of all ages.

- **Family physician.** Family practice doctors can be either MDs or DOs and, like pediatricians, also complete medical school and at least 3 years of "on-the-job" training (in a family medicine residency). Like pediatricians, family physicians must also pass an examination and meet several criteria to become board certified and then renew their certification.

Unlike pediatricians, however, family physicians do not limit their practice to the care of children from birth through adolescence. As their titles imply, they care for patients of all ages.

- **Nurse practitioner.** In some instances, you may find that your baby is scheduled to see a pediatric or family nurse practitioner. These health care providers are registered nurses with additional education. Those who specialize in pediatrics generally have specific advanced training in caring for children. Nurse practitioners may work in your doctor's office in conjunction with or under the supervision of physicians.

Whomever you choose, you'll want to make sure that they have the training and/or experience to offer guidance on the health- and illness-related matters you may encounter—many of which are unique to child-hood.

The Selection Process

Once you have found one (or a few) possible doctors, call the office(s) to see if it is possible to schedule a prenatal or "meet the doctor" visit. You might want to also ask if the visit is offered free of charge (because some doctors' offices do charge) or see if it's covered by your insurance. While just about all of the parenting books and magazines we've read suggest bringing along a standard set of questions for the doctor, we have found that most parents are left not knowing exactly what to do with the answers. Furthermore, you may find that the specific answers you do get are in reality less important in your decision-making process than the physician's personal style and whether you felt like you've clicked. Having said that, if you still feel the need to follow a checklist, we have included several points to consider under each commonly asked question that follows. Remember that you are not necessarily looking for the smartest doctor in your area, or the one with the most patients, but one who bases medical decisions on the best available information and at the same time is a good match for you, your family, and your parenting style. If at any point you feel this physician-patient relationship is not a good fit, even after you've already brought your baby home, we encourage you to discuss your concerns with your doctor and, if need be, to find another one.

The Issue of Insurance

Q: *Does your office accept my insurance?* This question is worth asking even before you set up an interview because the reality of managed health care these days is that your insurance carrier may well dictate which physicians and practices you can take your child to and which ones you can't. Given the ever-increasing costs associated even with routine doctor visits, it's a rare parent who decides it's worth going outside of the system and paying out of pocket to see a particular doctor. Even with the uncertainties of what will happen with health care reform at the time we are writing this, we strongly suspect that knowing what your costs and coverage will be up front will continue to be useful.

WE'VE GOT YOU COVERED

As you plan for the arrival of your newborn, don't forget to check with your insurance company to find out what you need to do or submit to have your baby added to your insurance policy. Then just be very sure to have any and all necessary forms submitted within the required number of days after your baby is born (usually 30 but double-check and then follow up)— a crucial task you will not want lost in the shuffle of new parenthood.

How Privileged Is Your Provider?

Q: *Do you have hospital privileges at the place where we plan to deliver?* While this information is worth knowing, we've found that it rarely factors into a parent's decision about their baby's health care provider unless they feel very strongly about seeing that particular person in the hospital. If you decide to take your baby to a health care provider who does not have hospital privileges where you plan to deliver, your baby will still be seen and evaluated by a qualified physician at the hospital. On discharge from the hospital, you can proceed to arrange all of your well-baby visits with your chosen provider.

Q: *Where do you admit infants and children in the event that they require hospitalization?* The answer to this question is important only if you (or your insurance company) have a strong preference for one hospital over another because your baby's physician will naturally admit your child to the hospital at which he or she has privileges. Some physicians have privileges at multiple hospitals, which may give you some flexibility.

Asking About Availability

Q: *What are your office hours and location(s)?* While you're probably like most parents in that you'd be willing to drive to the ends of the earth for your unborn or newborn child, chances are good that when given the choice, you'd rather not have to drive across town much less all over creation every time your baby needs to see the doctor. As with nearly everything from real estate to diaper pails, location will most likely play some role in your decision. You'll also want to find out whether the practice you're considering has office hours that actually suit your needs. If your schedule is flexible, extended hours may not be such an important factor. For those of you who can barely make it to the bank during banker's hours, much less set up camp in your doctor's waiting room on a work day, you may want to look around for a practice that offers weekend hours and/or stays open late on weekdays.

Q: *How does your office handle scheduling appointments, answering patient phone calls, and after-hours emergencies? How difficult is it to get an appointment for a sick visit? For a routine checkup?* We don't feel it's necessary to cross doctors off your list simply because they are not always available to answer your questions personally and in a timely fashion in the middle of a busy work day. You'll just want to make sure that qualified members of their staff are ready, willing, and able to help you during regular business hours. The office should have a well-defined mechanism to contact the doctor and clear instructions as to where to go in the event of an after-hours question or emergency. Again, this is some good basic information to have about your chosen (or considered) practice, but it's not likely that you'll be told something that makes you decide to look elsewhere. In reality, you're more likely to find out after you've started going to a particular practice whether your wait time is repeatedly and unacceptably long, whether you're able to get advice by phone or schedule appointments relatively easily, and if you're happy with the overall workings of the office.

Q: *Is Timeliness Next to Goodliness?* Here's what we can tell you from personal experience: Being a punctual pediatrician is *much* easier said than done. That's because pediatricians never really know how long any one visit is going to take until they are in the room. This makes scheduling a best-guess attempt. Having said that, factoring a doctor's visit into what is likely to be your own less-than-predictable and very demanding schedule is not any easier. That's why you and your doctor should each do your best to show up on time, and yet be willing to cut each other some slack every now and then in acknowledgment of the strenuous jobs you both have. That said, if your doctor routinely runs late—not just 15 to 30 minutes every now and then but regularly more than an hour—then it's worth considering if there is something wrong with the way your doctor is setting up the schedule.

Tricks of the Scheduling Trade

To give you your best shot at avoiding the pediatric practice rush hours, traffic delays, and peak travel days, we suggest the following:

- **Be the first out of the gate.** Ask for the first appointment of the day, or pick a time right after lunch whenever possible. These are the times when traffic is less likely to have backed up. We have no insider knowledge to share with you about how to avoid those days when your doctor arrives unexpectedly late from making rounds at the hospital in the morning or runs late despite working through lunch; in those situations all bets are off.
- **Schedule mid-week.** Mondays and Fridays are notoriously busy in the doctor's office because parents either come in anticipation of a weekend without convenient access, or as soon as they can on a Monday after going it alone with a sick child over the weekend.
- **Avoid holidays, vacations, and predictable events.** Rush-hour traffic on the road may slow down considerably on national holidays and during vacation times, but this is often a time when parents can opt to bring their kids into the doctor without having to take a day off from work. It's not that you shouldn't set out to visit your pediatrician on, say, President's Day—you are just not likely to be alone. On holidays

when your doctor's office is open, hours may be reduced and they may be short-staffed—both factors that increase your likelihood of a longer wait. For future reference, there also tends to be a bit of a mad rush at the end of the summer when kids all but flood in for mandatory school physicals.

- **Anticipate extended visits.** If you anticipate needing extra time with your baby's doctor, ask if you can be scheduled additional time for the visit. Consider taking the last appointment of the day when your doctor won't feel the pressure of lots of other parents stacking up behind you.

Training and Experience

Q: *What is your training background and level of experience?* Our first response to you on this one is to figure out how much you really care. As practicing physicians, we all have diplomas hanging on our walls and have had to go through the careful scrutiny of the state licensure board before hanging a shingle. And to be board certified in pediatrics, everyone has to pass the same test and meet the same requirements regardless of where he or she trained. While some new parents conclude that the older and more experienced a pediatrician is, the better, plenty of others find themselves interested in taking their babies to a younger provider—one that they feel shares more of their contemporary attitudes or perhaps has children of a similar age.

Going Solo?

Q: *Will other physicians in the practice see my baby?* This is a perfectly legitimate question, but it shouldn't surprise you if the answer is yes. While there are still a fair number of solo practitioners out there, there has been a definite trend toward group practice. If you are considering a group practice, you may be better off asking how many days a week the practitioner you're interested in seeing works and if you'll be able to request visits with that person whenever he or she is in the office. Given that pediatricians are just like everyone else and occasionally take days off, get sick, or go on vacations, you'll also want to make sure that you are comfortable with the other practitioners in the group who will take over when yours is not available.

Seeing Eye to Eye

Q: *What is your philosophy about particular medical treatments or parenting strategies such as circumcision, the use of antibiotics, spanking, or potty training? What is your approach to breastfeeding? Sleep problems? Colic?* If you don't have strong feelings about child rearing or definite opinions regarding your child's medical care, then you'll be able to focus your attention more on other factors such as those listed above when selecting a pediatrician that's right for you. More often than not, however, parents and pediatricians alike have strong feelings about certain approaches to raising children. If you are dead set against using formula or pacifiers, for example, you will definitely want to find out which providers in your area are the most supportive of and experienced in the practicalities of breastfeeding. For certain topics where the research and science are well established, such as the importance of immunizations, be aware that some pediatricians may find it difficult to support (or even accept into their practices) families who choose to go against well-established guidelines.

Personal Characteristics

Your search for a pediatrician need not be scientifically based or entirely logical. It is perfectly reasonable to take into account personal qualities in your quest. Depending on your own comfort level or the gender of your child, you may prefer a male pediatrician instead of a female (or vice versa). It may be a priority for you to have your child treated by someone who has firsthand experience as a parent, shares your cultural or religious background, or has an authoritative style instead of a collaborative one (or again, vice versa).

A Room of One's Own

It's worth discussing the feature of separate waiting rooms (separating those who are sick and those who are well) if for no other reason than because it seems to have become standard for parenting books and magazines to recommend finding a practice that has them. We wholeheartedly agree that in an ideal world (or at least in an ideal doctor's office) it would be very nice to keep those who happen to be coming to the doctor because of an illness away from those who have yet to catch one—especially when those who are well include you and your baby. We want to point out that it's not exactly realistic to think you can successfully dodge all illnesses—either in or out of the doctor's office. After all, people tend to be most contagious *before* they develop symptoms, and we all live in a world full of bacteria and viruses. To be honest, we've never actually known a parent to choose a practice based on whether it had one waiting room or two. In our experience, parents are usually more concerned with how long they have to wait to be seen than where.

Our thoughts on the matter: Ask if it's possible for you and your newborn to wait in an empty examination room if the waiting room arrangement doesn't allow for separation of the sick from the well children. Other than that, we suggest using common sense just as you would when taking your baby out anywhere in public, limit the amount that others are allowed to come in direct contact with him, shield him from the direct line of fire if someone nearby is coughing or sneezing, and use criteria other than architectural design to determine if a particular pediatrician/practice is right for you.

In the End

When it comes to the bottom line and making a decision, we hope we've persuaded you that there's more than one "right" answer to each question, and that you are well equipped to figure out your own right answers. When all is said and done and you've weighed all your choices, remind yourself that while you're not exactly searching for a new best friend, you certainly want to find a doctor whose style best suits your own needs and who is going to be a supportive partner in your exciting and educational journey through parenthood.

CHAPTER 26

head to toe and in between

Ever wish that parenthood came with a tour guide and your newborn came with an instruction manual? Given that we are determined to serve as helpful tour guides and this book is, in many ways, meant to play the role of an instruction manual, we certainly don't want to neglect any of the nuts and bolts of baby care. The following is an up close and personal look at all of the involved parts—a handful of which are unique to infancy, such as the shriveled up umbilical cord and the soft spot on the top of every newborn's head. Others we discuss not because they would otherwise be unfamiliar to you, but because the context has changed. Chances are good you've never paid so much attention to or been solely responsible for someone else's fingernails, tear ducts, or noses before. Without any further ado, we'll get on with the tour.

From the Beginning—How Far Things Have Come

A Quick Glance Back

You may find that part of the wonder of your beautiful new child is trying to comprehend just how he or she could possibly have come to be. Not just the birds and the bees stuff, but the fact that a single fertilized egg can grow and develop into a newborn baby in a matter of a few short months. When you think about it, becoming a parent is nothing less than miraculous. Yes, we know that referring to the many long weeks of pregnancy as "relatively short" may lead you to question whether we've actually experienced the joys of pregnancy before, but we assure you we have. It's just that in the grand scheme of things, the reality of what was once a microscopic blur now taking the form of a newborn represents the fastest rate of growth that we as human beings ever experience over the course of our entire lifetimes.

As you prepare yourself for what lies ahead, here's a quick look back at how far you (and your baby) have come.

- 4 weeks: your baby probably measured no more than a large grain of sand
- 9 weeks: about the size of an olive
- 14 weeks: about the size of a fist
- 24 weeks: around 1 pound
- 32 weeks: half of his ultimate birth weight
- Newborns: an average weight of 7 pounds 5 ounces and roughly 20 inches long.

Sizing Up the Situation

Many parents are greatly relieved to find out that it is perfectly normal for newborns to lose weight—up to 10% of their birth weight, in fact—before they start gaining it back again. This characteristic weight loss tends to be more pronounced in newborns who are breastfed (see "Breastfeeding" on page 5) than for those who are bottle-fed. In either case, all newborns are expected to turn the corner, stop losing weight, and start gaining back ounces all within the first week or so—ultimately regaining or exceeding their birth weight by 2 weeks. Monitoring day-to-day weight changes (and even comparing before- and after-feeding weights) serves as a relatively good indicator of whether newborns are getting enough to eat. You'll therefore find that your baby's pediatrician pays close attention to your baby's day-by-day numbers in the hospital and in the days after discharge. This will be especially true while you are waiting for your milk to come in and if your newborn gets off to a sleepy start, is uninterested in eating, or is simply a poky eater.

Parts Is Parts

Taking It From the Top

As you've undoubtedly noticed, newborns have little to no head control—at best mustering up their resolve to briefly pick up or turn their heads. In part this is because it requires a fair bit of strength, and the muscles involved simply need time to develop. Babies also have another factor working against them when it comes to holding their heads up high, and

WEIGHT LIST

In the first few days, most newborns lose several ounces, but usually not more than 10% of their birth weight. That means that a baby who weighs 7 pounds at birth may well drop the scales instead of top them—reaching a weight as low as 6 pounds 4 ounces or so before turning things around.

In the first few weeks, babies gain up to an ounce per day, or as much as a pound per week.

Your baby is likely to double her birth weight by 4 months of age and triple it by the time her first birthday rolls around.

In the spirit of looking ahead, you can estimate your baby's adult height by doubling her height at age 2 years.

that is their sheer size. While your baby's head may not seem all that big to you, take a moment and compare it to the size of the rest of his body. Now make the same comparison between your own head and body. Your baby's head is proportionately much bigger, making him unquestionably top heavy. On a practical note, we thought we'd point out a point of parental interest: Newborns' big heads don't require extra attention just by new parents. Clothing manufacturers have also taken note and subsequently figured out how to accommodate them as well, designing infant clothing with expandable and stretchy wide collars or adding snaps, zippers, or buttons to narrower necklines.

 HEAD HANDLING WITH CARE

On a more serious note, head size along with a distinct lack of head control leave babies very susceptible to injury. This is why it is so important never to shake a baby. Doing so has the potential to cause much more serious harm than it would in older children or adults. As for the soft spot, it's not as vulnerable as one might think, but it still warrants being handled with care (see "The Soft Spot" on page 277).

Room to Grow

The fact that the bony plates that make up your baby's skull won't join together for many months is quite fortunate. By remaining open and expandable, they allow your baby's brain to grow. You will find that your pediatrician routinely monitors this growth by measuring your baby's head circumference (the distance around the largest part of your baby's head) and recording it on a head circumference growth curve right alongside her weight and height. On average, your newborn's head should

- Increase in circumference by as much as 2 inches over the next 2 months
- Reach about 90% of adult head size by the time your child turns 2 years

 A BIG HEAD USUALLY MEANS...A BIG HAT

While there are certainly some instances when a big head can signify an underlying medical problem, it's reassuring to keep in mind that the most common cause of a big head is genetics; the tendency toward "big-headedness" simply runs in the family.

The Shape of Things to Come

This topic is particularly directed toward those of you who have been mistakenly led to believe that all newborns are born picture perfect with pretty little round heads. Let us just say that for anyone who has gone through or will experience vaginal delivery, it is nothing short of a blessing that a baby's skull is made up of soft bony plates that are capable of compressing and overlapping to fit through the narrow birth canal—a process referred to as molding. For some babies—such as those who "drop" well in advance of being born (in other words, settle themselves head first deep into their mother's pelvis well in advance of delivery), or those who must endure long labors and narrow birth canals—the result is often a newborn head shape that more closely resembles a cone than a nice round ball. If you run your fingers over your newborn's skull, you may also find that you can feel ridges along the areas where the bony plates of the skull have overlapped. In short, cone heads are quite normal. Fortunately, over the next several weeks the bones of your baby's skull will almost assuredly round out and the ridges will disappear, assuming, that is, that your baby doesn't spend too much time on his back with his head in any one position—a common but easily avoidable cause for the development of a flat back or side of the head known as plagiocephaly (see "Back to Sleep" on page 90)

The Soft Spot

You will notice 1 if not 2 areas on your baby's head that seem to be lacking bony protection. These soft spots, referred to as *fontanelles* (anterior for the larger one in the front, posterior for the smaller and typically less noticeable one in the back), are normal gaps in a newborn's skull that will allow your baby's brain to grow rapidly throughout the next year. Many parents are afraid to touch these soft spots, but you can rest assured that, despite their lack of a bony layer, they are well protected from typical day-to-day baby handling. Other things to know about the soft spot(s) include

- In young infants, a sunken soft spot (when combined with poor feeding and dry diapers) can suggest dehydration. Our advice to you: Don't read too much into this because it can be a subtle finding or sometimes be present in normal babies. Instead, make sure you have a good grasp on how to recognize dehydration (see "What Goes In Must Come Out" on page 61) and check with your doctor if you have any concerns—with or without a sunken soft spot.

- In some instances, the soft spot on the top of your baby's head may seem to be pulsating. There is no need to worry—this movement is quite normal and simply reflects the visible pulsing of blood that corresponds to your baby's heartbeat.

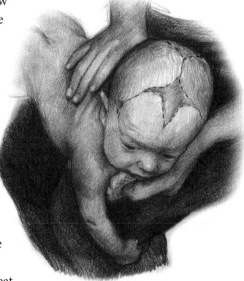

Soft spots or "fontanelles"

Cover-Up

Ever wonder who was in charge of determining what's the latest style in newborn head wear in the newborn nursery? Well before you spend too much time laying blame, we figured we'd point out that those typically unattractive polyester knit newborn caps aren't given out just for looks.

Newborn babies not only have proportionately bigger heads, but they don't regulate their body temperatures as well as adults or even older infants do and therefore stand to lose a significant amount of heat from their heads if left uncovered. This is the real reason that it's generally recommended that you put a hat on your baby's head during the first few weeks—especially in cool weather or drafty rooms.

Bumps and Bruises

In addition to molding, it is not uncommon for newborns to have a bit of swelling or bruising of the scalp immediately following delivery. The swelling usually is most noticeable at the top back part of the head and is medically referred to as a caput (short for *caput succedaneum*). When bruising of the head occurs during delivery, the result can be a boggy-feeling area, called a cephalohematoma. Bruising and swelling are usually harmless and go away on their own over the first days and weeks of life, but can be a contributing factor for jaundice (See "Seeing Yellow: Jaundice" on page 313).

Gone Today, but Hair Tomorrow

Sure, babies are sometimes born with full heads of hair, but it's far more likely for them to be born with little to none. And those with hair today are likely to find it gone tomorrow. That's because any hair your baby is born with is likely to thin out significantly over the next few months before ultimately being replaced with "real" hair. It is also entirely possible that whatever hair your newborn does have will change color by several shades and several times over his lifetime.

Cradle Cap

Although seborrheic dermatitis is the technically correct term for cradle cap, parents faced with scaly newborn scalps tend to agree that it is more appropriately called "cradle crap." Cradle cap resembles the baby equivalent of dandruff and, despite being harmless, nevertheless tends to drive some parents nuts. That's most often because cradle cap can be a nuisance to get rid of—especially for those babies who have a lot of it. While you can certainly try the standardly recommended approach of massaging affected areas with a little baby oil, mineral oil, or baby shampoo and then gently removing the flakes with a soft brush (some use soft-bristled toothbrushes), we strongly suggest you don't lose any sleep over it. Your pediatrician can give you additional advice regarding the use of a medicated dandruff shampoo if you're determined to conquer your baby's cradle cap. Otherwise, we've found it's best to simply let cradle cap run its course, as it usually goes away over the course of the first year.

The Eyes Have It

Do You See What I See?

When it comes to baby vision, the eyes don't really have it all until 3 to 5 years down the road—about the time when 20/20 color vision is thought to set in. That does not mean, however, that your newborn can't see anything. Here's a glimpse of what your newborn can see.

- **From a distance.** Because of their limited range of vision—estimated to be around 20/400—newborns tend to pay closest attention to objects near their faces. At birth, your newborn should be able to see a good 12 inches in front of him fairly clearly—the perfect distance at which to gaze at your smiling face while you hold him. By the time he reaches 3 months, he should be able to not only see, but also follow, objects you move in front of him.

- **In contrast.** Early on, babies are rumored to prefer items with contrasting colors. While this serves as a good explanation for the popularity and marketing of red-white-black infant toys, the truth is that you really don't need to go out of your way to offer your newborn a healthy daily dose of visual stimulation. Your everyday interactions and commonplace baby objects (such as books, pictures, or rattles) will more than suffice (See "Activities of Daily Learning" on page 161).

- **Gaining control.** While it is relatively common for babies younger than 4 months or so to appear cross-eyed on occasion, they should develop better eye-muscle control relatively quickly. Normal eye alignment and the ability to focus are key factors in developing normal eyesight, so be sure to mention any unusual eye movements you notice, especially if they continue beyond the first few months, to your baby's pediatrician.

 NO MORE TEARS...YET?

Anecdotally, newborn babies don't typically shed tears in the first month or two of life. As far as we could determine, however, even premature babies reportedly make tears. Best explanation we could find for their delayed appearance? Simply that making tears is different from shedding them. The amount of tears newborns typically make apparently isn't enough to send them rolling down cheeks until babies are several months old.

Duct Work

Your newborn has tiny tear ducts located in the inner corner of each eye that drain into the nose and, when functioning properly, play an important role in draining tears. We liken this drainage system to a sewer system; if and when babies become stuffy, those that happen to have been born with narrower than usual (or blocked) tear ducts—which applies to as many as 20% of all normal newborns—may experience a noticeable backup in the sewer system. Unable to adequately keep up with the normal ebb and flow, tears back up—resulting in a more watery and/or goopy eye (or eyes). If you and your pediatrician determine that your baby has a blocked tear duct or two, you can clean off any goop that accumulates around your baby's eyes by gently wiping the lids with a warm, damp, clean towel or tissue. We should point out that eye goop often seems to bother parents much more than it does newborns. When the going gets goopy, we recommend you resist the temptation and limit your wiping to when things get really nasty.

Tear duct

Although its usefulness has, in the past, been debated, the current first line of treatment is massage. By lightly pressing and then gently massaging the area between the corner of the eye and the nose downwards 2 or 3 times a day you can presumably help relieve any obstruction in the duct and get things moving. Most blocked ducts get better by the first birthday. Those that don't clear up on their own generally necessitate a trip to see a pediatric ophthalmologist, who may deem it necessary to use a small probe to carefully open up the uncooperative duct(s).

 PINK EYE

While blocked tear ducts end up being solely to blame for a good many goopy eyes, it is nevertheless going to be important for you to be aware of and on the lookout for pink eye. Although pink eye technically refers to any eye that appears pink (or red) regardless of cause, the term is most often used to describe eye infections. Although it's easy enough for us to tell you that true infections—especially those caused by bacteria— often have a thicker yellow or greenish discharge and are more likely to be accompanied by some degree of swelling and/or redness, distinguishing between the two is easier said than done. Since it is particularly important for eye infections in newborns to be diagnosed and treated without delay, any suspicions you may have should promptly be followed up with a phone call to your pediatrician. Even if your baby has already been diagnosed with a blocked tear duct, you'll still want to watch carefully for signs of infection, because infants who have blocked tear ducts are more prone to developing them.

What's Going to Make Those Brown Eyes Blue?

What you see when you gaze into your newborn's eyes is not always what you'll ultimately get when it comes to eye color. Not only are the genetics of eye color quite complex, but predicting a baby's future eye color before birth is relatively unreliable. We can tell you, however, that a baby's eye color depends on how much of a particular pigment there is in the colored part of the eye, or the iris. The more of this pigment—called melanin— there is, the darker brown a baby's eyes will appear. Conversely, babies with blue eyes have very little melanin. Anywhere in between results in varying shades of brown, hazel, or green. With that in mind, it will probably make more sense to you when we tell you that if your baby is born with brown eyes, nothing short of colored contact lenses is likely to change her eye color to blue. However, babies who are blue-eyed at birth have the potential to produce more melanin over time and end up with eyes of a different color (usually by 6 months of age or so) than they were born with. Interestingly, some older kids and adults also continue to see changes in their eye color as they age (even without the help of fashionable contact lenses).

Seeing Red

Ever end up with red eyes in photographs? If so, then you're already familiar with exactly the same reflex your pediatrician is looking for when he or she shines the light from an ophthalmoscope into your newborn's eyes—the red reflex. What may be a nuisance to photographers happens to be a very reassuring sign for pediatricians when it occurs in newborns. The red reflex not only reflects the presence of normal retinas at the back of your baby's eyes (appearing red because of the many blood vessels located there), but also tells us that light can make its way all the way in and back out again unobstructed. An absent (or white) reflex, in contrast, may mean there is a problem with the eye.

We're All Ears

Setting the Sound Stage

Did the latest music CDs for yet-to-be-born babies catch your attention? Perhaps you came across parents-to-be who religiously read books to the bulging belly that was soon to become their child. Well, as tempting as it may be to get a head start on a baby's education, we suggest that expectant parents sit back and relax during their pregnancies because there will be plenty of time for teaching later. Now with that said, if your idea of relaxing happens to include listening to a little classical music or taking a few practice runs through *Goodnight Moon* before bed, your efforts are not likely to fall on deaf ears—at least not after your sixth or seventh month. That's because the parts of the ear involved in hearing generally finish developing by 24 weeks, and by 28 weeks fetuses have been shown to respond consistently to sound in utero.

SOUND ADVICE FOR ALL NEWBORNS

Whereas an adult can typically hear sounds at around 13.5 decibels (the level of a soft whisper), a fetus between 27 and 29 weeks is able to detect sounds at a level closer to 40 decibels—the average sound of a running refrigerator or the flow of light traffic. By the time a baby reaches full term, his ability to hear will have matured to such an extent that he can hear sounds similar to those heard by adults. However, anywhere from 1 to 6 babies out of every 1,000 will have childhood hearing loss. Given these numbers and the fact that hearing plays such an important role in an infant's language and cognitive development, universal newborn hearing screening is recommended for all infants before they reach 1 month of age. This screening test should ideally be done in the newborn nursery before you and your baby are discharged from the hospital. Any baby who fails the initial screening test should get a full hearing evaluation by no later than 3 months of age. If true hearing loss is diagnosed, interventions are available and recommended as early as 6 months of age.

Accessorizing

It may (or may not) surprise you that one of the most frequent ear-related questions we get is "How soon can I get my baby daughter's ears pierced?" Our response: If you can wait until your child is less susceptible to infection, much less likely to swallow the tiny (and not generally size-appropriate for children younger than 3 years) parts inherent to wearing earrings, and better able to care for her own ear piercings—we highly recommend doing so even if it means waiting until she is in elementary school. If, however, you feel compelled to have your infant's ears pierced during infancy, then you'd be well-advised to wait for at least 2 weeks after she gets her 2-month shots, one of which will be an immunization against tetanus. Then try to find an experienced piercer who uses sterile equipment and, if possible, has experience piercing baby earlobes. As with many things, you'd be wise to check with your pediatrician first. A few actually provide this service themselves, while others may be able to steer you in the direction of someone they feel is careful and trustworthy.

Your Baby's Nose Knows

Despite the fact that mouth breathing seems as though it should be a perfectly reasonable alternative, newborns are, for the most part, "obligated" to breathe through their narrow little noses for a good 5 months or so. Knowing that, it should begin to make sense to you why many newborns develop noisy breathing with the slightest amount of stuffiness or dryness. Add a snotty-nose cold and congestion to the picture and the effects become much more noticeable and inconvenient—especially at feeding time. Below we have included some of the basic techniques recommended for ridding your baby of unwanted snot and congestion in the hopes of keeping everyone breathing easy.

THE AIR MOVES IN, THE AIR MOVES OUT

Every now and then, a baby's nasal passageway doesn't develop and open up the way it's supposed to. A quick and easy way to determine whether air is able to make its way in and out of your newborn's nose normally is to take a thin piece of cotton (stretch out the tip of a cotton swab or part of a cotton ball) and hold it just in front of one nostril while lightly pressing the other nostril closed. You should see the cotton move gently each time your baby breathes out.

- **Nose drops.** Often referred to as saline nose drops, they work by simply moistening and loosening up mucus. They are inexpensive, sold over-the-counter, and readily available just about anywhere that sells basic baby supplies. They can be used alone (to moisten or loosen up dried mucus) or followed by a bulb suction. If you are so inclined, you can even make your own by mixing ¼ teaspoon of salt in 1 cup of warm water. Use just a few drops at a time.
- **Bulb suction.** We've included this option not because we think it always works, but because some new parents are quick to reach for their bulb suctions when in search of fast relief. While we readily admit that they can and do serve a definite purpose for babies (and parents) in their more snotty times of need, we suggest you take a moment to consider what it feels like to have a piece of rubber or plastic shoved, however

gently, up your nose. After factoring in this not-so-comfortable thought, we recommend that you limit the use of a bulb suction to those times when your baby not only seems to be truly congested and has a big blob of mucus in clear view, but when the snot actually seems to be interfering with your baby's ability to eat, sleep, and/or breathe. If, on the other hand, the goober is just hanging out minding its own business and not really bothering anyone (save for its appearance), consider giving your bulb suction a rest and grab a tissue instead.

 SUCCESSFUL SUCTIONING

If and when you do need to use a suction bulb to remove mucus, it's generally a good idea to limit your attempts to about 3 times a day, as more frequent use can irritate your baby's nasal lining and make him even more congested. For best results, press down lightly on one nostril to hold it closed while you gently suction the other side, keeping in mind that the middle part of each nostril tends to be the most sensitive to probing.

- **Vaporize.** Running a vaporizer or a humidifier in your baby's room is almost a knee-jerk reaction of parents everywhere when faced with the challenges of a baby with a stuffy nose cold. While, to be perfectly honest, you may not always see a hugely noticeable response, there are definitely times (such as when your baby won't sleep or eat because she's congested and irritable) when you'll probably agree that every little bit helps. Adding moisture to the air is certainly one small step in the right direction. You may also find that running a hot shower with the door closed and then sitting in the steamy bathroom with your baby can also help improve the drainage.

Sneezing

Newborns typically sneeze a lot. You can save yourself a lot of unnecessary worry if you remember to chalk the sneezes up to sensitive reflexes rather than over-interpret them as a sign of illness. Most babies outgrow this tendency to sneeze in response to the slightest little tickle within a few months—at about the same time as they begin to gain control over their other reflexes (see "Reflexes" on page 301).

Mouth to Mouth

Most new parents have few, if any, concerns about their newborns' mouths—that is, unless they see something that they think doesn't belong there. If you find anything in your baby's mouth that surprises you or that you're just not sure about, be sure to bring it to the attention of your pediatrician. Typical in-mouth sightings can include everything from

- **White/clear bumps.** Whitish bumps are sometimes found or appear on the gums, lips, or roof of the mouth. Generally harmless, they often serve to fool parents into thinking that a tooth is erupting months before one pokes its way through the gum.
- **Newborn (or natal) teeth.** On rare occasion, infant teeth decide to erupt way ahead of schedule—sometimes even showing up right at birth. If your doctor doesn't notice them first, you'll want to point them out because they may, in some instances, need to be removed.
- **Sucking blisters.** Babies can develop blisters just from sucking—something they obviously do a lot of in their first weeks and months. They appear most often on the lips, but sometimes on fingers or even toes as well, if and when newborns manage to reach them and get them to their mouths. Sucking blisters generally require no treatment and end up going away on their own.
- **White coating.** If you start to see white on the inside of your newborn's mouth, you'll want to consider 2 major causes—either lingering breast milk/formula or thrush. The white of thrush (a yeast infection found in the mouth) tends to appear most often on the tongue and hidden in the nooks and crannies of the mouth—commonly tucked between the cheeks and gums. Thrush is often overlooked or written off as residual formula or breast milk until it persists and spreads. As a rough rule of thumb, any white spots or patches in a newborn's mouth that don't easily wipe off with a cotton swab should be evaluated for thrush and treated accordingly.

Thrush Attack

Thrush is caused by a type of yeast *(Candida)* that commonly lives in the intestinal tract and is also responsible for some diaper rashes. Unlike the red spots and patches it is known to cause on a baby's rear end, *Candida* forms spots and/or patches of white in the mouth that don't easily wipe away and slowly spread. While many parents consider thrush to be a pain in the butt, in most instances it is fortunately not a pain in the mouth—simply a nuisance. Your baby's pediatrician can help make the diagnosis and set you up to remedy the situation. Good ways of treating thrush include

- **Liquid yeast medication.** This comes as a prescription solution suitable for putting in your baby's mouth. While you'll want to follow your doctor's recommendations—typically putting one dropperful in each cheek 4 times a day—the underlying approach to treatment is even more straightforward: Look for white spots and try to get your medicated solution on them (we prefer to use a clean cotton swab).

- **Thinking outside the mouth.** You aren't likely to rid your baby of thrush unless you address the problem outside of her mouth as well as in it. It takes a good boiling to kill the yeast that hangs out on pacifiers and baby bottle nipples. And for those of you who breastfeed, be forewarned that *Candida* doesn't limit itself to artificial nipples. If your baby has thrush and/or you experience a burning, irritated feeling on your nipples, check with your doctor about treatment for yourself as well so that you don't pass the infection back and forth (see "What's Behind Burning Nipples" on page 20).

- **Persistence.** Thrush isn't always easy to get rid of. Not only does it hide out in hard-to-reach places, but it has an annoying habit of popping back up again just when you think you, your bottle of yeast medication, and your boiled pacifiers have conquered it. Even when the coast seems clear, keep your guard up and watch for any new white spots to appear.

- **The purple approach.** If your baby's thrush is widespread and/or persistent despite your best efforts, your pediatrician may suggest the use of a purple-staining, yeast-killing solution called gentian violet. While effective, we strongly suggest you anticipate a bit of a mess and be prepared to postpone baby photos for several days after gentian violet is applied to let the purple staining in and around your baby's mouth fade first.

Tongue Tied

We're all born with a little tissue called a frenulum that connects the bottom of our tongues with the floor of our mouths. Babies occasionally are born with a frenulum that extends as far out as the tip of the tongue—

seeming to "tie" a newborn's tongue, limit its ability to stick out past the lips, and potentially interfere with sucking and feeding. This condition (known as *ankyloglossia* or tongue-tie) is often harmless and generally requires no treatment. That said, some studies have shown that tongue-tied infants who were having difficulty latching on to breastfeed benefited from having the frenulum cut (typically a relatively simple office procedure called a *frenulotomy)*.

Smiling

No one knows exactly why newborns first begin to smile when they are sleeping—waiting a few weeks until they carry over to the daytime. Nor is it easy to say exactly when during the first month your baby's smiles will become more intentional. If you ask us, does it really matter? We don't find it very worthwhile to spend much time debating the meaning of a smile because we think any newborn smile is enough to melt a parent's heart. And by 3 months, your baby should have developed an undeniably social smile that he will happily share with those around him.

Chest

A Breath of Fresh…Fluid?

Take a moment and consider the fact that babies actually practice breathing well before they're born. It is not exactly intuitive, given that their lungs are filled with amniotic fluid right up until the day when they decide to leave their cozy uterine surroundings, enter the outside world, and take their first big breath of fresh air. This fluid, found in all babies' lungs throughout pregnancy, is essential for normal lung development. So is time. For the first month and a half of pregnancy, fetal lungs take on their basic shape and structure. If you think of the lungs as a tree, this is the period where the trunk and major branches are formed. Up until the 25th week, smaller branches form and then the smallest "leaves"—known as alveoli—start to develop and take on the structure ultimately necessary to breathe in oxygen. By the time a baby reaches full term, he is estimated to have anywhere from 50 to 150 million alveoli. This number actually continues to increase over the first several years of life, burgeoning to a total of about 300 million alveoli in adulthood.

Baby Breaths

For anyone not already familiar with some of the notable differences between the way adults and newborns breathe, some of the characteristic newborn breathing habits may make you more than a little nervous. In the interest of sparing you unnecessary angst, we wanted to familiarize you with 2 of the more common (and normal) tendencies.

- **Picking up the pace.** Perhaps one of the most common questions we get about the newborn breathing style is if it's normal for them to breathe so fast. The answer is yes—even at rest, infants breathe considerably faster than adults in addition to having faster resting heart rates.
- **Taking a break.** The tendency of newborns to take several breaths in rapid succession followed by a few seconds of rest—referred to as periodic breathing—is common and often disconcerting to parents caught previously unaware. As long as newborns remember to limit their pauses to no more than a few seconds and experience no accompanying color changes—especially any resembling a shade of blue—then periodic breathing is considered a normal, harmless habit.

Breasts

We're willing to bet that there are many of you out there who were hoping that there were going to be at least a few body parts that you could put off thinking about until puberty. In addition to recommending a great book for you to read when you aren't quite so sleep deprived (called *From Diapers to Dating: A Parent's Guide to Raising Sexually Healthy Children* by Debra Haffner), we wanted to be sure to mention that baby girls and baby boys alike are, on occasion, born with enlarged breasts. That's right, the swelling of one or both breasts can vary from subtle to fairly pronounced and is thought to be the result of babies' exposure to their mothers' hormones during pregnancy. Some newborns even have some milky white breast discharge to go along with the swelling—something you may have heard referred to as witches' milk. The good news: You don't need to do anything about the swelling or discharge. Swollen newborn breasts generally disappear on their own within a few weeks to months.

"IT'S A NUBBIN"

Nubbins, extra nipples, supernumerary nipples, accessory nipples—whatever you want to call them—these so-called third nipples are extra breast tissue found on the chest below the level of a baby's 2 normal nipples (and as low down as on the abdomen). Brought into the national spotlight on a memorable episode of *Friends* (Chandler had one), they're hardly ever of any medical significance, rarely change during puberty, and in most cases are small enough and flat enough either to go unnoticed or to look like birthmarks. Some babies, however, are born with a third nipple that more closely resembles a normal nipple. If an extra, out-of-line nipple becomes a source of embarrassment later in life, take comfort in knowing that it can be removed.

The Care and Keeping of the Cord

The umbilical cord is one of the new-baby body parts that seems to get the most attention. After serving for so many months as a vital connection between mom and baby, it quickly becomes unnecessary once your baby is born and starts breathing and eating on her own. You can expect your newborn's umbilical cord stump to dry up and fall off within a few weeks (typically anywhere from 1 to 3, to be more precise). In the meantime, you may be relieved to know that the blood vessels that once ran through it are now closed off, and your baby's umbilical cord and belly button are no longer a direct connection to anywhere.

Letting Go

Many new parents are very tentative when it comes to caring for their newborn's umbilical cord. For the most part, dealing with the umbilical cord actually means keeping it clean and waiting for it to fall off. While a particular infection-preventing purple dye and/or rubbing alcohol used to be the standard of cord care, the currently recommended routine involves applying absolutely nothing. That's because when left alone, most umbilical cords will just fall off by themselves. We've found that intermittently and gently pushing down the skin surrounding the umbilical cord so that the base of the stump gets some exposure to air can help speed up the drying process a bit. In case you're worried about hurting your baby, you'll be relieved to know that there are no nerve endings on the cord itself, and babies don't feel any pain or discomfort with careful handling. Every now and then you might see a little blood at the base of the cord—an admittedly disconcerting sight that is usually the result of a cord stump becoming detached a bit too soon (in other words—sort of like pulling off a scab before the underlying skin is entirely healed). The most useful approach to cord care is to let the cord fall off all on its own, and until it does, avoid undue moisture to the cord (see "Prelude to a Bath" on page 137). Be sure to call your doctor in the unlikely event that you see any signs of infection, including yellow drainage and/or any redness or tenderness of the skin around the cord.

 ## UNCOOPERATIVE CORDS

Some of you may benefit from a little forewarning: Not all cords cooperate according to plan. Some of the more common inconveniences we come across include

Hanging on. Some cords are persistent, clinging on for dear life despite daily encouragement to fall off. While the range of normal is as long as 5 weeks, it's worth discussing an obstinate cord with your pediatrician to see if there's something that can be done about it (see Oozing).

Oozing. After the umbilical cord stump falls off, the belly button tissue may take its own sweet time to heal. If it continues to ooze or develop a little pink moist bump that doesn't dry up, your pediatrician may apply a touch of a chemical called silver nitrate to quicken the healing process. Rarely, pus may ooze from the belly button and/or the surrounding skin may become red and swollen. If this happens, show your baby's doctor without any delay because any and all potential infections warrant immediate attention at this age. True infections of a newborn's umbilical site generally require medical management, antibiotics, and close observation.

Bleeding. When your newborn's cord comes off, don't be surprised if there is a little bleeding to go along with it. The best way we've found to explain the bleeding: It's like when a scab comes off and pulls a bit at the normal skin as well. There's bound to be a little short-lived bleeding.

Innies Versus Outies

Ever look at your own belly button and wonder why it was that your doctor didn't do a better job of giving you a cute little innie when you were born? Well you'll soon discover, if you haven't figured it out already, that the innie versus the outie status of your newborn's belly button is completely out of anyone's control. Ultimately, how much or little your newborn's belly button sticks out depends on how the umbilical cord scar heals.

 BANKING ON CORD BLOOD

Cord blood—blood that courses through the umbilical cord right up until a baby is born—has been found to contain cells that can successfully cure a wide range of genetic, blood-related, and immune system disorders as well as some types of cancer. This makes cord blood of great interest in the medical world, offering the hope for treatment of such potentially devastating diagnoses. Fortunately, collection of cord blood is relatively quick, easy, and pain-free, and is typically done just before or just after birth.

Several types of cord blood banks, including both public and private, now exist worldwide and allow for the long-term storage of these life-saving cells. With the existence of cord blood banking, expectant parents are now faced with an important decision: whether to invest what can be a significant amount of money in storing their babies' cord blood in a private, for-profit cord blood bank. While the idea of reserving your baby's cord blood exclusively for potential personal or family use in the future is understandably tempting, the actual likelihood of needing to do so is medically unlikely. Unless you already have a child with a known medical condition that could directly benefit, private storage is therefore not currently recommended. That said, allowing your baby's cord blood to be collected and stored in a public blood bank and made available in a national registry is recommended, should the option be available to you.

Back to Basics

Sacral Dimple

It's adorable to see babies with dimples on their cheeks, but on occasion they show up on a baby's backside in the area just above the buttock crease, called the sacral area. Most sacral dimples, when present, are very shallow and simply look like a little indentation in the skin. They are still quite cute, but it is well worth making sure they're carefully evaluated by a health professional because every now and then they serve as a sign that what lies underneath didn't develop quite accord- ing to plan, because they have the potential to extend deeper below the surface.

Sacral dimple

Genitals

Now to get down to business and address those parts of your newborn's body that new parents tend to have questions about but often hesitate to ask. When it comes to learning about your newborn's genitals, we strongly believe that (1) "down there" just won't suffice (for long, anyway) and (2) there's bound to be information that's new to you regardless of whether you have a baby of the same or opposite sex as you.

 BOY OR GIRL

Along with pregnancy comes the inevitable question, "Are you going to find out?"—a question that refers to the modern-day luxury of being able to find out months ahead of time by ultrasound, or even more definitively by chromosome testing, whether you're destined to have a boy or girl. Even though you may not be, the early period of genital development is re- ferred to as the "indifferent" stage for good reason. That's because there is no difference in the appearance of the external genitals between boy and girl fetuses until around the 14th week. So if you, like we, are among those who couldn't wait to get a sneak peak, rest assured that your obstetrician was not just trying to teach you a lesson in patience by making you wait until somewhere between your 16th to 20th week to get an ultrasound.

Baby Girls

Keeping Clean

Unless poop is involved, there is no need to scrub thoroughly in all the nooks and crannies that make up your newborn girl's vulva. In fact, when cleaning your baby girl, soap is not necessary. You can use plain water, a baby

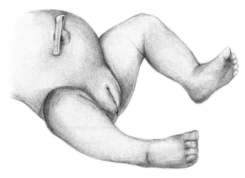

Vulva, labia

wipe, or a damp washcloth or cotton ball to wipe from your baby's front to her backside. Too-vigorous cleaning can irritate the labia and actually cause the flaps of skin to stick together.

LABIAL ADHESIONS

Infants and young girls sometimes develop what are called labial adhesions. This is a condition where the folds of the labia minora fuse together. This usually starts from the bottom and extends up. In most instances, a large enough opening remains to allow pee to come out normally. Labial adhesions are caused by irritation of the labia with subsequent fusion of the tissues during the healing process. This condition usually goes away on its own once a girl reaches puberty because the higher estrogen level helps to lubricate the tissues. For newborns, your pediatrician may advise you to apply Vaseline or a prescription estrogen cream to help separate fused labia.

Vaginal Discharge

Newborn girls often have clear or white discharge from the vagina. This discharge helps to protect the vaginal area from sticky poop and the like. During diaper changes you can gently wipe away excess discharge, but you don't need to dig deep or scrub hard to get rid of it all. Call your pediatrician if the discharge becomes yellow or green or develops an odor because such changes may suggest the need for further evaluation and/or treatment.

Vaginal Bleeding

Many newborn girls seem to have mini-menstrual periods with bloody discharge from the vagina. Although you may find it disconcerting, this is a normal effect of mom's hormones and usually goes away within a few weeks.

Baby Boys

Penis Care

Whether or not you decide to circumcise your baby boy, the routine newborn care is the same—gently clean the penis during baths, pulling the foreskin back only as far as it will go. For uncircumcised boys, you will only be able to see the opening at the tip of the foreskin. It will be a few years before the foreskin will loosen enough to pull behind the head (or glans) of the penis for cleaning. For circumcised boys, your goal is to keep the head of the penis clean and prevent any foreskin from causing adhesions by sticking to the glans.

 HYPOSPADIAS

In this condition the foreskin won't look quite right, and the opening of the urethra (where the pee comes out, also called the meatus) may not be right at the tip of the penis where it's supposed to be. Recognizing hypospadias at birth is especially important for parents who plan to have their newborn sons circumcised, because the circumcision procedure should be delayed and performed by a urologist at the same time as the correction of the hypospadias.

To Circumcise or Not to Circumcise

Because there is no medical necessity to circumcise an infant boy, the decision to remove the foreskin of the penis should be made based on your personal, religious, and cultural beliefs. While there are reports that circumcision may further decrease the already low risk of cancer of the penis, urinary tract infections in men, and spread of sexually transmitted diseases, the American Academy of Pediatrics has weighed in by stating that you need not base your decision to circumcise on health benefits or concerns. Good hygiene can usually prevent these conditions.

Except for those babies born with a hypospadias, prematurely, or very small, circumcisions are generally done within a week or two of birth. This procedure may be done in the hospital or your doctor's office and is typically performed by either your baby's doctor or your obstetrician. Babies do feel pain, so be sure to ask about options for limiting the pain of the procedure, as sugar water, acetaminophen (Tylenol), and a local injection of lidocaine are routinely given. Insurance companies may or may not pay for this procedure. Outside of the newborn period, a urologist may perform medically necessary circumcisions. These may require general anesthesia in the hospital because older babies are thought to have more pain sensors and are apt to bleed more.

Following a circumcision, the head of the penis may appear purple-red and/or swollen for up to a week. You can also expect a moist or even goopy-looking scab to form and remain on the head of the penis while it heals. A little Vaseline, Bacitracin, or KY Jelly often helps keep the scab from sticking to the diaper, and is therefore most useful while the circumcised area is still raw. In general, parents should avoid giving their newborns full baths until the penis has healed completely (see "Prelude to a Bath" on page 137). Contact your pediatrician if you think you see pus or notice any bleeding that leaves a spot of blood bigger than a quarter on your baby's diaper.

When to Call a Foul Ball

There are a few commonly mentioned conditions involving a baby boy's scrotum and testicles with which you may want to familiarize yourself. If your baby's testicular area doesn't look quite right, he may have

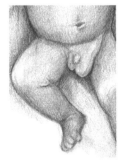

- **A hernia.** Hernias tend to be more common in premature babies and are 10 times more likely to occur in boys than in girls. This is a condition

where there is a small opening in the belly wall that allows part of the intestine to creep down into the scrotum, or testicular sac. This can actually occur in the groin area of girls as well. When a baby boy has a hernia, his scrotum and/or groin area may appear full and larger than normal. The bulge of a hernia tends to appear or enlarge when babies cry because crying puts more pressure on the belly. If you suspect that your baby has a hernia, contact your pediatrician. Surgery will usually be required to make sure the intestine doesn't become stuck, twisted, or swollen.

- **A hydrocele.** Excess fluid surrounds the testicle(s) and will make the scrotum look large. This fluid will transilluminate, meaning if you hold a flashlight against the scrotum, it will "glow" and appear fairly translucent (reminiscent of ET's glowing index finger). Hydroceles usually disappear by 1 year of age without any intervention. They occur in about 10% of baby boys.

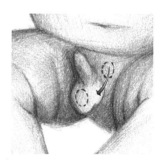

- **Undescended testes.** Over the course of fetal development, a baby boy's testicles move down from the abdomen and ultimately settle themselves in the scrotum. Sometimes the testicles (one or both) are slow to descend—taking their own sweet time to move down into the scrotum during the first few months. Other times the testicle does not descend and therefore does not develop as it should and won't function properly if left to fend for itself in the abdomen. If and when surgery is indicated, it is recommended as early as 6 months of age, but no later than 18 to 24 months.

On the Surface—Your Newborn's Skin

Visualize what happens to skin that has been soaked for a long time in a tub full of warm water. It gets shriveled and soft and has a tendency to become a bit dried out afterward. Now if you consider the fact that your newborn has been soaking in an amniotic fluid bath for 9 months, you'll better understand why her skin looks like it does—most likely dry, cracked, and/or peeling. If you think about it, it's actually amazing that a newborn's skin doesn't look worse than it does after delivery. While we find that almost all new parents come to us in search of a way to remedy the dry skin situation, there's really not much to be done except exercise patience. Moisturizers only serve to temporarily slick down the dead, flaky skin that is destined to be sloughed off anyway, and given that some young babies have sensitive skin to begin with, we suggest avoiding the unnecessary use of lotions in the first month unless otherwise directed by your doctor.

Rashes

Newborns frequently develop rashes on the skin, most of which are common and harmless. In an effort to familiarize you with what you may be faced with (because many newborn rashes tend to show up on the face), we have put together the following list. Whether due to maternal hormones or tiny pores that are easily clogged, these common newborn rashes rarely require anything more on your part than patience and a hands-off approach, with the exception of an occasional wipe with a wet washcloth.

- **Baby acne.** Although baby acne doesn't tend to show up until a month or so of age, we're listing this first because it tends to be the most concerning for parents. Just as in puberty, these pimples appear due to the effect of hormones on the oil glands, only this time it's mom's hormones from pregnancy that are the culprit. Baby acne tends to last for a few months before going away and may get worse before finally getting better.
- **White bumps (milia).** These tiny bumps are usually found on newborn noses and usually disappear within a few weeks without requiring anything on your part.
- **Erythema toxicum.** This red, splotchy, bumpy rash with little blister-like lesions in the center can make newborns look as if they've been attacked by fleas. E tox, as it is often called, often appears shortly after birth—within hours or days—and can be expected to go away within about a week. Individual spots can actually come and go within hours (similar to hives) and should not be poked, prodded, or popped. Because any blister-like rash needs a doctor's evaluation, be sure to get confirmation that it's erythema toxicum you're dealing with.

- **Heat rash.** Warm clothes or sweat can cause fine pink pimples on your baby's skin—most commonly on the face and in and around skin folds. Try to keep him cool and dry to avoid heat rash or get rid of it once it appears.

Birthmarks by Color

- **Pink or red.** Splotchy, flat red or pink spots on the eyelids, forehead, or back of the neck and scalp are called angel kisses, salmon patches, or stork bites (the technical term is nevus simplex). These often fade over the first few years and they tend to get brighter when your baby cries. Darker red areas on the skin are called port-wine stains, or nevus flammeus. Hemangiomas are bumpy strawberry-like collections of blood vessels that may be found anywhere on the body and can be of any size. They may not appear until after birth, and typically grow in size during the first year before gradually shrinking over the next several years. Most disappear on their own, while a few may require laser or steroid treatment or even surgery.
- **Blue.** Mongolian spots are bluish-green flat birthmarks often seen in babies with darker skin. They are frequently located on the lower back or buttocks but can be found on other body parts as well. They tend to fade with time, but until they do, it's a good idea to make sure their presence is documented in your baby's medical record to decrease the likelihood that they will be mistaken for unexplained bruising.
- **Brown.** Flat, light-brown birthmarks are called café au lait spots. These usually require no intervention, but on occasion (usually when someone has 6 or more of them) can be associated with other symptoms or rarely be associated with neurologic conditions. Spots called moles or nevi may also be brown but tend to be darker and in some cases raised.

Blue or Mottled

Because babies don't have great circulation, you may well see your fair share of mottled or even bluish skin, especially of your newborn's hands and feet. If you notice this, simply make sure your baby is warm enough by covering up cool extremities and repositioning her to get the blood flowing. Should your newborn's lips, gums, or skin around the mouth appear blue, on the other hand, contact your pediatrician without delay because this more centrally located blueness may mean your baby is not getting enough oxygen.

Fingers and Toes

Not a whole lot to say—it's usually a matter of counting 10 of each and you're done. Well, almost. Every now and then a baby is born with an extra digit or with a toe that curls a bit more than normal—neither of which are likely to be a big deal in the grand scheme of things and both of which can tend to run in families. If either situation applies to you, just discuss it with your pediatrician. We've found that the real story from a practical standpoint is not your newborn's fingers and toes, but what lies in store for you on the tips of them. What really throws some parents for a loop is the recurrent challenge of nail management.

Nails, Nails Everywhere

Did you know that fingernails grow an estimated 0.1 mm each day and that they grow faster in young people, in males, and in the summertime? Well, neither did we until we looked it up, but that is apparently the case, and it certainly doesn't surprise us. While that may not seem like much on the surface, let us assure you that it will keep you busy. Keeping up with your newborn's nails as they continuously grow can be a very demanding task. As far as we're concerned, the real purpose baby nails serve is to break you into parenthood. They will likely require trimming or filing at least once a week because long nails on the hands of newborns with little to no control of them predictably result in stray scratches. If you happen to fall behind on your nail clipping, your baby will inevitably remind you (and make you feel guilty) by scratching his face when his nails get too long (or if you leave sharp corners or points when clipping).

Hand Exploration

Many parents cover their newborn's hands with baby mittens or socks to prevent wayward nails from scratching their faces. As your baby develops over the next several weeks (and you become more skilled at nail clip-ping), it's a good idea to allow your baby plenty of time during which he can freely explore with his hands. If scratches continue to be a problem, we suggest limiting covered time to when your baby is sleeping.

Curved Legs and Feet

After being curled up in her mother's body for 9 months, it's not surprising to find that a baby's legs and feet come out a bit footloose and fancy-free—

THE BABY MANICURE-PEDICURE

A handful of parents are intimidated by the prospect of having to cut their baby's nails and would probably opt for a professional manicure-pedicure if only they were generally available. No such luck. If you're lucky, your hospital nurse will be able to help demonstrate the correct technique, but some hospitals actually discourage their personnel from doing so, we can only presume because any unintentional injury may be a liability problem. And while we aren't exactly recommending it (or admitting to doing it ourselves), we're well aware of the fact that some parents opt to bite or peel off their newborn's nails rather than fiddle with clippers or scissors. Because clippers and scissors can trim nails in a more controlled fashion, you'll be better off using one or the other (or both), or simply using a nail file to keep things under control. For best results, trim or file your baby's nails when she's asleep and her hands are less of a moving target.

Push down on the fingertip skin so you can get the clipper or scissors around both sides of the nail and avoid cutting your baby's finger (or toe).

Then, just as a professional manicurist would, finish off any sharp or rough edges with an emery board and…Voila! Not so bad after all once you get the hang of it.

appearing to be curved. These positional effects will gradually improve over the first months and years of life. A few babies will have more significant problems with the bones of their feet, which may require casting or surgery. Make sure your pediatrician checks your baby's feet, especially if they seem rigid or curved and can't be straightened out.

Reflexes

Reflexes are actions that happen automatically. Newborns are born with several of them, many of which they will grow out of as their nervous systems develop and take control over the next several months. We've listed some common normal reflexes that you'll probably come across.

- **Grasp.** We consider the newborn grasp reflex to be one of the most endearing. It causes your baby to grasp tightly to your finger if you place one into the palm of his hand. Pressing on the bottom of his feet will also cause his toes to curl up.

- **Sucking.** The sucking reflex is present even before birth, as witnessed in many a prenatal ultrasound. You'll find the reflex is so strong that your baby may want to suck even if he's not hungry. Rather than overfeed him, consider offering a pacifier or clean finger to satisfy his urge (see "Sucking Sense and Sensibility" on page 57).

- **Moro or startle reflex.** When newborns are startled by loud noises or sudden changes in position, they may well throw their arms and legs out and even start to cry. You can chalk up this entire sequence to what is known as a startle reflex.

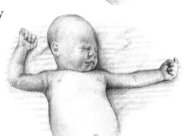

- **Fencing pose.** We included this reflex only as a point of general interest. Watch your newborn as he lies on his back. Whichever side his head is turned to is likely to be the side he reflexively extends his arm, while the opposite arm will bend at his side (resembling the pose of a fencer).

CHAPTER 27

fever: trial by fire

As you're probably well aware, fever is a hot topic that applies to everyone—young and old. We all get plenty of firsthand experience with it long before we reach parenthood, yet there's nothing quite like a baby's first fever to make even the most well-prepared parents feel a bit hot and bothered themselves. Whether it happens at 1½ weeks, months, or years, fever can admittedly be quite unnerving. While as pediatricians we are committed to making sure that you develop a healthy respect for fever—especially in the first few months after your baby is born—as parents we're convinced that having a good understanding of what causes fever, its implications, and what may (or may not) need to be done about it will help prepare you to manage your baby's first and future fevers safely and confidently.

Fending Off Fever

Before you read up on what to do in the event that your newborn gets a fever, let us first offer you some simple strategies for putting off your first run-in with fever for as long as possible.

- **Limiting exposure.** You may find that you have many well-wishers waiting in the wings even before you get home from the hospital. While you should be sure to express your gratitude for their support, be selective about whom you allow to share their best wishes in person. By coming over to see and/or hold your baby, they may share their viruses as well.

- **Hand washing.** Now is not the time to be shy about requiring that anyone and everyone who wants to lay hands on your susceptible bundle of joy has to wash them (their hands, that is) first. All rules of in-law etiquette aside, don't hesitate to postpone all hugs and pinches as long as possible, but at least long enough to ask for a show of clean hands first.

- **Don't go looking for trouble.** There's nothing inherently risky about taking an appropriately dressed newborn out of the house, but it's wise to be a bit choosy about where you go. Crowded areas and small closed-in spaces are perfect places to come into contact with unwanted germs. Taking a walk outdoors or sticking to wide open spaces will decrease the likelihood that your baby will be coughed on, sneezed at, or touched by people who are sick.

- **Help is only a wipe away.** Despite all your best fever-fighting efforts, you may find at some point in the not too distant future that someone somehow has managed to break through all lines of defense and touch your baby with the same hand recently used to hold a snot-filled tissue or cover a cough. Given that this can and has happened to the best of us, we suggest keeping a handy supply of baby wipes nearby to wash off the "contaminated" area at your earliest convenience. Even though we don't have hard-core evidence proving that this works, the basic principles of infection control strongly support such a simple effort and we therefore consider it well worth a shot.

Fever in Newborns

Instead of venturing into great detail about what causes fever and whether it truly warrants your fear and respect, we first want to point out what we consider to be our most important take-home message: Discussing what needs to be done about a newborn with a fever is *very* different from fever considerations in older infants and children. The reason is straightforward: The younger the infant, the less prepared their immune system is to fight infection. Therefore, the best way to sum up a new parent's healthy approach to fever is that it's *always* better to be safe than sorry. You should never wonder about whether to bother your newborn's doctor about a fever: Just make the call. Sure, most fevers during the first few months are likely to be caused by the same common cold viruses that plague the rest of us, but a newborn's risk of having a serious underlying infection, while relatively small, is nevertheless real. It is for this reason that *any infant with a fever during the first few months of life should be brought to the immediate attention of a doctor.* What happens from there depends on the age of the baby and the circumstances. In some cases, young babies with fevers simply need close observation. In others (especially in the first month of life) you should be prepared for your baby's doctor to check blood, urine, and even spinal fluid for signs of infection. In general, the younger a baby is and the sicker she seems, the more likely she is to require hospitalization and treatment with antibiotics in addition to the tests listed above.

 IN THE ABSENCE OF FEVER

While new parents are routinely warned to take fevers very seriously we know that some serious types of infections have the potential to cause little or no fever in newborns. In the absence of fever, babies who seem to be less responsive than normal—anywhere from a bit listless to downright lethargic—or are having problems eating need to be taken just as seriously as those with fevers and evaluated to determine the cause. If you ever find yourself concerned about your baby's health, don't waste any time sitting around waiting for a fever to show up before consulting with your baby's doctor.

Overcoming the Fever Fear Factor

Now that we've done our duty in delivering the "take all fevers seriously in your newborn" warning, we also feel obliged to give you a bigger picture perspective and point out that there's a fine line between taking fevers seriously and living in constant fear of a rise in your baby's temperature. We hope that the information that follows will help eliminate the fever fear factor and better prepare you to rise to the occasion.

The Body's Built-in Thermostat

You've probably heard it on the news or read it in print—fever serves a purpose. While we won't belabor this point and make you suffer through all we learned on the subject in our own medical training, it's worth reminding yourself every now and then. Fever not only acts as a warning sign for infections, but it is actually thought to help the body in its effort to fight them. A part of the brain called the hypothalamus is responsible for regulating body temperature—similar to the way a thermostat controls the temperature in your house. In general, infants and young children have much more sensitive "thermostats" than adults. When viruses, bacteria, or other fever-causing agents trigger the hypothalamus to raise the body's set point, body temperatures rise. You can therefore think of fever as the body's equivalent of having its thermostat setting turned up.

Fever Defined

The natural question that begins most discussions involving fever is: Exactly what temperature is considered a fever? You'd think you could get a straight answer to such a seemingly straightforward and commonly asked question, but chances are good that if you asked around you'd get a wide range of answers starting anywhere from 99°F on up to 100.4°F or more. That's because several factors go into defining fever.

 IT'S A MATTER OF DEGREE

Normal body temperature is generally defined as 98.6°F. A rectal temperature of 100.4°F or higher is typically used to define a fever in newborns. How the numbers that fall in between are interpreted tends to vary considerably. In part, that's because body temperature fluctuates normally over the course of any given day—generally rising a bit in the afternoon and evening. The degree of variation is thought to increase with age; while a child's or adult's temperature can vary as much as 2°F (1.1°C) over the course of the day, you should expect your newborn's range of normal to be much smaller.

Using Thermometers for Good Measure

Back in the days when we were kids, pretty much everyone used a glass mercury-containing thermometer. While we'll spare you a long-winded discussion of the potential dangers of broken glass and the risks associated with exposure to spilled mercury, suffice it to say, these thermometers are not just out of style, they are not recommended. From a practical standpoint, it's also a good thing; we have yet to talk to anyone who found mercury thermometers easy to read. In contrast, the readily available digital thermometers currently in vogue are (almost) foolproof—put them in the right place and the numbers just appear.

Hot Spots—Fever by Location

The easiest way to categorize thermometers is according to the part of the body where the temperature is taken (axillary = underarm, tympanic = ear, oral/pacifier = mouth, temperature strips = forehead, and rectal = self-explanatory). Temperature strips, albeit temptingly easy, are generally frowned on as being notoriously inaccurate. Even when using some of the more accepted temperature-taking routes, such as placing a thermometer in a child's mouth or armpit, the resulting temperatures can vary quite a bit. That is why the definition of fever usually includes some reference to the location in which the temperature was taken.

 FEVER ON LOCATION

The following represent the temperatures typically used to define fever:

99°F (37.2°C) axillary

100°F (37.8°C) oral

100.4°F (38°C) rectal

When reporting a temperature to your pediatrician, there's really no need for you to add, subtract, or otherwise mathematically manipulate the results based on where you took the temperature. Instead, just be sure to mention how/where you measured it.

You should be aware that almost all doctors recommend *only* using rectal thermometers for newborns up until the age of at least 3 months (with many recommending continued use until up to 3 years) because the resulting readings are considered the most accurate measure of a newborn's core body temperature.

Bottoms Up: Taking a Rectal Temperature

While you're certain to find plenty written about the ins and outs of using each type of thermometer, we decided that your time and ours would be best spent focusing on the rectal approach. There's no way around it: Rectal temperatures are considered the gold standard of temperature taking, especially in infants younger than about 3 months. When it comes to figuring out whether your newborn has a fever, you should settle for nothing less. If

LOOKING AHEAD: INNOVATIVE
THERMOMETERS

Ear and temporal artery thermometers are marketed to parents as quick and easy alternatives to rectal thermometers and have both been shown to be relatively accurate methods of measuring temperature— just not in newborns. The temporal artery thermometer simply involves sliding the thermometer across the forehead, while ear thermometers require a good fit in the ear. If you already happen to have one of these types of thermometers, you don't need to get rid of it. Just be aware that it's a good idea to steer clear of them and reach for the rectal thermometer until your baby reaches about 6 months of age.

you are now squirming at the thought (which we're pretty sure some of you are), take a minute to get used to the idea and then we'll walk you through the process. Despite the dread many new parents seem to experience, you just have to believe us that taking an infant's rectal temperature is not all that difficult or uncomfortable—for the baby or the parent. In fact, many parents sweat their way through taking their first temperature only to be pleasantly surprised when their babies don't seem to mind. Some even sleep right through the whole "ordeal"!

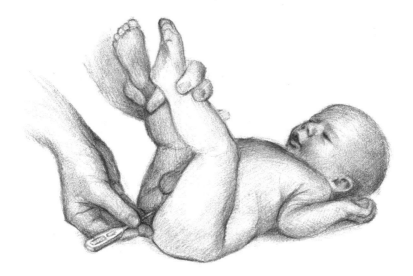

The easiest way to get set up is to lay your baby on a comfortable but firm, flat surface. Place him across your lap if you like, or consider using a changing table, sofa, or the floor—whatever you find easiest and most convenient. You can either put him on his belly or lay him on his back. If you opt for the back, then hold up your baby's legs just as you would if you were changing his diaper. Be forewarned that regardless of how you approach it, taking a rectal temperature has the potential to trigger pooping—especially in young infants—so you might want to place a towel or changing pad underneath your baby in advance. Disposable probe covers are optional but can make cleanup that much easier. You may also want to dab a little lubricating jelly (such as Vaseline or KY Jelly) onto the short, round metal tip of the thermometer. Then carefully insert the tip into the rectal (anal) opening just until the metal tip is no longer showing (between ½ and 1 inch). Then all you need to do is keep the thermometer in place by gently squeezing your baby's butt cheeks closed around it until a reading has been made. Once you're done using the thermometer, remember to give it a quick rinse with some hot soapy water (especially if you didn't use a probe cover) and be sure to put it away somewhere handy along with a mental note that this is now designated "for rectal use only"—not that it couldn't technically be used for any other type of temperature taking, but the thought of mistakenly doing so really causes people to cringe!

Over-Bundled = Overheated?

It is a commonly held belief that over-bundled infants can end up with an elevation in their temperature. There is a certain degree of truth to this belief because babies' skin temperatures have been shown to rise noticeably with bundling and cool down again once they are unbundled and their temperature rechecked. Rectal temperature, on the other hand, is thought to be relatively unaffected by bundling, especially if you get a reading of 100.4°F or above. Bottom line: Never write off an elevated rectal temperature as simply the result of too many layers of clothing or blankets—especially if it doesn't come down.

Getting a Feel for Fever

Foregoing a thermometer in favor of feeling your baby's forehead is never considered an acceptable measure of fever in a newborn. Even for older children, for whom this thermometer-less method of temperature taking

CLIMATE CONTROL

Interestingly enough, there doesn't seem to be a definitive answer to the question of what temperature to set your thermostat at for the sake of your newborn's health and well-being. In general, however, there seems to be consensus among parenting experts that a comfortable room temperature for babies is anywhere between 68°F and 72°F. When it comes to what is appropriate indoor attire for the youngest members of the household, some feel that babies are adequately dressed wearing the same number of layers as everyone else, while others recommend an additional layer of clothing. We really don't think it makes that much difference either way and simply suggest that if your baby seems to be uncomfortably warm or cool, just be sure to adjust her clothing and/or your thermostat accordingly.

has been shown to be a decent way to tell if they are hot or not, you still cannot rely on your hand alone to determine just how hot. In other words, parents may well be accurate in saying that their older children have fevers simply because they feel hot, but estimating just how hot—101°F versus 103.5°F—is always best left to a thermometer.

TOO MUCH OF A GOOD THING

Having done our best to inform you about the gravity of fever, let us now do our best to spare you and your newborn a lot of unnecessary probing. Given that most newborns actually make it all the way through the first several months of life without ever needing to have their temperature taken, there is definitely such a thing as taking a baby's temperature too often. Quite a few new parents have come to our offices having paid heed to all of the abundant cautionary advice about fever in the newborn period, and consequently are under the impression that they need to take and record their babies' temperatures on a daily basis (or even more frequently). We can think of very few (if any) reasons that would warrant such routine measurements in the absence of any suspicious symptoms. Big picture perspective: Some of you may benefit by giving your new thermometer a break (figuratively speaking, anyway)—whipping it out only for good reason (ie, make sure you didn't skip the beginning part of this chapter).

Understanding Febrile Seizures

Febrile seizures are seizures caused by fever. While approximately 95% of all children *never* have a febrile seizure, we've nevertheless found that the very idea causes most parents a certain degree of anxiety—much of it unnecessary—now and throughout parenthood. And that's why we thought we'd give you a bit of perspective on the subject to carry with you in the months and years to come. For purposes of easing your current state of mind we want to start by pointing out that the statistics are quite reassuring: Newborns are unlikely to experience this type of seizure because they typically occur between the ages of 6 months and 5 years. Furthermore, and contrary to popular opinion, the likelihood of having a febrile seizure is not based on how high a fever gets but rather on how fast it rises. If a child is destined to have a febrile seizure, it will most likely occur early on in the course of the fever(s), not days into an illness. And finally, to set the record straight, febrile seizures by themselves don't cause permanent damage and are rarely predictive of a long-lasting seizure disorder. That said, seizures in babies always need to be fully evaluated in order to determine if there are any underlying causes before concluding that it was a febrile seizure.

Treating a Fever

It is short and easy to tell you how to treat a newborn's fever: If you suspect your newborn has a fever, your immediate course of action is to seek medical advice and/or attention. Everything you may know or have heard about fever medications, lukewarm baths, or the potential benefits of fever all take a back seat at this age. End of discussion.

OK, so we aren't really going to leave it at that, but we definitely do mean it when we say that you don't have to bother yourself with the information on page 312 right now if you don't want to. In fact, we seriously considered not including it at all because we didn't want to give any of you the impression that there is any room for interpretation of fever in newborns without involving your pediatrician. Then we gave it a second thought and decided that when it comes to parenthood and fevers, there are a lot of inquiring minds out there who undoubtedly want to know more—if only for future reference.

Fever Medications

We don't intend to tell you when and how much fever medication you should use for your newborn because (a) this book is not about our practicing medicine; (b) we've already told you the golden rule—that you should first and foremost be talking to your baby's doctor; and (c) your baby's doctor, in turn, will tell you which medicine to use and how much, if any (all of which will depend on your baby's age and weight). Instead, we've listed below some of the basics of fever medications that we think every parent should know.

- Just about all medications commonly used to treat fevers in infants contain either acetaminophen (eg, Tylenol, Tempra, Feverall) or ibuprofen (eg, Advil, Motrin).
- Fever medication meant for use in infants comes in either liquid form (concentrated drops or suspensions) or as rectal suppositories.
- Fever medications are always dosed according to a baby's weight.
- There are different sizes of droppers used to measure liquid fever medication. As a result, "one dropperful" can mean different amounts depending on which type and brand of infant drops you're using, so always pay very close attention to the markings and only use the dropper that came with the bottle.
- Infant drops are much more concentrated than the children's suspension form. Always make yourself double-check that the dose you are using is correct for the type of medication you're using.
- Be sure to read the fine print on the label about how often the medicine can be given and take it very seriously! Acetaminophen is not to be given more often than every 4 to 6 hours. Ibuprofen (not generally recommended for infants under 6 months of age) should only be repeated every 6 to 8 hours.

CHAPTER 28

seeing yellow: jaundice

In our humble but medical opinion, all new parents should add the color yellow to their list of newborn traits to be familiar with, watch for, and be poised and ready to bring to medical attention if and when it shows up. That's because most newborns stand a good chance of turning at least a light shade of yellow—in other words, developing some degree of jaundice—during the first weeks of life. In most cases, jaundice is harmless; in some cases, it requires treatment. In any case, you'll want to be prepared to recognize jaundice and discuss its appearance with your pediatrician without delay. While jaundice is not, in fact, a disease, it is a visible indication that there is extra bilirubin in a baby's bloodstream.

Behind the Scenes

We thought it would be quite useful to first provide you with a basic understanding of what lies just below the surface of yellow-tinged skin. To do that, it helps to understand what bilirubin is. From birth and throughout our lives, our bodies are responsible for continually breaking down and getting rid of old red blood cells while all the while replacing them with new ones. Bilirubin is simply a normal breakdown product of red blood cells. Our livers are given the ongoing task of processing bilirubin, which is ultimately disposed of by the intestines in the form of poop. Jaundice results when, for whatever reason, too much bilirubin accumulates in the body.

Who Gets Jaundice?

There are several straightforward reasons why healthy, full-term newborns develop higher than normal levels of bilirubin and end up looking yellow. Not only do newborns have a proportionately larger number of red blood cells than adults—inevitably requiring more in the way of breakdown and processing—but it may take a baby's liver several days or even weeks before it is able to rise to the occasion and function at full speed. Ultimately, the 2 main factors involved in bilirubin removal include how much of it there is, and how efficiently it's being cleared out. Examples for each are listed below.

It's in the blood

- **More blood.** As we mentioned, babies are born with a higher concentration of red blood cells than adults and older children, increasing the demands placed on a newborn's liver.
- **Bruising.** Many newborns experience some degree of bruising or even develop what is called a hematoma (an egg-like swelling of blood, most commonly in the scalp) from the pressure of childbirth (see "Bumps and Bruises" on page 278). As these additional collections of blood cells are broken down, there is a resulting increase in bilirubin that must then be cleared from the body.
- **Blood type differences.** Jaundice is sometimes caused when mom and baby have different blood types. For the most part, a mother's blood remains separate from her fetus's throughout pregnancy. During delivery, however, some of it manages to pass through the placenta and umbilical cord and make its way into her baby's bloodstream. Recognizing these stray red blood cells as foreign, the baby's body swiftly reacts against them by breaking them down—posing the potential for a more rapid accumulation of bilirubin.

Getting the All-Clear

- **Catching on.** Babies tend to have slow liver function at first and may have some evidence of jaundice as they wait for their livers to mature and catch up.
- **Slow to go.** Newborns who are slow to figure out how to eat or not getting much fluid in the early days of breastfeeding may in turn be slow to poop. There may be other medical reasons a baby may have problems with pooping. Either way, the end result is that bilirubin stays in the body rather than being pooped out.

- **Problems with processing.** Far less commonly, a baby may have a more serious problem with the liver. Certain disorders can cause the liver not to function properly, resulting not only in a buildup of bilirubin but the appearance of pale-colored (almost white) poop.

Taking It From the Top

Whenever bilirubin builds up in the bloodstream, regardless of cause, more of it inevitably makes its way into the skin and causes a baby to appear yellow. Interestingly, the yellow tends to show up in a fairly predictable head-to-toe fashion—first on the face and then gradually spreading down toward the toes. How far down on a newborn's body the yellow goes is thought to be roughly indicative of how high the bilirubin levels are in the blood. In other words, the lower down on the body the yellow extends, the higher the bilirubin level is likely to be. On a side note, the actual shade and intensity of the yellow can be deceiving, and can't be relied on to offer any sort of definitive clue as to just how high the bilirubin level is.

Time Course

Most term babies reach their peak levels of jaundice at 3 to 5 days before improving completely; premature babies peak a few days later. After peaking, the jaundice should resolve within a few weeks. Newborns who appear jaundiced earlier or stay jaundiced much longer than typically expected may have an underlying medical problem that should be evaluated by a pediatrician.

- **Early jaundice.** Any jaundice that appears within the first 24 hours after birth needs medical evaluation. Sometimes it can indicate a problem with the liver or a baby's blood cells that needs to be addressed, but in all instances it suggests that the bilirubin level needs to be watched closely and treated appropriately.
- **Typical jaundice.** Regular newborn jaundice (also called physiologic jaundice) appears gradually after the first couple days. The bilirubin level generally peaks by about 5 days for full-term babies and about 1 week for those born prematurely.
- **Late jaundice.** Babies with what is referred to as breast milk jaundice may not reach their most yellow until 2 weeks of age, and may take anywhere from 3 to 12 weeks to return to normal. Fortunately, breast

milk jaundice in an otherwise healthy baby who is breastfeeding and gaining weight well does not require that mom stops breastfeeding, but you'll certainly want to talk to your pediatrician before coming to any conclusions about whether you think your baby might have this type of jaundice.

- **Persistent jaundice.** Regardless of when jaundice sets in, babies whose livers can't keep up, for whatever reason, get progressively more yellow. In some liver conditions a baby's poop can also lose its color and become pale in color. This is one of the many reasons why pediatricians routinely express sincere interest in the color of baby poop (see "The Many Colors of Poop" on page 67). Another symptom to be on the lookout for in conjunction with jaundice is poor growth, because just about any underlying medical problem can cause newborns to gain weight more slowly than expected. On occasion, red blood cell abnormalities are also known to cause the type of jaundice that lasts longer than a few weeks. Before you assume the worst, read on because good old-fashioned, run-of-the-mill jaundice can certainly take a while to fade away.

 EASY COME, SLOW TO GO

Jaundice appears fairly predictably from head to toe while bilirubin levels are rising. However, the yellow color does not always disappear in reverse as bilirubin levels subsequently fall, and it can take weeks for jaundice to fade away completely. In general, the whites of the eyes are usually the last things to return to normal.

Spot-Checking for Jaundice

Just as with fever in the newborn period, trust us when we say that your doctor will want to know if you're seeing yellow in your baby's eyes or on her skin. While some babies become unmistakably yellow, easily alerting parents and pediatricians alike that they need to be evaluated, we have found that others pose more of a challenge. That's because the color changes of some newborns' skin can be more subtle—whether due to varying underlying skin tones, ruddy complexions, dim room lights, sleep deprivation, or simply because jaundice has a way of gradually creeping up on new parents unnoticed. To be more effectively on the lookout for jaundice, we suggest you

- Move to a well-lit area, preferably one that offers you natural light.
- Gently press on your baby's skin and then remove your finger.
- Before blood flow returns and makes the skin appear pink again, take a look to see if the underlying area appears yellow. If you're not sure, compare it to a spot much farther down on the body using the same technique.
- If the first area you check appears to be yellow, make your way down your baby's body—the upper chest, at the nipple line, then the belly— continuing to spot-check until you find a level at which the jaundice stops. Report (or show) your findings to your baby's pediatrician.
- You can then keep a watchful eye to see if the jaundice increases.

Measuring Bilirubin Levels

Skin color changes offer parents and/or pediatricians the first hint that bilirubin is on the rise. Subsequently, the rate at which the yellow color spreads from head to toe can give us a vague idea of how fast the bilirubin level is increasing. Whenever the degree of jaundice is in question, a simple blood test currently is considered the most accurate way of determining where things stand. If your baby becomes jaundiced, don't be surprised if he is subjected to one or more heel pokes or blood draws to collect the necessary sample(s) to determine how much bilirubin is in his bloodstream. How many bilirubin levels your doctor decides to check will depend not only on what's causing your baby's jaundice and how many days old your baby is when it appears, but also how high the first level is, how fast it seems to be rising, and how likely it is to be effectively cleared. Also available is a technology called transcutaneous bilirubin monitoring (TcB) that determines bilirubin levels using a special form of light applied to the skin's surface. Although some studies have shown TcB to be equally accurate, and it is generally more readily accepted because of the fact that it is noninvasive (ie, no blood-letting involved), when in doubt, the blood test is still considered to be the gold standard.

Taking Care of Business—Treating Jaundice

Getting Pooped Out

Because we know that bilirubin is primarily cleared out of the body in poop—something that some newborns produce in much more abundant supply than others—it only stands to reason that those newborns who get off to a slower start pooping may, in turn, become a bit more yellow than those who fill their diapers early and often. When it comes to jaundice, the more you can do to encourage feeding (and, therefore, pooping) the better. You may have been advised to feed your baby at least every 3 to 4 hours, but if your baby is interested in eating even sooner, go ahead and feed her more frequently as this can help clear out the bilirubin. If possible, feed your baby slightly more milk at each sitting (a few more minutes per side, for example, if breastfeeding, or by offering an extra ounce or so if bottle-feeding) to help increase the poop output.

 LET THE SUNSHINE IN

Rumor has it that in the 1950s an observant nurse noticed that babies placed near the window in the newborn nursery were less likely to become jaundiced than their (relatively) in-the-dark colleagues on the other side of the room. Whether this story is actually true, we're not sure, because we didn't devote any time to checking it out. What we do know is that sunlight plays a useful role in changing bilirubin into a form that the body can dispose of more easily. In fact, "sunbathing" your baby with few clothes on in the indirect sunlight that streams through the (non-tinted) windows of your home for as little as 15 minutes a few times a day can help keep jaundice in check. However, exposure to direct sunlight is not recommended because of the risk of sunburn.

Let the Lights Begin

On further study of the "let the sunshine in" principle of treating jaundice, a particular wavelength of blue light has been shown to speed up the bilirubin breakdown and elimination process without causing sunburn. Phototherapy simply makes use of this blue wavelength in the form of a "bili blanket" and/or special lights to treat babies with high bilirubin levels easily and effectively. This lighting is often done in the hospital, but sometimes the equipment can be sent to your house for the few days your baby might need it.

A Positive Perspective on Rising Bilirubin

While we have done our best to prepare you for the possibility of jaundice in your newborn, we are well aware of the fact that facing a yellow newborn with rising bilirubin levels requiring repeated trips to the pediatrician's office (or blood work in the hospital) all in the first week or so of parenthood can be quite challenging. In fact, we have found it enough to make concerned new parents actually feel that their babies are unhealthy and themselves ill-equipped for the demands of parenthood. We therefore wanted to make sure to give you a more positive big-picture perspective. Remember—jaundice is not a disease. While it is certainly true that very high levels of bilirubin can have serious effects on babies (by affecting and potentially causing permanent damage to areas of the brain—a condition known as *kernicterus*), we are fortunate that modern-day medicine allows us to recognize and treat rising bilirubin levels long before they ever reach dangerous levels. In addition, severe jaundice is rare and tends to occur in premature or critically ill newborns. Any poking, prodding, repeated doctor's visits, phototherapy, or hospitalization necessitated by bilirubin levels that are on the rise are done to keep the levels from ever getting to the point where a baby would be at risk.

getting to the points: vaccines, your baby, and you

We'd like to think this chapter won't be your first exposure to vaccines. If nothing else, we hope to convince you that it shouldn't be your last. That's because your child will receive plenty of vaccines over the next several years (and on into adolescence and adulthood, for that matter) all of which will help prevent the serious and life-threatening diseases of decades past. The fact of the matter is that vaccines have been recognized as one of the most life-saving public health achievements of the last century, and have become a mainstay of modern medicine, pediatrics, and parenthood. Whether you have recent memories of getting a flu vaccine, or older recollections of your own childhood immunizations, there's a lot that has changed with today's vaccines. Here's an overview you won't want to skip—starting with a look at vaccines and ending with a sobering reminder about the devastating diseases themselves—diseases we now have the power to prevent.

What Exactly Are Vaccines?

In order to answer this fundamental question, we're going to need to start with a brief background on the immune system and how it works. In all but a very few unfortunate instances, we are all born with an immune system made up of cells, glands, organs, and fluids. These components work together throughout the body to fight bacteria and viruses and other threats to our health. The immune system's job is to be on the lookout for any germs that enter the body, recognize them as foreign invaders (commonly referred to as *antigens*), and make weapons specifically to fight against them (*antibodies*). One of the most important features of the

PUTTING VACCINES IN PERSPECTIVE: HOW FAR WE'VE COME

1796: Edward Jenner notices that milkmaids exposed to cowpox seem to be protected from getting smallpox—an extremely deadly disease that at the time accounted for up to 10% of all deaths worldwide. His observation leads to the development of the first successful vaccine.

1955: Dr Jonas Salk develops the first polio vaccine.

1963: The first measles vaccine is licensed, followed in 1967 by the MMR (measles, mumps, and rubella) vaccine.

1964: A committee of experts is created by the Centers for Disease Control and Prevention (CDC) to provide up-to-date advice on the use of vaccines—a role that the Advisory Committee on Immunization Practices (ACIP) has played ever since.

1979: The world sees its last case of smallpox. Its eradication is heralded as one of the greatest achievements of modern medicine.

1988: The World Health Assembly launches a global attack on polio at a time when the virus was still found in 125 countries on 5 continents and paralyzed more than 1,000 children each and every day.

1990: A national system is created to monitor vaccine safety. Known as VAERS (Vaccine Adverse Event Reporting System), this system still exists today.

1991: Hepatitis B vaccine is recommended for all infants.

1999–2001: As a precautionary measure, thimerosal is phased out of use as a preservative in the routine childhood immunization series. Thimerosal is later found not to cause any harmful effects. Today, only a few childhood vaccines even use thimerosal in the manufacturing process (which is then removed), and most contain no thimerosal at all.

2006: Fewer than 2,000 cases of polio a year are reported worldwide. This is attributed to the monumental polio eradication effort that began in 1988 and resulted in the immunization of more than 2 billion children.

immune system is its memory. Not only is your body capable of making antibodies against a whole host of antigens, but your immune system learns from its experiences, allowing you to better defend yourself in the future against antigens you've been exposed to in months, years, and even decades past. Simply put, this is how we develop *immunity.*

Vaccines—also commonly referred to as immunizations—help prevent dangerous germs from causing diseases by preparing the immune system to recognize them. In fact, vaccines are composed of the very same antigens (or parts of them) that cause disease. Unlike the germs themselves, however, vaccines are made of either "killed" or significantly weakened "live" antigens that are significantly weakened. The whole trick to making vaccines is making sure they're strong enough to teach the immune system to create antibodies, memory cells and, therefore, immunity, but not strong enough to cause disease. While a majority of vaccines are given as shots, certain vaccines can be given by mouth (orally, such as the rotavirus vaccine) or in the nose (nasally, such as some of the current flu vaccines). And for those of you who are needle-averse, be aware that scientists continue to search for new ways to give vaccines that are just as effective but do not require a shot. As for us, we're still wistfully awaiting the long-rumored vaccine-producing banana plant (which, in case you're wondering, is an innovative shot-free alternative that has actually been proposed and is being researched).

Getting Right to the Point

At this stage, we should probably get to the point that many new parents seem to worry about most. The point we're referring to: the one at the tip of the needle that is used to give shots. Yes, it's a needle. And no, we don't personally find the actual process of getting a shot to be exactly pleasant. Given the fact that shots' reputation almost invariably precedes them, it only makes sense that every compassionate pediatrician we know s-p-e-l-l-s it, tiptoes around it, and does her very best not to say the word "shot." But to put things in perspective for you (and for all of the parents who've brought their babies to our pediatric practices), we'd like to point out that a quick needle poke is actually preferable to many well-tolerated discomforts we can think of, such as a paper cut, for example. And unlike a paper cut, the poke of a needle serves a very clear and potentially life-saving purpose.

A BOOST BEFORE BIRTH

Did you know that mothers can take credit for giving their babies' immune systems their very first antibody boost? Although a newborn's immune system can take a good 6 months after birth to get up to full speed, antibodies can cross over from mother to baby through the placenta months before birth. While antibodies shared between you and your baby during your pregnancy will provide your newborn with valuable protection against many infections, they unfortunately don't protect against some serious and vaccine-preventable illnesses, such as whooping cough. Additionally, their ability to protect wears off within 1 month to 1 year. These are both good reasons why vaccines are given as early as possible in childhood and why it's so important for moms and other caregivers who are in close contact with babies to also get themselves vaccinated against influenza and get the Tdap vaccine. It is also the reason why breast milk (which also contains antibodies) helps keep breastfed babies healthier during the first year of life (see "A Breast a Day Keeps the Doctor Away" on page 10).

With that in mind, we want to focus our attention, and yours, on ways you can support and soothe your baby in the process.

- **A show of support.** We have observed over the years that how babies react to getting shots often reflects how their parents react. If you tremble and quake, your baby will definitely be able to sense your stress. Our suggestion? Take a deep breath, remind yourself that shots are over and done with quickly, and offer your baby a strong show of support by simply staying calm, close by, and ready to hold and console her. Not only will this serve you well for the many shot-visits that lie ahead, but you should apply the same principle of calm when your baby turns into a toddler and spends her days toddling, tripping, and bumping into things. When she feels any pain, she will undoubtedly look to you for a reaction. If you can remain relatively cool and supportively collected, you'll help ensure that each and every head bump or up-and-over attempt at walking (of which there will be many) doesn't turn into an unnecessarily melodramatic experience.

- **Hold tight…**not only figuratively, but literally as well. Realize that your physical contact, whether it's holding your baby in your lap, holding her hands, or stroking her head, can go a long way toward making the actual shot much more bearable. Helping to make sure your baby doesn't move during the process can also ensure that the shots are over and done with more efficiently *and* safely.

- **Be soothing.** While getting a shot is no walk in the park, the procedure itself is over very quickly and typically leaves babies surprised and a bit indignant, more than anything else. After your baby receives a shot, we recommend holding, talking, singing, or otherwise soothing him right away, and then moving on to something else such as breastfeeding or taking a bottle, or going for a brief walk outside the exam room.

Taking the Edge Off

One dose? Two doses? Three doses? Four? One of the most immediate questions parents typically pose after all the shots are said and done is whether or not they can, should, or need to give their newly vaccinated infants any acetaminophen (most commonly Tylenol). In our experience, any pain from injections is usually short-lived, although some babies do have soreness at the site of the shot for a day or two. After receiving any vaccine, there's also a chance of a low-grade fever (up to 100°F or 101°F), and some babies may be a little fussier or sleepier than usual for the rest of the day. If you are so inclined, you should discuss with your baby's doctor whether to give any pain reliever, because while we have our own opinions (ie, we both tend to fall into the wait-and-see camp), parents and pediatricians alike vary in their philosophies regarding whether the potential for aches and pains warrants any anticipatory treatment. Methods of medicating range from all or nothing, to somewhere in-between.

- **Wait and see.** This means you choose not to give any acetaminophen in anticipation of unwanted symptoms, but rather sit tight and wait to see if any signs or symptoms warrant it.
- **A dose for good measure.** This middle-of-the-road approach involves giving a single dose of acetaminophen "just in case," and then waiting to see if any additional doses are needed according to the wait-and-see plan. Some parents opt to preemptively pre-medicate before the shots. Others give a dose right after. We've known some parents to wait hours after a shot visit without giving any acetaminophen, but then give a bedtime dose as a precautionary measure.

- **Covering your bases.** As far as we know, not too many parents these days opt to give their babies acetaminophen every 4 to 6 hours for the 24 or so hours after shots. And if you ask us, that is probably a good thing. Although acetaminophen has been shown to decrease the degree to which babies get fevers after shots, a recent study also raised the question of whether acetaminophen has the potential to lessen the effectiveness of shots. Given that a majority of babies really do seem to do well without the benefit of any medicine at all, we recommend minimizing how much medication you give unless your baby shows signs of being fussy, feverish, or uncomfortable (in which case you should discuss the symptoms with your baby's doctor).

Regardless of the approach you choose, we want you to always be sure to consult with your pediatrician (and the vaccine information sheets, see "VIS = Very Important Sheets" on page 329) about side effects your baby may experience, ask whether giving acetaminophen would be appropriate, and find out the proper dose for your baby based on his current weight (see page 312).

 YOUR FIRST SHOT AT PREVENTION: **HEPATITIS B**

Most newborns are offered their first shot at vaccines even before leaving the hospital, as the first dose of hepatitis B vaccine is recommended at birth. Although a baby's risk of infection with hepatitis B virus (HBV) is relatively low, it is a risk well worth protecting against. HBV is known to cause serious disease of the liver that can lead to liver failure or cancer later in life. Fortunately, the vaccine is considered to be one of the most effective vaccines available, and has been shown to be both safe and effective when given as a first or "birth" dose. If you want to put hepatitis B vaccine's protective powers into perspective, consider this: Since routine vaccination began in 1991, infection rates among children (and adolescents) have dropped by more than 95%.

The Childhood Immunization Schedule

Each year leading pediatric and infectious disease experts put together the standard childhood immunization schedule. This schedule is admittedly a busy one, involving a master multiyear rollout plan for your baby's many vaccines. While this would be the time when we'd ideally proceed to lay out a nice, simple timeline for you to follow, the reality is that this timeline changes a little bit each year based on the latest scientific information available, and the schedule is created with a certain degree of flexibility. What we can tell you is that you can pretty well expect at least one—and probably more—immunization at each of your baby's routine well visits, typically scheduled at 1, 2, 4, 6, 9, 12, 15, and 18 months. Here are some additional factors that play a role in scheduling vaccines.

- Vaccines are given early in childhood based on the principle that the sooner we protect our babies from vaccine-preventable diseases, the better. That's because many of the infections they prevent are deadliest during infancy.
- Figuring out when to give each vaccine is dependent on scientific research that tells us when children's immune systems will be able to rise effectively to the challenge.
- Vaccines that are given in combination, such as for measles, mumps, and rubella in the MMR vaccine, have been shown to be at least as effective (if not more so) than when they are given separately.
- Most childhood vaccines require more than one dose to ensure that your child develops immunity. There is always a required wait time between one dose and the next.

The bottom line on the timing of your baby's vaccines: We suggest maintaining a healthy respect for all of the science and research behind the current vaccine schedule. The official childhood immunization schedule is a good starting point for most children, but there are exceptions. Should you have any questions or concerns, we suggest you discuss them with your baby's doctor.

For the Record

What we can share with you from experience, both as pediatricians and as parents, is the advice to keep good records about each and every vaccine your baby gets, starting from day one. Sure, this may seem like stating the obvious and, yes, your baby's doctor is required to document all of them as well. But given the fact that you will be asked to provide this information many, many times over the upcoming years—for your child's entry into everything from child care to elementary school to a new doctor's office, a foreign country, college, and beyond—we can't stress enough how glad you'll be to have handy a neatly documented, up-to-date list of the names and dates of all your child's vaccines in one easy-to-track-down-later place. Whether it's in your baby book or online, stored for safe-keeping in your computer files or on a state registry, having a backup of your child's meticulously maintained immunization record will prove to be exceptionally useful, if not downright mandatory.

 ## CREATING A CUSTOMIZED SCHEDULE

If you like to stay on top of things and want to create your very own, customized immunization schedule, you need look no further than the Centers for Disease Control and Prevention (CDC) Web site. The only part of the process that requires your patience will be entering the Web address needed to take you directly to their very cool instant immunization scheduler (http://www2a.cdc.gov/nip/kidstuff/newscheduler_le/). Once there, all you have to do is enter your baby's birth date (which, for the record, is not shared or stored) and voila!—a printable schedule of all of the currently recommended vaccines and the calculated date on which your baby will be due to get each of them. There is even a column for you to record the actual date your baby receives each vaccine.

Reliable Resources

It's only natural that parents want to know as much as possible about the safety and effectiveness of vaccines. The trick to staying informed about all of your child's future vaccines is for you to know where to get the most current information. We suggest you start by making it a habit to discuss vaccinations with your baby's doctor, and taking the time to read the Vaccine Information Statements (VIS) you will receive every time your child gets a vaccine.

If you'd like additional information, here are some of the reliable resources we share with our own patients, friends, and family members.

- **The American Academy of Pediatrics immunization Web site.** The AAP and its over 60,000 members play an integral role in assessing, revising, and delivering information about vaccines, and have created a parent-friendly Web site in order to give you direct access to this useful information. www.aap.org/immunization

- **The Centers for Disease Control and Prevention.** Here you'll find a wealth of information you can trust about everything from safety and schedules to details about the diseases themselves. www.cdc.gov/vaccines

- **The Immunization Action Coalition.** This national nonprofit organization is dedicated to the prevention of disease through immunization by way of creation and distribution of educational materials for the public (as well as for health professionals). www.vaccineinformation.org

- **The Vaccine Education Center at The Children's Hospital of Philadelphia.** Here you'll find a program called Parents PACK (which stands for Possessing, Accessing and Communicating Knowledge) to give parents access to up-to-date information and a place to go to ask questions and have an informed dialogue about vaccines. www.vaccine.chop.edu/parents

---

 VIS = VERY IMPORTANT SHEETS

OK, so technically VIS stands for *Vaccine Information Statements,* but these highly informative vaccine summary sheets are unquestionably important. So important, in fact, that federal law requires that VISs be handed out before each dose of most vaccinations are given. Written by the Centers for Disease Control and Prevention (CDC), they conveniently contain the most current information about the benefits and risks of each vaccine, as well as a convenient description of any potential side effects, condensed into a relatively easy-to-read single sheet of paper. While you will certainly have plenty of VISs provided to you over the next several years, you can access them for yourself at www.immunize.org/vis.

Out of Sight, but Never Out of Mind

While we hope you will now be better prepared to oversee your child's immunizations, we want to close out our overview with a quick reminder of why it is that vaccines are so important. The fact that most new parents (and younger pediatricians) in the United States today have never seen much less experienced a case of measles, mumps, or rubella, for example, is both good and bad: Good because it means we've been incredibly successful in combating devastating diseases of the past. Bad because it has become all too easy to get swept up in the day-to-day details of new parenthood and forget about diseases that are now largely out of sight. But with the exception of smallpox, they are not gone. In order to keep them from being out of mind, we're leaving you with a brief look at just some of the diseases we're all working together to prevent.

- **Polio**. This is a contagious viral illness that affected up to 20,000 Americans a year prior to widespread vaccine use. Some people infected with this virus (including President Roosevelt) were left with paralyzed arms and/or legs. In others, however, the virus paralyzed the muscles necessary to breathe and resulted in death.
- **Measles.** The measles virus causes rash, cough, runny nose, eye irritation, and high fever but can also lead to ear infections, pneumonia, and—most concerningly—seizures, brain damage, or death. Before a vaccine was available, nearly everyone in the United States could be expected to get measles, and 450 died each year from the disease. While there has been a truly dramatic decrease in measles cases in the United States (from millions down to hundreds of cases per year), rates of infection run the real risk of surging every time vaccination rates go down. If the vaccine was no longer available, there's every reason to believe that this highly contagious virus would return to infecting US children by the millions and cause an estimated 2.7 million annual deaths worldwide.
- **Mumps.** In addition to the more common symptoms of fever, headache, and swollen glands, the mumps virus is known to cause deafness, meningitis, painful swelling of the testicles or ovaries, and (more rarely) infertility or death.

A CONCERNING BUMP IN MUMPS!

With a documented mumps outbreak in the United States as recently as February 2010 and an 11-state outbreak that occurred between December 2005 and May 2006—both of which sickened thousands of people—to say that mumps is "out of sight" is simply not true, and allowing it to become "out of mind" is a risky proposition. Outbreaks such as these serve as a reminder that ensuring our children get the benefit of the measles, mumps, and rubella (MMR) vaccine is as important as ever.

- **Rubella.** While the rash, mild fever, and arthritis characteristic of rubella infection may not seem too serious, this virus poses a great risk to unborn babies. If a pregnant woman gets infected, a miscarriage or serious birth defects can result.
- **Diphtheria.** Diphtheria is caused by bacteria that have the ability to create a thick covering over the back of the throat and cause breathing problems, paralysis, heart failure, and death—particularly in infancy.
- **Tetanus.** This potentially fatal infection results when bacteria get in the body through open cuts or wounds. It doesn't take more than stepping on a rusty nail or cutting yourself with a dirty knife to become infected. Tetanus is commonly referred to as "lockjaw" because it causes painful tightening of the muscles, including the jaw, and can make it impossible to open one's mouth or swallow. Two out of every10 infected people die from tetanus.
- *Haemophilus influenzae* **type b.** You probably are familiar with this bacteria only by its abbreviated name, *Hib*. It can cause pneumonia; severe swelling in the throat; infections of the blood, joints, bones, and heart; and it used to be the leading cause of bacterial meningitis in children under the age of 5 in the United States. Before Hib vaccine became available in 1985, this bacteria was responsible for more than 20,000 severe infections and 1,000 deaths a year.

While there are many more diseases science can claim to have conquered, we'll stop here and let you learn more about them, and vaccines, using the resource list we've provided.

PART VII

thanks for the memories

Time Flies—So Catch It!

Time certainly may not seem to fly by when you're anxiously awaiting the birth of your child or buried knee-deep in diapers and facing your umpteenth night of interrupted sleep, but one of the almost universal insights parents gain with time is just how fast the days, weeks, months, and years go by. A cliché? Yes, but definitely worth taking note of at the start of your parenting career.

Reality Check

Before we jump right into our advice about how you can creatively archive your parenting memories, we feel the need to add a short disclaimer: Neither of us comes close to qualifying as Martha Stewart disciples when it comes to craftiness (although Laura on occasion has to curb her urges). Nonetheless, we've found that our own relatively simple creations and those suggestions we've collected and shared over the years about preserving childhood memories rank high on the list of our most popular advice—especially because they don't require a lot of artistic talent, immense creativity or, for that matter, time. The most important ingredient, in fact, is foresight. Some of the following suggestions may not strike your fancy, but at the very least we hope they help you to think up your own ideas that may be even better than ours. Our goal is simply to keep you from joining the ranks of countless numbers of parents who have found themselves regretfully saying, "What a great idea—If only I'd thought to do it myself!…Sooner!…With my first child!…When I had time!"

birth memories

Whether the birth of your child has yet to become a reality or is an event so recently ingrained in your memory that the possibility of forgetting any of the details seems quite unlikely, we want to forewarn you that even birth memories fade and blur over time. That's fine for those of you content with simply remembering the date and time of the big event along with a few random details interjected into the picture. If you aim to remember more—for your own sake and to share with your child some day—you will want to continue reading this section. The ideas we've included are simple and straightforward, yet while you're swimming in all the novelties of parenthood, you might not otherwise think of them.

Keys to Photographic Success in the Delivery Room

The birth of your child will undoubtedly be a momentous occasion—one worthy of capturing for posterity—however, it's one thing to envision the perfect shot of your baby in the delivery room and another to get it. Short of signing up to be the next featured delivery on The Learning Channel's *A Baby Story*, it is going to be up to you to figure out exactly how much of "the moment" you want to capture and how you're going to go about doing it.

- **Plan ahead.** If and when you fall into delivery preparedness mode and pack your suitcase in anticipation of your trip to labor and delivery, don't forget to include your camera and/or your video camera and whatever accessories they may require. Even beyond showing up with your camera equipment, we suggest you take a few minutes between breathing exercises and OB appointments to discuss a simple photographic game plan. First and foremost, be sure to find out if your hospital has any photographic restrictions. If there are any, you'll want to be sure to factor them in as you think about your photographic goals. If you've got your heart set on capturing a particular shot, the odds of getting it will be better if you make your wishes known ahead of time. Don't forget to figure out a place to keep your camera that's out of the way but easily accessible. While all of this advanced planning may seem a little extreme to some of you (especially those of you less "into" photography than we are), trust us when we say that the resulting photos will speak for themselves.

- **Delegate.** If you don't consider yourself much of a photographer, have no desire to rise to the occasion and focus your efforts on capturing the moment, or just plain anticipate having too many other things on your mind when you deliver—don't hesitate to delegate. If you plan on having any family or friends in the delivery room, pick the one you consider to be the best photographer (and the one least likely to be overcome with emotion when it's time to click the shutter or start the tape rolling), and make it clear what shots you hope to have captured when it's all over. Whichever type of camera you choose, make sure you or your designated photographer is comfortable using it, as well as prepared to swap out memory cards, and/or replace batteries. In short, the delivery room isn't a great place to sit down with a new camera and an instruction book.

- **Use discretion.** You don't have to have gone through labor and delivery or witnessed one before to realize that there's not a whole lot of privacy involved in the process. That does not, however, mean that you can't control the degree of exposure evident in the commemorative photographs. I'm sure you all know what we're talking about because you inevitably have to give at least some thought to how to take pictures of a baby being born *without* getting the infamous crotch shot. Fathers-to-be (or other family members or friends) who might otherwise find themselves caught up in the moment often do quite well in their role as photographer if you've not only delegated the job ahead of time, but made it very clear what you would and would not like to see revealed in the family photo album or posted on YouTube for all of eternity.

- **Consider composition.** Now you may be thinking to yourself "who has the time to consider composition? I'm just focused on maintaining some degree of composure," but that's why it's worth mentioning the concept to you now and not in the delivery room. After all, many a new parent has regretted not discussing photographic discretion in advance of the big event, much less having the designated photographer give some quick thought to such photographic challenges as the fact that open curtains on a bright sunny day can ruin the best of pictures. How much forethought you choose to devote to this subject will depend purely on how important the photographic end result is to you.

 THE PERFECT POSE

Before you deliver, you may want to set your sights on what continues to be our favorite delivery room picture. While not all deliveries are conducive to being captured on film, the cutting of the cord is definitely a pose well worth a shot. Now, before you laugh this photographic feat off as an impossibility, let us assure you that it can be done—if not by you, then at least by someone else in the delivery room. Long before I (Laura) went into labor, someone suggested that I try to take a photo of my baby on the delivery room scale so I could use it as my birth announcement photo. Having made that my personal goal, I instructed my husband to keep track of our camera and to give it to me as soon as I delivered. Little did I know I'd find myself armed with a camera well before my son made his way to the scale—in time to snap photos of my squawking baby in the obstetrician's arms as his father did the honors on the cord. Thrilled with what I considered to be the ultimate once-in-a-lifetime photo, I decided to try again with my next child. Two years later I ended up with an even better photo of my husband cutting the cord—this time complete with a clock in the immediate background bearing witness to the momentous cord-cutting event.

- **Digital distribution.** There's no question that as a society, we're now fully embedded in the digital age. When it comes to sharing the joyous news (and photos and videos) of your baby's birth, this means the opportunity to do so almost instantaneously. That said, you may want to figure out your game plan ahead of time. Some parents prefer to simply compile an e-mail address list ahead of time and send out a message to the group announcing the arrival. Others find it easier to upload photos to a password-protected photo-sharing Web site, or make use of Facebook, YouTube, or other ready-made venues for sharing the news and accompanying photographic documentation. If you are a little more digitally adept and commit to a bit more effort, you can even create your baby's very own Web page—something that will represent his very first digital footprint and is sure to be cherished for decades to come.

Video

Video recorders have made their way up to the top of just about every expectant parent's wish list. Whether you decide to have the tape rolling in your delivery room or ban all live coverage of the event is purely a matter of personal preference (unless there is some related hospital policy, of course). Just remember that the photographic considerations we discussed for photographs in the delivery room apply to video as well—only more so. Unless you plan on doing a whole lot of editing, whoever is in charge of the video camera should be well versed in discretionary limits, not to mention the use of common sense when deciding when to put the camera down and get out of the way. If nothing else, we suggest putting a ban on instant uploading, since it is our firm belief that those being filmed as the events of delivery unfold should have the ultimate say (as well as absolute veto power) when it comes to sharing the associated sights and sounds.

CHAPTER 31

commemorative creations

Saving Time in a Bottle

Even if you've never dried and preserved flowers before, here's your chance to create a great keepsake that is inexpensive to make and priceless. If you happen to receive roses or other flowers in recognition of your baby's birth, remember to take them home with you and hang them upside down (or put someone else in charge of doing so) until they are *completely* dry. Especially if you have no prior experience with flower drying, please pay particular attention to our emphasis on the words "completely dry." Trust us when we tell you from experience that anything short of fully dried flowers have a very high likelihood of turning into a progressively moldy bunch of old flowers sealed in a jar. Fortunately, most flowers can be left drying for as long it takes you to come up with a few spare minutes (which, from personal experience, can easily be a couple of months). Then simply get a glass jar that has a tight-sealing lid, cut the stems off the flowers, and carefully place them in the jar along with any additional small mementos you might have saved or purchased (such as pink or blue confetti or ribbon), and then seal the jar so it's airtight. A pink or blue ribbon and bow around the outside of the jar makes for a nice finishing touch. While quick and easy to make, this keepsake is likely to become far more valuable than the minimal time and effort you put into it. We hope you'll be thanking us for years to come.

Tipping the Scales

We haven't met a parent yet who hasn't appreciated the suggestion of taking a picture of their newborn on the delivery room scale—capturing baby and his official birth weight in one shot. This is a relatively easy to get and likely to be treasured picture that makes a great stand-alone keep-sake, but better yet makes the perfect choice if you're considering a photo birth announcement.

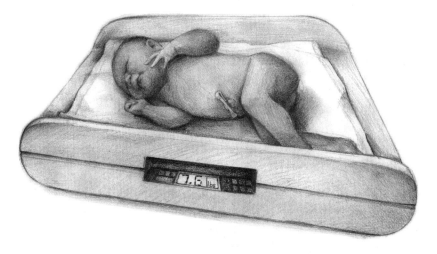

On the Day You Were Born

It may seem hard to imagine as you settle into a routine of caring for a newborn that one day, in the not too distant future, this same child will ask you as many questions as she can come up with about more subjects than you can presently imagine—including the day she was born. As we mentioned at the beginning of this chapter, your memories of childbirth and the events surrounding it may seem so vivid immediately following the grand event that you'll figure you can afford to wait a while before taking the time to write them down. Well, we suggest you learn from our mistakes and spend a few minutes writing down for your child what will certainly become a cherished gift—your account of the day she was born. Include as many details as you can, no matter how trivial they may seem now. You'll be surprised to find out which details your 4- or 5-year-old considers to be the most entertaining, whether it's the pre-labor dinner that didn't sit so well during delivery or the fact that she peed on her daddy the first time he held her. We do suggest, however, that you censor out any inappropriate language that may have found its way into your delivery room and simply stick to what was wonderful about the day.

Putting the Day on Display

The beauty of creating a shadow box frame that displays all of the paraphernalia you collect from the day your child is born is that just about anyone can do it quite easily with only a little forethought, at very little expense, and in a relatively sleep-deprived state. It also gives you something to do with all the hospital and delivery-related odds and ends you otherwise don't quite know what to do with but can't quite bring yourself to throw away.

- **Collecting memorabilia.** This is where the forethought part comes in, because you'll want to remember to gather together as many small items as you can think of that relate to the day your baby was born. Some suggested items include
  — Baby hat from the hospital
  — Hospital clothing or outfit your baby wears home from the hospital
  — Cord clamp
  — Hospital name card (usually attached to baby's crib throughout hospital stay)
  — Wrist ID bracelets
  — Birth announcement
  — Dried flowers
  — Recent ultrasound picture
  — Headlines and date cut out from the local newspaper
  — An issue of your favorite magazine from that week to remind you of news and current pop culture
  — Any souvenirs of the day, such as movie ticket stubs, a take-out menu or matchbook from a restaurant (with matches removed, of course), or even a greeting card from the President of the United States. That's right—if you are so inclined, you can send a request to the White House Greetings Office with your baby's name, address, and date of birth and get a personalized keepsake in return for your efforts.
- **Supplies.** You can either decide to wait and purchase the necessary supplies after your baby is born, or plan ahead and purchase them when your hands aren't yet so full. We've found that the latter option certainly increases the likelihood that you'll have your project hanging on the wall before your baby's first birthday. Either way, as long as you man-

age to gather together the memorabilia, it's not important *when* you get inspired to actually sit down and work on putting together your shadow box display. When you do, useful supplies to have on hand include

— *A shadow box frame.* While there's no reason you can't get this whole project done professionally, it's really quite easy (and less expensive) to buy a shadow box from a craft store or frame shop. Choose your frame size based on how many mementos you intend to include.

— *Decorative paper.* Many of the craft store shadow boxes simply come with an inset made of white cardboard. If you're partial to a plain white background, you can skip decorative paper. Otherwise, look for some non-fading craft paper—pink or blue checkered paper seems to be quite popular—or even gather up some fabric or new baby wrapping paper to line the inside of the shadow box.

— *Scissors*

— *Tape, glue, and/or staples.* Check with your local craft store regarding which types of tape and glue are best suited for this type of project.

— *Additional decorations.* Using additional items such as ribbon, tiny decorative pink or blue flowers, or even new-baby confetti (which comes in the shape of tiny little rattles and baby bottles) can definitely help spruce up your shadow box.

The rest is really quite easy. After figuring out what you want to use as a backdrop—whether it's plain white, the day's newspaper headlines, your baby's birth announcement, or decorative paper—and preparing the inside of your shadow box accordingly, play with the layout of your trinkets until they look good to you. You may want to consider using photocopies of newspaper headlines or ultrasound photos because the originals will run the risk of yellowing over time. Regular tape may do the same thing, so consider asking an associate at any scrapbooking store what your longer-lasting options are for securing your assorted items for posterity. Then simply secure your memorabilia, along with some decorative ribbon, confetti, and/or flowers, and voila! Without requiring much in the way of artistic skills, you'll have a commemorative creation worth displaying in your home for years to come.

CHAPTER 32

capturing the moments along the way

Before going any further, we feel obliged to tell those of you who aren't already aware that there are entire craft books and Web sites too numerous to count dedicated to the subject of preserving childhood memories, and many who profess to be expert in this field. While expert we are not, we have more than enough experience dealing with the regrets and missed opportunities of other parents (and, at times, of our own) that we decided to offer you a sampling of suggested ways you can continue to preserve in time some of your child's proudest (or most amusing) moments.

A Word About Baby Books

Perhaps one of the easiest ways to start out is with a baby book. Our advice to you is this: Get off to a good start by documenting some of the early details of your child's life for posterity, and then simply continue the habit later in life. Those of you who didn't already get one (or two or three) as baby gifts should have no difficulty finding one that suits your tastes—anything from a calendar-style book (where you can fill in the blanks for everything from the birth weight and head circumference to the first visitor, first smile, first tooth, and first birthday) to a book with blank pages that you can fill in as you please. Those of you who are more technologically inclined and have come to embrace the digital world we now live in may wish to keep an online baby journal instead. Fortunately, there has been a virtual explosion of parenting Web sites in recent years offering new and seasoned parents alike an unlimited number of templates, creative ideas for digital baby books, and even virtual scrapbooking communities. Explore your many options (ideally ahead of time) and go with what best suits you.

Big Before You Know It

The reason we thought to so prominently include the suggestion of preserving your child's footprints and handprints is because we can't tell you the number of times parents have thought the idea of doing so was great, marveled at another parent's footprint creation, but never got around to doing it themselves. After all, who hasn't looked at a little pair of shoes, a birth certificate with imprints from a newborn's tiny feet, or a toddler's handprints on a piece of construction paper and wistfully remembered the days when they were that small. It's quick, it's easy, and there are more than a few retail products out there that eliminate any need for creative talent. Some suggestions include

- Simply frame a piece of paper with your baby's handprints or footprints on it. Adding your baby's name and birth information or putting the prints onto decorative paper is an easy way to embellish your work of art. We suggest making the extra investment in non-fading paper.
- Place your baby's first pair of shoes in a shadow box alongside a footprint made when the shoes were worn.
- Make an imprint or 3-dimensional plaster mold of your baby's hand or foot. Mold kits, some of which will allow you to adorn, paint, or otherwise enhance your creation, are readily available at most craft shops or stores that sell baby products.
- Go to a pottery painting store and use baby-safe paint to preserve your baby's handprint or footprint on a dish, serving plate, tile, or any of the large number of other pottery pieces generally available.
- Create a handprint (or footprint) photo frame.

 HELPFUL HANDPRINT HINTS

It's easiest to get a good handprint if you wait until your baby is asleep before attempting it. You may also find the activity less challenging if you wait a few weeks or months before choosing hand over foot, because newborns are notorious for keeping their hands in a tight fist—when awake and asleep—much to the dismay of their handprint-seeking parents.

Journaling

While many of you may not have ever contemplated the idea of keeping a journal and most of you probably don't consider yourself to be writers, this paragraph is still worth reading. Perhaps one of the cutest things we've seen when it comes to capturing the memories created during new parenthood comes from my (Laura's) newborn nephew. OK, really the weekly e-mail updates he sends me come from his mother's e-mail address, but they offer up in first-person narrative all sorts of details about his preceding week of acclaimed accomplishments, memorable milestones, and amusing mishaps. Not only do family and friends (especially those who live too far away to share in the day-to-day experiences) enjoy reading and receiving these weekly journals, but down the road they are sure to become an invaluable (and highly entertaining) compilation of preserved memories. If you've never been much for journaling before, maybe this idea will be as compelling a reason as any to start!

 PRESERVING YOUR CHILD'S DIGITAL FOOTPRINT

In this day and age of high-tech everything, it is often said that our children start creating a digital footprint from the day they are born. With that in mind, we want to share with you one of the most practical tech-savvy-new-parent tips we've heard of, courtesy of Laura's twin sister. Once your baby's name has been set in stone—either by mutual agreement or birth certificate or both—simply check to see if it is available as a domain name and register it—thus staking your baby's first claim to a dedicated space in the digital world.

Photo Clubs

The point of mentioning photo clubs to you now is to make sure you are aware that they exist. While there are many variations on the theme, the basic idea behind photo clubs is that you pay a membership fee (often in the $25–$35 range) that buys you a full year of no sitting fees. Having this type of membership is great if you're not particularly handy with a camera, but in our opinion well worth considering even for those of you who fully intend to take your own shots. In our experience, new parents with photo club memberships (ourselves included) find themselves getting pictures of their children and families taken not only more economically than by a costly professional photographer, but also more regularly and frequently—whether at the local JCPenney, Sears, or any of the other participating photographic studios in your area.

CHAPTER 33

sharing the memories

Although you're undoubtedly familiar with the abundance of jokes made about having to watch someone else's home videos or look through old photo albums, as a new parent living in a highly digitally connected world, you're not likely to find a shortage of interested parties when it comes to sharing in your child's progress. Of course this may be truer with some friends and family members than with others. We've found that grandparents and other relatives generally rank at the top of the "marvel at the new baby" list. Finding a few simple ways to share captured moments with them—especially when close family and friends aren't able to share them directly—is generally much appreciated. When it comes to showing off your child in style, some recent gadgets as well as some time-tested ideas, may serve you well as a new parent.

(Almost) Instant Access

- **Internet viewing.** The use of e-mail, YouTube, Facebook, and Web pages for showing off your baby has become quite popular. If you're already set up with your own Facebook page, or at least adept at upload-ing pictures to your computer and e-mailing them, then you're already ahead of the game. If not, having a new baby in the family may be what it takes to finally convince you to learn. The beauty of it is that the actual process is really not all that hard to master; it's fast and inexpensive, and it doesn't take much advanced planning. And for those of you with parents or grandparents who are easily flustered by such modern-day conveniences as e-mail and the Internet, accessing Web pages or e-mailed photos requires little more than the basic hardware and a 2-minute tutorial. Many free Web-based companies also allow you to store your photos in a password-protected album. You can allow access to your family and friends by giving them the site and password information. And printed photos can still be ordered and then sent to friends and family as well.

- **Digital photo frames.** Although definitely more pricey than a simple Web page, this photo-sharing gadget is quite popular. After investing in the actual frame, signing up, and paying a fee for monthly service, interested friends and family simply need to register a frame and plug it in to a power source and a phone jack (unless they've upgraded to a wireless version). This arrangement is particularly convenient for grandparents or others who may not spend as much time on the computer, but cherish the opportunity (with no effort on their part) to wake up to new photos you've uploaded to be displayed on their frames. Although it takes a little bit more work on the part of the frame owner, a basic digital photo frame allows users to display slideshows from a memory card and doesn't require an ongoing fee.

 MEANINGFUL THANK YOUS

Once you've had a child, you'll find that the gifts just keep on coming with the passing of each holiday and birthday. While your baby can't exactly be counted on to deliver the proper thank you, as his parent you can help to provide his gift givers more meaningful thanks by photographing or filming him lying on, wearing, reading, or using each gift and then sending the photo/video clip to whichever friend or relative was kind enough to give it. As your child gets older and can play a more active role in expressing his appreciation, continue in the tradition of capturing special moments, events, trips, or gifts from others and remembering to send the photos/videos as a more meaningful way of saying thank you.

PART VIII

parting insights

You have now reached the end of this book, but you are only just starting your lifelong adventure. We thought long and hard about what parting insights we wanted to leave with you because in the end—all diapers and joking aside—we love being parents and we want you to enjoy this noblest of professions as much as we do. When we tried to think of how to finish things off in a meaningful way, everything that came to mind seemed to have been said before—mostly in the form of clichés. The one we feel is nevertheless worth repeating is that you will soon become the person who knows your baby best—what she wants, needs, likes, and dislikes. This expertise will come naturally over time, so it is worth reminding yourself every so often that parenthood is not a race. As for the rest of the clichés, you're certain to hear from others that your baby will grow big before you know it and how they're only young once. Instead of elaborating, we thought we'd lighten things up a bit by leaving you with a few thoughts that occurred to us while writing this book—all of which relate to a concept that has become all the more apparent to us over the past several years since we first wrote it: Becoming a parent is really quite a lot like writing a book on parenting.

- It seems like everyone's doing it.
- It's a guaranteed adventure.
- If you're lucky you fall right into your new role, but for most of us it takes a good bit of time, effort, and patience.
- It has a way of taking over your life, but you find that you wouldn't want it any other way.
- It serves as a reminder that everything is always easier said than done.
- You are bound to run into obstacles along the way. You will be the exception to the rule if you don't have days when you doubt yourself.
- Having faith and sticking with it always pay off in the end.
- People are going to judge you. Regardless of what they think, if you do your best and remain committed to learning new things along the way, you'll always have something to be proud of.
- Striving for perfection is great, but expecting to achieve it is a setup for failure.
- And finally…

this end is really only the beginning!

index